New Approaches to Qualitative Research

Qualitative research has seen a surge of growth during the past decade. This is in large part because positivist approaches have not yielded the kinds of results that had been anticipated, and more researchers are seeking alternative perspectives to understand phenomena. The number of researchers using qualitative approaches continues to grow, yet there are few up-to-date guides to assist thinking broadly about qualitative research as a field of inquiry.

Over the decades the range of approaches has increased, which has led to an even greater lack of certainty about how to think about doing qualitative research. In considering key issues while offering practical guidance on how to work within the face of uncertainty, this book will be a valuable resource to this next generation of researchers.

New Approaches to Qualitative Research offers:

- a clear understanding of the range of issues related to researcher stance, the way that researchers position themselves in relation to their subjects, their participants, and their own belief systems, and the way in which they locate themselves across the qualitative paradigm

- an overview of some of the most cutting-edge qualitative techniques in use today: from the exploration of visual texts to the concept of inquiry to synthesis methods, this section lays out the state of the art in methodology

- specific information regarding processes of data analysis, synthesis and interpretation that are employed in these various approaches.

In this book, the authors take the stance that qualitative research is a broad approach that encompasses and even encourages difference and uncertainty, and here at last they provide a route-map to this uncertain but fruitful line of inquiry. This vital text is ideal for professional researchers, final-year undergraduates and postgraduates in a range of subject areas.

Maggi Savin-Baden is Professor of Higher Education Research at Coventry University, UK.

Claire Howell Major is Professor of Higher Education at the University of Alabama, US.

New Approaches to Qualitative Research

Wisdom and uncertainty

Edited by Maggi Savin-Baden and
Claire Howell Major

Routledge
Taylor & Francis Group

LONDON AND NEW YORK

First edition published 2010
by Routledge
2 Park Square, Milton Park, Abingdon, Oxon, OX14 4RN

Simultaneously published in the USA and Canada
by Routledge
711 Third Avenue, New York, NY 10017

Routledge is an imprint of the Taylor & Francis Group, an informa business

© Maggi Savin-Baden and Claire Howell Major for selection and editorial
material. Individual chapters, the contributors.

Typeset in Galliard by
Saxon Graphics Ltd, Derby

British Library Cataloguing in Publication Data
A catalogue record for this book is available from the British Library

Library of Congress Cataloging-in-Publication Data
New approaches to qualitative research : wisdom and uncertainty / edited by
Maggi Savin-Baden and Claire Howell Major.

p. cm.

1. Education—Research. 2. Education—Research—Methodology. 3. Qualitative
research. I. Savin-Baden, Maggi, 1960- II. Major, Claire Howell.

LB1028.N364 2010

370.72'1—dc22

2009050241

ISBN10: 0-415-57240-1 (hbk)
ISBN10: 0-415-57241-X (pbk)
ISBN10: 0-203-84987-6 (ebk)

ISBN13: 978-0-415-57240-8 (hbk)
ISBN13: 978-0-415-57241-5 (pbk)
ISBN13: 978-0-203-84987-3 (ebk)

Knowledge would be fatal; it is the uncertainty that charms one. A mist makes things beautiful.

Oscar Wilde, The Picture of Dorian Gray (1891)

When one admits that nothing is certain one must, I think, also admit that some things are much more nearly certain than others.

Bertrand Russell, *Am I an Atheist or an Agnostic?* (1947)

… you are come to meet your
trouble: the fashion of the world is to avoid
cost, and you encounter it.

William Shakespeare, *Much Ado about Nothing*, Act 1 Scene 1 (1600)

Contents

Figures and tables

Figures

Tables

Acknowledgements

Many thanks to John Savin-Baden for correcting and proofreading this text, for our husbands, John and Ted for managing the children while we write, Skype and think; and to all those who have contributed to this volume for their hard work and commitment to the project.

Notes on the contributors

Julia Colyar is an assistant professor in the Department of Educational Leadership and Policy at the University at Buffalo (UB), State University of New York. At UB she teaches courses on cultural diversity, student affairs administration and the impact of college on students. Her research focuses on access and transitions to college for underrepresented students; she also writes about qualitative research methodologies. She received her PhD in higher education from the University of Southern California.

Glynis Cousin is director of the Institute for Learning Enhancement and of the Centre for Excellence in Teaching and Learning at the University of Wolverhampton. She joined the university from her previous role as senior advisor at the Higher Education Academy in York. Glynis has worked in adult, community and higher education. Her research is in the fields of diversity, internationalization, curriculum inquiry and research methodology. Her recent book *Researching Learning in Higher Education* was published by Routledge in February 2009.

Madeleine Duncan, MScOT, DPhil (Psychology) is a senior lecturer in the School of Health and Rehabilitation Sciences, University of Cape Town, South Africa. Committed to the advancement of contextually relevant occupational therapy education and practice in a developing country, her service, research and publication interests focus on undergraduate teaching and learning, the impact of chronic and structural poverty on humans as occupational beings and psychiatric disability.

Lesley Gourlay is a research fellow in the Learning Innovation Applied Research Group at Coventry University. She received her MSc and PhD in applied linguistics from the University of Edinburgh, before moving into research in higher education. Her interests include academic and digital literacies, transitions into higher education, internationalization, policy discourse and critical approaches to educational research and development. She has published in *Language Teaching Research, London Review of Education* and *Teaching in Higher Education*.

Karri Holley is assistant professor of higher education at the University of Alabama. She received her MA and PhD from the University of Southern California, and her BA from the University of Alabama. Her research interests include interdisciplinarity, graduate education and qualitative inquiry. Her monograph on interdisciplinary challenges in higher education was recently published by Jossey-Bass. She has also published in *Educational Studies,*

Educational Researcher, Higher Education, Innovative Higher Education and *Studies in Higher Education*.

Adrian H. Huerta is a student services advisor at the University of Southern California. He earned an MA in higher education and student affairs from Ohio State University and a BSc in counseling from the University of Las Vegas, Nevada. His research interests include post-secondary access and equity for traditionally underrepresented groups, gender issues, institutional accountability and qualitative methods. He has presented his research to national and international audiences.

Heather Kanuka is academic director of university teacher services and associate professor of educational policy studies at the University of Alberta, Canada. Prior to her recent appointment to the University of Alberta, Heather was a Canada Research Chair in e-learning at Athabasca University. Heather's research interests are academic development, e learning and philosophies of educational technology.

Aaron M. Kuntz is assistant professor of qualitative research methods at the University of Alabama. He received a doctorate from the Department of Educational Policy, Research, and Administration at the University of Massachusetts at Amherst. His research interests include sociocultural contexts of education, organizational culture, qualitative inquiry, materialist methodologies, identity theory, critical geography, academic citizenship and program evaluation. His most recent work appears in *Higher Education: Handbook of Theory & Research* (2009), *Journal of Higher Education* (with Berger) and *Review of Higher Education* (with Gildersleeve, Pasque and Carducci).

Theresa Lorenzo is an associate professor in occupational therapy and disability studies in the School of Health and Rehabilitation Sciences, Faculty of Health Sciences at University of Cape Town, South Africa. Her experience has led her to publish in the fields of disability, rural development, community-based rehabilitation and service learning for occupational therapy students. She is a strong advocate of action learning and participatory research of disability inclusion in social policy processes. She has a PhD in public health. Her passions outside work are cycling, watching films and being outdoors, especially if it involves travelling.

Bruce Macfarlane is professor of higher education and head of academic development at the University of Portsmouth (UK). His research interests are in the ethics of academic practice and leadership, and his publications include *Teaching with Integrity: The ethics of higher education practice* (RoutledgeFalmer, 2004), *The Academic Citizen: The virtue of service in university life* (Routledge, 2007) and *Researching with Integrity: The ethics of academic enquiry* (Routledge, 2009). He is a vice chair of the Society for Research into Higher Education and a senior fellow of the UK Higher Education Academy.

Claire Howell Major is a professor of higher education at the University of Alabama. Her research focuses on teaching and research methods in higher education as well as on higher education in popular culture. Her first two books focus on instructional approaches: *Foundations of Problem-Based Learning* (with Maggi Savin-Baden) and *Collaborative Learning Techniques* (with Elizabeth Barkley and K. Patricia Cross). Her most recent book, *An*

Introduction to Qualitative Research Synthesis (with Maggi Savin-Baden), is a research methods book describing this process for integrating qualitative information. She has published more than thirty journal issues, articles or book chapters, the most recent of which appear in the *Journal of Higher Education, Teachers College Record, Higher Education* and *Research in Higher Education*.

Paddy O'Toole is associate dean, community and international engagement in the School of Education at Flinders University in South Australia. Paddy's research area involves the construction and retention of knowledge in organizations. Her research has involved her in the corporate sector, the military, schools and universities. She is the director of the Doctor of Education programme and teaches in qualitative research methods and educational leadership and management.

Rebecca Ropers-Huilman is a professor of higher education and an affiliate of the Gender, Women and Sexuality Studies Program at the University of Minnesota. After completing her doctorate at the University of Wisconsin-Madison in 1996, she served as a faculty member at Louisiana State University (LSU) for eleven years. She has published four books and more than thirty articles or book chapters focusing on equity, diversity, gender and higher education. She served as the Women's Center director and the director of Women's and Gender Studies while at LSU, and is the current editor of *Feminist Formations* (formerly the *NWSA Journal*).

Johnny Saldaña is a professor in the School of Theater and Film at Arizona State University's Herberger Institute for Design and the Arts. He is the author of *Longitudinal Qualitative Research: Analyzing change through time* (AltaMira Press, 2003), *The Coding Manual for Qualitative Researchers* (Sage Publications, 2009), the forthcoming *Understanding Qualitative Research: The fundamentals* (Oxford University Press, 2011), and the editor of *Ethnodrama: An anthology of reality theatre* (AltaMira Press, 2005). He has also published chapters on research methods for such titles as *Handbook of the Arts in Qualitative Research*, and entries for *The Sage Encyclopedia of Qualitative Research Methods*.

Maggi Savin-Baden is professor of higher education research at Coventry University, and director of the Learning Innovation Applied Research Group. As someone who has always been interested in innovation and change, her current research is focusing on the impact of virtual worlds on learning and teaching. Over the last three years she has been developing the method of qualitative research synthesis and has gained funding to develop problem-based learning in immersive virtual worlds. To date she has published six books on problem-based learning; and another entitled *Learning Spaces* (McGraw Hill). *An Introduction to Qualitative Research Synthesis* (Routledge), with Claire Howell Major, was published in early 2010. In her spare time she is doing an MSc in e-learning and learning to snowboard.

Cathy Tombs is a research assistant in the Learning Innovation Applied Research Group at Coventry University, and is involved in the subject of learning in innovative and new technologies, particularly in virtual worlds such as Second Life. Her work includes the research and development of virtual learning scenarios in various disciplines, and she has had involvement in several projects including the JISC-funded PREVIEW (Problem-based Learning in Virtual Immersive Educational Worlds) and OCEP (Open-Content Employability) projects.

Lana van Niekerk completed her Bachelors and Masters degrees in occupational therapy at the University of the Free State, South Africa. After working in mental health for some years she joined the University of Cape Town where she was appointed associate professor and head of the Occupational Therapy Division in 2002. For her PhD thesis she used interpretive biography to explore the influences that impact on the work-lives of people with psychiatric disability. Her current research is focused on supported employment, with the ultimate goal to develop supported employment services in South Africa.

Kristan M. Venegas is an associate clinical professor and research associate in the Center for Higher Education Policy Analysis at the University of Southern California. Her research interests include college access and financial aid for low-income students of colour and qualitative research. She has authored and co-authored journal articles, book chapters, technical reports and policy briefs using qualitative research. Venegas's work has been published in the *Journal of Higher Education, Readings on Equity in Education* and *American Behavioral Scientist.*

Ruth Watson, BSc, OTMed, PhD, is a retired emeritus associate professor of the University of Cape Town, Department of Health and Rehabilitation Sciences, South Africa. She continues to research, write and teach graduate occupational therapists about what she is learning. This work has become concentrated on occupation-based practice in all aspects of service delivery, and is particularly motivated by a concern for the impact that chronic and structural poverty have on human endeavours. Ongoing research is revealing how much marginalization and vulnerability restrict human development throughout the lifespan and undermine the fulfilment of human potential.

Katherine Wimpenny, PhD, MSc, DipCOT, Cert Ed, has worked in a variety of professional practice settings prior to her present role as a senior occupational therapy lecturer at Coventry University. She specializes in occupational therapy theory and professional development, and is currently involved in partnership work with occupational therapy colleagues in practice. She contributes to the delivery of occupational therapy degree programmes at undergraduate and postgraduate level, including the support of student research. She has published work and presented at COT national conferences.

Kelly T. Winters is a doctoral student in higher education and a graduate research assistant with the Postsecondary Education Research Institute (PERI) at the University of Minnesota. Her research interests are in the social contexts of higher education access and equity policies, and in critical and feminist theories and qualitative inquiry. She holds a BA in English from St Catherine University (St. Paul, Minnesota) and a Masters degree in higher education from Harvard University.

Preface

Although we live in different countries, Maggi in the United Kingdom and Claire in the United States, we have written together for nearly a decade now. We began our association when we were 'introduced' to each other virtually by a mutual colleague who asked us to co-edit a special issue of the *Journal on Excellence in College Teaching*. As we worked through editing that work, reading and weeding through research articles and sharing ideas and information about research and research processes, we realized that our work had much in common, not only subject-wise but also from a methodological perspective, and that we had much to gain from an ongoing association. We soon realized that we would know each other for a long time.

During 2007–09 we developed an ever-evolving approach to qualitative research synthesis, a methodology that involves synthesizing and interpreting research from existing qualitative studies. In our earliest efforts, we realized that we really had no idea how to go about it. We were completely starting from scratch and we had to build our approach from the ground up. We eventually found models that improved our thinking about synthesis, and shared what we learned with others through our first article together (Savin-Baden and Major, 2007) and our later book (Major and Savin-Baden, 2010). It was undertaking such a project that prompted us to consider the shift in method and methodologies occurring. The breadth and depth of new qualitative approaches seemed to us to be undocumented in one volume, and our conversations turned towards this.

This text then reflects a component of a decade-long conversation about research, why to do it, how to do it, who should benefit from it, and so on. Over time, we came to the conclusion that we were not satisfied with the status quo of research, even of the most exploratory forms of research. This conclusion has led us to reconceptualize what we were trying to accomplish and to try new approaches to scholarship that extended beyond 'discovery'. This book's contributors have been included because their approaches, methods and values extend what it means to be a qualitative researcher, and both of us hope therefore that this book extends not only those who read it, but also the field of qualitative research, too.

References

Major, C. H. and Savin-Baden, M. (2010) *An Introduction to Qualitative Research Synthesis: Managing the information explosion in social science research*, London: Routledge.

Savin-Baden, M. and Major, C. H. (2007) 'Using interpretive meta-ethnography to explore the relationship between innovative approaches to learning and innovative methods of pedagogical research', *Higher Education*, 54(6), 833–52.

Chapter 1

Introduction

The uncertainty of wisdom

Maggi Savin-Baden and Claire Howell Major

Beginning in the twentieth century, philosophers and researchers began to speak out, taking a critical view of positivistic approaches to research, which, they argued and continue to argue, were and are not serving knowledge well. The underlying assertion was that positivist approaches that sought to discover 'truth' had missed the mark, largely due to the non-existence of a universal 'Truth' that could be objectively, and with certainty, known. These arguments gathered steam, and many scholars began to consider questions about the purpose of research, ways to accomplish research, sources of data, and so forth.

Many of these post-positivists argued that the emphasis of research should be upon interpretive understanding, for example the *verstehen* of Weber (1949), rather than the Comtean-type positivism of observable, objectively defined phenomena. Instead they argued, for example those in the Chicago School, that truths held by individuals need to be uncovered and unpacked in order to shed light on multiple, and often competing, realities. The emergence of fieldwork methods and the evolution of the interview as a central research strategy in Chicago in the 1950s furthered methodological development in the qualitative paradigm. Dewey was perhaps one of the first to raise the issue about how our various knowledge claims are warranted, arguing that for truth claims to be taken seriously they must be supported by appropriate arguments or evidence. He maintained that there was no difference in principle in the warranting of scientific and other types of claims (Dewey, 1916).

These and attending arguments have changed the way that many researchers approach their work. The trend for those who have found validity in these claims has been towards more naturalistic, interpretive and critical inquiry, and such studies often have been published under the moniker of 'qualitative research'. In social science and professional fields, thousands of articles resulting from the studies that these researchers have produced have been published in numerous journals. In addition, a variety of tomes describing approaches to qualitative research have been developed (for example, see Denzin and Lincoln, 2000).

Despite these important efforts to establish qualitative studies as a legitimate approach to research, however, uncertainty as to how to undertake qualitative research still seems to exist, especially as new models, approaches and conceptual frameworks emerge. Researchers still are struggling with what it means to be a qualitative researcher, what various qualitative designs entail, and how qualitative research plays out in the face of a number of environmental and cultural variables. This is perhaps epitomised in the overuse of approaches termed 'grounded theory', terms such as 'fine-grained research' and arguments that something is necessarily ethnographic, when often what is being referred to is just a few interviews. Such difficulties and struggles were the impetus for developing this text.

Guiding concepts for the book

The guiding concepts for this book are wisdom and uncertainty. These two terms in some ways seem incompatible with each other. Yet we see that they can and likely should be viewed as complementary. We make the argument through the selection of chapters that comprise this text that uncertainty is a part and parcel of wisdom. We further explore this notion prior to providing an overview of the text.

Wisdom

The concept of wisdom has received attention since the ancient Greeks sought to discover its basis. For example, in the fifth and fourth centuries BC the Sophists became the first to consider the epistemological question, 'what is the nature and reliability of human knowledge?' The Sceptics in this tradition believed that the human mind was incapable of taking in knowledge without distorting whatever it perceived or conceived. The metaphysical perspective peaked in this period, when the trio of Socrates, Plato and Aristotle fundamentally changed views of knowledge acquisition. Socrates, the first of these famous Greek philosophers, believed knowledge was unattainable. To prove his claim, he used dialogue and questioning approaches to probe student understanding of moral concepts such as justice, and applied formal logic to their ideas to show inconsistencies, inadequacies and weaknesses of their beliefs. He wanted students to think harder and search to discover truth within themselves. His method evolved into the current notion of the Socratic method or Socratic dialogue. This questioning and probing of assumptions and beliefs is inherent in research methodologies today, but often the whole issue of wisdom is sidestepped. Certainly, few research methods texts tackle the issue of wisdom, and perhaps our stance here is best demonstrated though the combined effort of Plato and early Christian texts. Knowledge according to Plato could not be gained through sensory perceptions alone; rather, knowledge must also involve a form of intuition. Similarly Solomon, king of Israel, when asked by God what he wanted did not ask for riches, but instead asked for wisdom – something that was later seen in action as a strongly intuitively guided decision-making process.

Wisdom in qualitative research seems to us to be not only associated with knowledge but also with virtues, as suggested by Macfarlane in Chapter 3 and Duncan and Watson in Chapter 6. The early Greeks, who perhaps were the first to consider the concept of wisdom, often associated it with a virtue. So one must have knowledge, in order to be wise, but it must be a knowledge of what is true and right. Yet wisdom, as in the case of Solomon and Job, also requires a capacity for intuition, as demonstrated by Kanuka, Major and Savin-Baden, and O'Toole in Chapters 11, 12 and 13 respectively. Other scholars have extended the concept of wisdom to being able to apply knowledge into different contexts, as exhibited by Ropers-Huilman and Winters in Chapter 5, Gourlay in Chapter 9, Lorenzo in Chapter 14 and Venegas and Huerta in Chapter 16. However, whether arising from virtue, intuition, knowledge or expansion of consciousness, the concept of wisdom seems to involve a further move beyond knowledge and understanding, onto the capacity to make good decisions, as Savin-Baden and colleagues note in Chapter 17 concerning research in immersive virtual worlds. Further, many believe that wisdom can and should be sought, and that it can be taught, yet we suggest that perhaps wisdom emerges best through managing uncertainty in research.

Uncertainty

Uncertainty is a term that has been used in a variety of disciplines, from philosophy to finance to engineering. Subtle nuances appear to distinguish the term from one discipline to the next, as Cousin notes in Chapter 2. Noteworthy, however and somewhat relevant to this text, are the concepts of uncertainty in statistical research. From probability to Bayesian statistics, the notion of uncertainty is well developed in statistical fields. As one of the advocates of Bayesian statistics notes:

> There are some things that you know to be true, and others that you know to be false; yet, despite this extensive knowledge that you have, there remain many things whose truth or falsity is not known to you. We say that you are uncertain about them. You are uncertain, to varying degrees, about everything in the future; much of the past is hidden from you; and there is a lot of the present about which you do not have full information. Uncertainty is everywhere and you cannot escape from it.
>
> (Lindley, 2006: xi)

Interestingly, the concept of uncertainty has not yet been fully explored in qualitative research. Perhaps what is more often referred to, however, is ontological security or insecurity, which derives from the phenomenological work of the philosophers Husserl, Merleau-Ponty and Sartre. In the early part of the twentieth century, investigations by these philosophers into a sense of being in the world produced various differently expressed disjunctions, from received experience to the uncertainty of labelling, naming and dealing with that experience, which was itself related to a sense of relationship between the self and whatever counts as shared reality. Such disjunctions are seen by van Niekerk and Savin-Baden in Chapter 4, Saldana in Chapter 7, and Kuntz in Chapter 15. Questioning the sense of the relationship of self to the real world leads to ontological questioning and can result in insecurity. This ontological security or insecurity fundamentally relates to a sense of identity and stability, although such senses differ at different times in context and between different people, as Colyar and Holley suggest in their discussion of narrative inquiry in Chapter 7. As the literature suggests, some people relish and some are undermined by certain levels of insecurity of self in the world.

Wisdom and uncertainty: interrelated concepts

In understanding that both wisdom and uncertainty are states of being, we believe that one can lead to the other. There is a level of uncertainty inherent in wisdom, particularly if one accepts that a judgement or decision must result from it and that actions in turn result from those judgements or decisions. We see uncertainty unfolding in qualitative research in several ways, as Wimpenny notes in Chapter 10, leading to several key considerations that ultimately influence scholarly approach. We depict them in the taxonomy shown in Figure 1.1, which we describe more fully in the following sections that lay out the organization of the text.

Likewise, there is wisdom in accepting that not all can be known, that there are some things simply beyond human capacity for understanding.

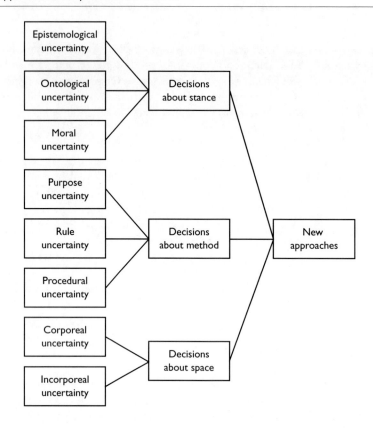

Figure 1.1   Taxonomy of wisdom and uncertainty in qualitative research

Organization of this text

This text is designed to present positions, designs and practices that recognize the complexity of qualitative research in a late modern age. In this book, we take the approach that qualitative research is a broad field of inquiry which encompasses and even encourages difference, which is apparent even within a given design, and that such difference often is not made explicit. This book seeks to make difference and difficulty explicit while also offering suggestions and guidance for practice, developed from experience in the face of uncertainty. Contributors to this book have meddled with uncertainty and wrestled with difficulties that arise from the level of complexity in a qualitative approach. The result is that we have a body of work to celebrate and share, through both successes and failures. We present this book in three parts: Part I, Stance; Part II, Methodologies and methods; and Part III, Places and spaces.

Stance

We see stance as the way that researchers position themselves in relation to their subjects, their participants and their own belief systems, and the way in which they locate themselves across the qualitative paradigm. Throughout the text, we acknowledge the many different ways to view stance, and recognize that researchers who must acknowledge an uncertain position face many unique challenges. We present five chapters that critically depict ways in which modern researchers can engage with uncertainty of stance.

Methodologies and methods

The development of a number of new methodologies has led to both the development of knowledge and the increase of questions about ways to go about discovery or integration of knowledge. The contributors in the methodologies and methods section have engaged with the notion of uncertainty in terms of the relationships between different theoretical designs of research, and have worked through the challenges of relating practices to often idealised theories of research. The six chapters included in this middle section describe new approaches, while articulating challenges in understanding and undertaking them.

Places and spaces

Space is a concept that has received recent attention in qualitative research, and perspectives of what the notion of space entails have ranged widely. For this reason, we have a broad definition of space. From notions of culture, voice and social space, and how they shape approaches to inquiry, and then onto virtual spaces as a medium for conducting research, this third section highlights advances in conceptions of space in the book's final five chapters. These advances too though are approached with a measure of uncertainty, as new spaces and new conceptions of space challenge the very ground on which we teach, learn and research.

Conclusion

Our aim has been to highlight uncertainty, to celebrate researchers who have engaged with it, and to encourage future researchers to continue to embrace but at the same time wrestle with it. In so doing, we believe that we highlight the wisdom that underlies uncertainties in stance, approach and space. We hope that our book helps to develop this important field of inquiry. We believe that our contributors have much to add to the conversation about uncertainty in qualitative research, and how embracing this central concept can help us all to develop wisdom.

References

Denzin, N. K. and Lincoln, Y. S. (2000) *The Handbook of Qualitative Research*, 2nd edn, Thousand Oaks, CA: Sage.

Dewey, J. (1916) *Democracy and Education. An introduction to the philosophy of education*, 1966 edn, New York: Free Press.

Lindley, D. (2006) *Understanding Uncertainty*, New Jersey: John Wiley.

Weber, M. (1949) *The Methodology of the Social Sciences*, New York: Free Press.

Part I

Stances

Chapter 2

Positioning positionality

The reflexive turn

Glynis Cousin

Many contemporary researchers, particularly qualitative, adhere to a notion of 'trustworthiness' to replace that of validity and reliability. Within this notion, the emphasis is on the reflexive process, which largely involves the extent to which the researcher has problematized their positionality in the research. My concern is that some of the reflexive accounts that address this question offer a kind of 'positional piety' in which either moral authority is claimed through an affinity with subjects (such as working-class woman) or through a confessional declaration of difference and relative privilege (such as white middle-class man). While researcher reflexivity does indeed include attention to the biographies we bring to the research setting, I shall argue that we need an expansive view as to what we might mean by this.

Addressing subjectivity

There is nothing new about researchers' thinking about their own bias on the basis of biography, or more broadly, insider/outsider status. With the growth of interpretivist frameworks across the social sciences and cultural anthropology (notably from the post-war symbolic interactionists associated with the Chicago School), there was a strong acknowledgement that all researchers into human activities brought their own subjectivity to the research table. The first wave of interpretivism is often called post-positivist since the problem set was that of minimizing subjectivity, of setting aside one's own baggage (bracketing in phenomenological perspectives) rather than forgoing the idea of objectivity.

Rolfe (2006: 307) has argued that early interpretivists shared with positivism the notion that there is a truth 'out there' to be got at. For instance, he writes that faith in the move to ask an independent researcher to check findings rests on a notion that '"categories" or "essences" are somehow already lodged in the data, waiting for the objective researcher'. This is an important point particularly for the phenomenographic tradition in higher education research, where the effort to find the essence of a thing in the data is the declared goal (but for a reflexive phenomenography, see Dortins, 2002). That said, getting others to see whether they see what you see is not necessarily going to drag the research into a positivist logic, because it depends on what you make of divergent or convergent interpretations. This can also be a reflexive move. It is also worth saying that the interpretivists often had more subtle ways of addressing truth claims than the label post-positivist captures. Indeed much of their work is deeply reflexive – see Foot-Whyte's (1943) comprehensive appendix to his study *Street Corner Society* for an indication of this.

Whatever qualification one wants to make, however, it is broadly true that the debate has shifted from minimizing subjectivity to thinking more about how to bring oneself into the research process through notions of reflexivity and in the light of fresh understandings about language. These notions are informed by an acknowledgement that our knowledge of the world is always mediated and interpreted from a particular stance and an available language, and that we should own up to this in explicit ways. The self is not some kind of virus which contaminates the research. On the contrary, the self is the research tool, and thus intimately connected to the methods we deploy. Added to this acknowledgement is the social construc- tionist insight that language cannot be treated as a technical means by which we articulate our findings. Language itself is value laden.

Re-presenting research

Researchers, then, should not strive to be wholly detached from their research. This does not mean they abandon carefulness, or what Bentz and Shapiro (1998) have called 'mindfulness' in the research process. It simply means that our view of the world is always from within it, and what we see, or what we erase from view, will be framed by our cultural resources, par- ticularly our language. Accordingly, the neutral research report, scripted into a 'smooth scientific narrative' which denies our investment in the research process (Law, 2004) is giving way to a new mode of representing research. This is exemplified by the shift from the passive to the first person in research reports. Foley objects that the former creates a fictive form of science:

> To evoke an authoritative voice, the author must speak in the third person and be physically, psychologically and ideologically absent from the text. That lends the text an aura of omniscience. The all-knowing interpretive voice speaks from a distant, privileged vantage point in a detached measured tone.
>
> (Foley, 1998: 110)

Similarly, Eisner (1991: 4) writes, 'I want readers to know that this author is a human being and not some disembodied abstraction who is depersonalized through linguistic conven- tions that hide his signature.'

There is a growing acknowledgement that the use of the passive is a rhetorical move that functions to suggest rather than to demonstrate rigour. Shank (2002: 10) invites his readers to ponder on the difference between a report that says *these effects were observed* and one that declares *I observed these effects*. Both describe the same observation of effects, but the lan- guage move in the first gives off a greater air of 'science'.

A second angle on language draws our attention to how the language we acquire plays an important role in shaping our worldview. The thinkable is constrained by our vocabulary. I would caution against linguistic determinism here, because it is also the role of a researcher to extend what is thinkable. Language is best seen as paradoxically capable of both enabling and inhibiting understanding. Perhaps the key thing to remember about writing research reports is that whatever our chosen genre, it is always going to be adrift from the actual experience about which we write. We are always *re-presenting* experiences through text or other media. In this sense all research is fiction, yet it is not the same as fiction. Researchers strive to tell a story from evidence whereas creative writers have a licence to play, distort and ignore evidence. The challenge for researchers is to write plausible, useful 'fiction' as well as to display a reflexive engagement with how we gather and analyse our evidence. Our notion of a 'field identity' (Srivastava, 2006) is part of the way in which we meet that challenge.

Aull Davies (1999: 4) defines reflexivity as a 'turning back on oneself, a process of self reference'. Typical reflexive questions might be: what is my power relationship with the people I am researching? How is 'respondent' disclosure problematic? Am I researching *with* or *on* people? What is my emotional investment in this question? Am I finding what I am looking for? The first three of these questions are pivotal for my discussion because they relate to what Macbeth has called 'positional reflexivity', which concerns the examination of 'place, biography, self and other to understand how they shape the analytic exercise' (Macbeth, 2001: 35 in).

A common way in which positional reflexivity is addressed is through the categories of 'race', ethnicity, class, gender, disability and sexuality. Arguably, the assumption that these are the salient factors in shaping who we are and how we view the world came initially from forms of Marxism which claimed that the structural position of workers offered them the potential to 'see' the source of their exploitation more fully than the capitalist exploiters. Standpoint feminism (Harding, 1991) took up the baton for women in making the claim that women-centred research would invite gender-sensitive ways of exploring, gathering and analysing data. As I discuss below, critical race theory is a popular advocate (Milner, 2007) of this perspective; it argues for a colour-conscious epistemology according to which, if white researchers do not problematize colour, they will think from an unarticulated power position of 'whiteness'.

Basically, these perspectives suggest that a special pair of glasses comes with an oppressed position. This is not an absurd proposition because those with an investment in privilege may well repress understandings of its effects on others; and those with an investment in losing their exploited status may well see more clearly sources of exploitation. The purpose of my discussion is to suggest qualifications to this view. First, I will sketch two cases of positional reflexivity as an illustrative resource for this discussion. Both cases offer researchers some helpful pointers about this issue, but my focus is on the ways in which I think each writer risks unduly clamping people into social boxes, assigning to them an unproblematized privileged standpoint and voice.

Class positionality

Hurst's methodological reflections of a working-class researcher on class begins with a fairly long introduction about her own class background. Her first sentence offers the flavour of this: 'By the numbers, I probably never should have made it to college. I was the oldest daughter of teen parents who struggled to survive economically' (Hurst, 2008: 334).

Having elaborated at some length on her own background, Hurst proposes that she was particularly well placed to interview working-class students because she could build rapport on the basis of common experiences. This shared terrain is thought to increase respondent trust and disclosure. A third into her report, Hurst returns to an account of herself: 'I am a White educated woman from the working class. It is important that I be clear about exactly what this means, as it is important for explaining the interview relationships I developed in this study' (Hurst, 2008: 340). In then discussing the kinds of responses she received from her working-class respondents, Hurst concludes that 'those cases reaffirmed my belief that it matters a great deal who the researcher is in relation to those being interviewed' (Hurst, 2008: 342). She adds that the respondents 'Were concerned that some facts, descriptions, stories might reinforce negative working class stereotypes' (Hurst, 2008: 342).

Hurst offers the image of the classical Greek figure of Echo in order to describe how she thinks that shared positionality supports or threatens the research enterprise:

> There was a real danger for me … that I would be listening for Echo, and that the students I interviewed would respond Echo like to my questions. As a working class academic myself, I was predisposed to believe that I knew what it was like to be a working class college student. I had to be very careful when crafting my questions and soliciting my interviewees not to let these preconceptions initiate the study.
>
> (Hurst, 2008: 339)

In the myth Echo was 'never able to initiate a conversation, or dialogue, but always to be consigned to repeating what others said before her' (Hurst, 2008: 339). Hurst suggests that by her giving voice to her working-class respondents, they were finally able to find 'someone who wanted to have a conversation with them' (2008: 349), namely herself.

To summarize, Hurst argues that her working classness facilitated trust and functioned to allay any suspicions that she would misrepresent her respondents. Her felt positional advantage or insider status encouraged authentic disclosures, untroubled by otherizing questions or readings of responses from non-working-class researchers.

Coloured positionality

Milner's 'Race, culture and researcher positionality: working through dangers seen, unseen and unforeseen' (2007) is framed by critical race theory. First, Milner offers the following position statement:

> I do not believe that researchers must come from the racial or cultural community under study to conduct research in, with, and about that community. It seems that researchers instead should be actively engaged, thoughtful and forthright regarding tensions that can surface when conducting research where issues of race and culture are concerned.
>
> (Milner, 2007: 388)

Milner is clearly saying here that engagement with issues of race and culture is what matters. He then offers what he describes as the three key 'tenets of critical race theory' which should inform that engagement. The first tenet he offers (2007: 390), following a leading proponent of the theory Ladson-Billings, asserts the pervasiveness of racism: 'race and racism are endemic, pervasive, widespread, and ingrained in society and thus in education. From a critical race perspective, race and racism are so ingrained in the fabric … of society that they become normalized' (Ladson-Billings, 1998).

A second tenet 'is that knowledge needs to emerge from the narratives and counter-narratives of people of color' (Milner, 2007: 391). This epistemology of experience gives voice to the oppressed and to the 'naming of their reality'. There are clear echoes here with Hurst's proposal that people who experience class oppression need to be able to talk about it without the noise of middle-class audiences.

A third tenet concerns 'interest convergence', in which white people are said to resist disowning their status as whites even when they are formally committed to anti-racism. Being white always produces an inherited privilege that will drive oppressive behaviour towards black people, even when the declared behaviour is anti-racist.

To summarize this second case, Milner has argued that racialized identities, conscious or not, will always determine the interview encounter; that knowledge comes from the narratives of the victims of racism, and that white people only act with black people when it is in their interests to do so.

Greying positionalities

As a first conceptual response to these cases, it could be said that both Hurst (2008) and Milner (2007) give primacy to a 'master status' (working-class, white or black). It was criminologists who first used this term to denote the tendency of people to label convicted people as 'thieves', 'larcenists' and so on, as if particular episodes in their lives exhausted explanation of them. So it is with some theories of oppression. Hurst's master status is working-class, although from her biography, she could equally label herself and her family as upwardly mobilizing, or as a class hybrid. Milner's master status is either white or black, with a similar suppression of the ways in which this status might be 'greyed', to use Srivastava's (2006) term.

It is important to clarify here that both Milner and Hurst are likely to protest that they do grey their categories through the concepts of intersectionality and multiple identities. See for instance Ropers-Huilman and Winters in Chapter 5 for an interesting discussion of how this is conceived in 'critical race feminism'. My suggestion is that even with these qualifying concepts the rhetorical drive of these theories of positionality returns them to anchorage in a master status. There is a tension between declaring complexity in the making of humans and in privileging one particular aspect of that complexity as stable and overarching. A key problem here lies in the very reliance on the notion of 'identity' which is not resolved by an act of multiplication.

Malesevic (2006) urges a radical rethink of how we approach issues of discrimination through the concept of identity. Malesevic lived through the shocking episodes of ethnic cleansing in former Yugoslavia, and is thus understandably anxious about identity politics. Identity, argues Malesevic, is a mathematical concept which has been thoughtlessly transferred to social science. While grouping units with common properties and differentiating them from other units might work for numbers, it clearly cannot work for humanity, not least because you always risk repressing the paradoxical relationship between humans. That is to say, every human, be they male, female, Welsh, black or white, can say to any other, 'I am the same as you and I am different from you.' I shall return to this point later.

In particular, the concept of 'interest convergence' in critical race theory presents a resistance to a thorough fracturing of the master categories of white and black in favour of colour-coded determinism which centres on its insistence that white supremacy permeates social relations. First, this resistance means that racisms that cannot be explained through a white–black opposition are not read as undermining this binary. In the case of anti-semitism, Gilroy (2004) has argued that if we analytically split this from anti-black racism, we impoverish our understandings of the workings of racism. This point stretches to racisms against Irish, Roma, Armenians, Bosnian Muslims, Rwandans, Poles, Rumanians and so forth – none of which yield to a black–white binary. A further relevant complexity is presented by the growing numbers of people who are of mixed inheritance.

Second, for critical race theory a concern for variation in value positions (anti-colonial and so on) is subordinated to an assumption that skin colour always trumps ethics. The moral energy of critical race theory is fuelled by the claim that white supremacy determines human behaviour. A person is either a victim of white supremacy or a carrier of its privileges. Although variation in ways of living blackness/whiteness is asserted through the concept of intersectionality, this assertion ultimately collides with a structuralist sociology and a *j'accuse* morality which largely excludes any common meeting place between black and white.

Third, what we bring to the research table is context-sensitive, mobile and interactionally determined. Research encounters vary enormously, and social positionality is one element among many that shape them. Quite banal factors such as the time of the day and the heating can be as facilitative or inhibitive of disclosure as are the biographies in the room. Some of the discussions on intersectionality in critical race theory might meet this view halfway, but again its moral and analytical pull towards a commitment to the pervasiveness of white supremacy inhibits a more fluid sense of positionality.

In the case of social class, like many upwardly mobilized academics, I could produce a formative story of social class 'lack', and I do not want to suggest that these stories are unimportant sources of influence. Nor do I want to charge Hurst with this error, but we have to take care that we are not going for the easy win of an Orphan Annie status. We also have to guard against writing a research report that is more about us than the research we have conducted. Finally, we have to ensure that we do not repress a complexity of factors that go into our making. We are both a social category and not. We are both determined and determining.

Thinking about your positionality through your social category as a starting point is no bad thing. We are all formed through social processes and institutions that classify, affirm or deny us according to factors such as class, ethnicity, religion and gender. Indeed, a prime purpose of sociology is to draw out the ways in which this operates in unequal and unfair ways. But at the same time we should heed Gorz's caution:

> The sociologists ... makes it impossible for himself to understand that each individual is also for himself a reality which exceeds what society gives him the means to say and do and that no one actually coincides with what the sociologists call their social 'identity'.
> (Gorz, 1989: 176)

The point Gorz is making is that we are all caught up in structures that are determining but we have some measure of freedom, however small, to respond to them. In short, human beings have agency, and are often disinclined to see themselves exclusively through a vulgar sociological lens. We must not forget that identities are also an outcome of negotiation and moral orientation (Dhanda, 2008).

Researchers have to consider whether they are inviting accounts that are overdetermined by a single identity position. The epistemological slant offered by Hurst and Milner risks such an invitation because they locate the production of knowledge in identity-based narratives. Collecting such narratives can be extremely important, but they will not give us unmediated access to experiences or knowledge. Reflexivity includes a concern for the extent to which we are making realities within a settled paradigm. It is important to remember that no one has easy, stable access to the naming of their reality. As Potter and Weatherall (1987) argue, we are likely to draw on an available 'interpretive repertoire' of language and inherited explanation with which to name 'our' reality. If, for instance, we are in the grip of a single 'ism' (Marxism, feminism or something similar), it will structure our explanations or the kind of questions we ask.

A strong thread in both the cases presented, then, is that if you have experienced a problem, you can speak with greater authority on it. As with Milner's notion of 'naming one's reality', in Hurst this is expressed in terms of prompting stories that do not 'Echo' class-based otherizing ones. Starting with our story seems to me a good idea, but finishing with this story without dialogue and challenge can produce confirmatory rather than insightful findings. Another way of looking at the notion of interpretive repertoire is through that of textual experience, as Rosen explains:

> A person's knowledge can only exist by virtue of a vast range of past experiences which have been lived through, often with the most intense feelings. These experiences, including textual experiences (books, lectures, lessons, conversation, etc.), we have been taught to disguise so that our utterances are made to seem as though they emerge from no particular place or time or person but from the fount of knowledge itself.
>
> (Rosen, 1998: 30)

So we are what we have read (and seen, touched etcetera), and this means that at least vicarious experience is available to us all. We might not have experienced racism personally, but as Milner (2007) writes, we can immerse ourselves in the scholarship to expand what we are alert to in our own assumptions and those of others. If we are the research tool, we need to be intellectually sharp and emotionally open. We also enter the research terrain with theoretical perspectives and ideas about what to look for on the basis of our textual experience. If that experience is limited, we will limit both the questions we ask and the responses we hear. If, for instance, we restrict our reading to one 'ism', be it postmodernism, feminism or critical realism, and if we only read rival accounts for what is wrong in them from our perspective, or if we do not read rival accounts to our own readings, we reduce the thoughtfulness with which we approach the research. Textual experience, then, is of obvious pertinence to the issue of positional reflexivity.

A further dimension to this question is well described by recalling Friedan's (1971) research into post-war suburban housewives in the United States. This study offers a classic example of respondents who could not 'name' their reality; they had no access to a facilitative discourse and it took an outsider to articulate what she famously termed the 'problem with no name'. These women's sense of guilt about the domestic comforts they enjoyed and the lack of an enabling vocabulary about human entitlement inhibited them from seeing themselves as more than wives and mothers. Reflexivity in the research process also includes suggesting to subjects 'possible horizons of meaning' (Holstein and Gubrium, 1997: 125), and perhaps the skill of the researcher to do so may be more important than their personal biography and status as insider or outsider.

It is particularly argued in Hurst (2008) that if the researcher has a shared biography with the researched, this will facilitate trust and disclosure. This is a defensible proposition, particularly where the 'researched' feels part of a vulnerable minority. But this cannot be a fixed rule of research because as Srivastava (2006: 219) puts it, 'too much insider status may be just as problematic to easing exchange as too much outsider status'. There is also the risk of what Foss (1996) has called 'symbolic convergence', by which she means that when a group of people get together with a common experience and goal, they often develop into a rhetorical community which produces a shared narrative. This narrative is often organized around a commonly felt wound.

Reflexivity would include thinking about the danger of asking questions that suggest common anchorage in a single identity script. Sometimes the people being researched sense from the questions asked that the researcher wants wound-based narratives, and obligingly deliver these. Unwittingly, then, we might ask respondents to limit self-analysis to what is socially bequeathed to them. Over-identification with 'inherited' positionality can produce intellectual and emotional laziness rather than invite reflexivity; this is so particularly where testimonies take a victimist stance. In making this point, I am not suggesting that subjects are never victims, but simply that few of us are only victims. Nieztsche's (1956) view of 'ressentiment' is relevant here. Our sense of injustice about our treatment can incline us to see only that injustice as the key formative experience in our lives. This creates a kind of emotional economy, famously characterized by Nieztsche as 'ressentiment', in which we replace ownership of our own agency with otherizing and despising the people whom we charge with otherizing and despising us.

Generally speaking, we have to be careful not to invert the problem we are addressing. Thus racists racialize particular groups of people into a unitary otherized category, and the temptation, to which I think critical racism falls, is to respond with an act of reversal in its commitment to an overarching black–white opposition. This reversal does not get us very far down the reflexivity road because no human being is entirely 'other' than another, even where unequal social structures make this very hard to see. Reflexive space has to include a concern for our common humanity alongside a concern for inequality and power.

The first tenet cited by Milner argues that the deeply ingrained nature of white on black racism overwhelms our positionality as that of white or black, suggesting no 'grey' meeting point, shared predicament or ethical space. The philosopher Rose (1993: 8) put the problem well in arguing against representing the 'other' as 'sheer alterity': *'the other' is equally the distraught subject searching for its substance, its ethical life.*

This is a humanist position which has lost voice under the noise of sociologies of difference and identity. Critiques of humanism draw attention to the partial nature of enlightenment humanism; it is charged with representing white, middle-class European man as humanity, arrogantly translating the rights of men into universal ones. This critique of enlightenment humanism is not groundless, although it needs to be acknowledged that others (women, the enslaved, working class and so on) seized upon its universal logic to extend its reach. We also need to acknowledge that humanism is more than a European enlightenment idea. Humanist values are traceable to all corners of the world and to many historical moments. This should not be surprising. It is absurd to imagine that only Europeans have spotted that as humans we all have shared predicaments, nor should it surprise us that various forms of humanism have failed the challenge to be inclusive. Humanism is best understood as a working concept. I am not here arguing against a regard for what makes us different, but I am suggesting that we include in our view of human complexity a regard for what we share or can potentially share. My argument joins with the growing literature that is revising cosmopolitan approaches to this question (see Fine, 2007 for an introduction).

In her very helpful discussion of 'negotiated identities', Dhanda (2008) argues that when we look at others, we must assign to them the same capabilities to be self-critical and ethical that we feel we have ourselves. Dhanda argues that this is how we acknowledge the other as a person who is shaped by context, by moral formation and by resources (however small) for self-reinvention. It seems to me that anyone can research anyone or anything on the basis of this acknowledgement. This does not, of course, create an even playing field, but it offers a humanist positionality which can cohabit with one that is mindful of power differences.

Srivastava's (2006) approach to the question of positionality offers another promising perspective. Using the Lacanian notion of 'lack' in the formation of human identity, she argues that we come to the research setting with some form of lack, such as that of not being an insider. From this standpoint, the research encounter is a negotiation of a shared space in which we assume 'field identities' which often involve adjustments of voice, dress, language and posture that are mindful of how we will be received.

In exploring her own very malleable 'field identity' as a researcher in India (Hindi speaker, English speaker, young woman, middle-class, Oxford scholar, Canadian, Indian, secular), Srivastava (2006) argues for a notion of 'currency' to inform researcher positionality. This notion acknowledges that identities are always in flux, and that we do not have a single way in which we present ourselves to others. Following Mullings, she suggests that the art of qualitative research involves finding a 'shared positional space based on the fluidity of our experiences that 'should not be viewed as simply a process of "racial and gender matching" (but incorporating) the dynamism of individual identities' (Mullings, 1999).

Srivastava's (2006) idea of striving for a shared positional space on the basis of dynamic, individual identities broadens the scope of reflexivity because it expands what we view as our experience. In particular, it deters us from entering the research terrain with a fixed master status, allowing for our malleable 'grey' elements to support the negotiation of what we might share. It also allows for our textual experiences to be part of who we are and what we bring to the field.

Conclusion

In offering a discussion on researcher reflexivity, my aim has been to challenge the appeal of identity positionalities from a number of directions. I have questioned whether the concepts of intersectionality and multiple identities adequately address how sociologies of identity cleave towards an original master status. I have also questioned a stark view of alterity in which the other is always other. My proposal is that researcher reflexivity is as much about our textual experience as it is our social positioning; that, following Srivastava (2006), it is best shaped by a fluid, negotiated view of positional space. In short, researcher reflexivity is grey.

References

Aull Davies, C. (1999) *Reflexive Ethnography: A guide to researching selves and others*, London: Routledge.

Bentz, V. M. and Shapiro, J. J. (1998) *Mindful Inquiry in Social Research*, Thousand Oaks, CA: Sage.

Dhanda, M. (2008) *The Personal Negotiation of Identity*, Saarbrücken, Germany: Vdm Verlag.

Dortins, E. (2002) 'Reflections on phenomenographic process: Interview, transcription and analysis', pp. 207–13 in *Proceedings of the 30th Annual Conference of the Higher Education Research and Development Society of Australasia (HERDSA)*, Perth.

Eisner, E.W. (1991) *The Enlightened Eye: Qualitative inquiry and the enhancement of educational practice*, Oxford: Macmillan.

Fine, R. (2007) *Cosmopolitanism*, London: Routledge.

Foley, D. (1998) 'On writing reflexive realist narratives', pp. 110–29 in G. Shacklock and J. Smyth (eds), *Being Reflexive in Critical Educational and Social Research*, London: Falmer Press.

Foot-Whyte, W. (1943) *Street Corner Society: The social structure of an Italian slum*, Chicago, IL: University of Chicago Press.

Foss, S. K. (ed.) (1996) *Rhetorical Criticism: Exploration and practice*, Prospect Heights, IL: Waveland Press.

Friedan, B. (1971) *The Feminine Mystique*, London: Victor Gollancz.

Gilroy, P. (2004) *Between Camps: Nations, culture and the allure of race*, London: Routledge.

Gorz, A. (1989) *Critique of Economic Reason*, London: Verso.

Harding, S. (1991) *Whose Science? Whose Knowledge? Thinking from women's lives*, Ithaca, NY: Cornell University Press.

Holstein, J. A. and Gubrium, J. F. (1997) 'Active interviewing', pp. 113–29 in D. Silverman (ed.), *Qualitative Research: Theory, method and practice*, London: Sage.

Hurst, A. L. (2008) 'A healing echo: methodological reflections of a working class researcher on class', *Qualitative Report*, **13**(3), 334–52 (online) <http://www.nova.edu/ssss/QR/QR13-3/hurst.pdf> (accessed 20 September 2009).

Ladson-Billings, G. (1998) 'Just what is critical race theory and what's it doing in a nice field like education?' *Qualitative Studies in Education*, **11**(1), 7–24.

Law, J. (2004) *After Method: Mess in social science research*, London: Routledge.

Macbeth, D. (2001) 'On reflexivity in qualitative research: two readings and a third', *Qualitative Inquiry*, 7(1), 35–68.

Malesevic, S. (2006) *Identity as Ideology: Understanding ethnicity and nationalism*, New York: Palgrave Macmillan.

Milner, R. H. (2007) 'Race, culture, and researcher positionality: working through dangers seen, unseen and unforeseen', *Educational Researcher*, **36**(7), 388–400.

Mullings, B. (1999) 'Insider or outsider, both or neither: some dilemmas of interviewing in a cross-cultural setting', *Geoforum*, **30**, 337–50.

Nietzsche, F. (1956) *The Genealogy of Morals*, New York: Doubleday.

Potter, J. and Weatherall, M. (1987) *Discourse and Social Psychology*, London: Sage.

Rolfe, G. (2006) 'Validity, trustworthiness and rigour: quality and the idea of qualitative research', *Journal of Advanced Nursing*, **53**(3), 304–10.

Rose, G. (1993) *Judaism and Modernity: Philosophical essays*, Oxford: Blackwell.

Rosen, H. (1998) *Speaking from Memory: The study of autobiographical discourse*. Stoke on Trent: Trentham.

Shank, G. D. (2002) *Qualitative Research: A personal skills approach*, Columbus, OH: Merrill Prentice Hall.

Srivastava, P. (2006) 'Reconciling multiple researcher positionalities and languages in international research', *Research in Comparative and International Education*, **1**(3), 210–22.

Chapter 3

Values and virtues in qualitative research

Bruce Macfarlane

Introduction

The history of 'research ethics' is practically synonymous with medical and scientific research. Prominent high-profile scandals in the United States and United Kingdom, which have helped to shape this history, include the ill-fated testing of the thalidomide drug during the 1960s, the four-decade-long Tuskegee syphilis study which ended in the early 1970s, and the retention of the hearts of dead children at hospitals in Bristol and Liverpool in the 1990s. Increasing regulation of research since the 1960s has been largely prompted by these high-profile scandals, and has impacted significantly on professional perceptions of what 'research ethics' means. This tends to be defined, almost exclusively, as about the (mis)treatment of human 'subjects'.

This historical legacy means that research ethics has, in effect, been 'captured' by the health and biomedical sciences research community. Their definition of what 'research ethics' means is dominant. The bioethical principles of beneficence, nonmaleficence and justice have been universalized in scope and may be found, regardless of discipline, in the research ethics codes of research councils, professional societies and universities throughout the world (Macfarlane, 2009). Bioethics has become a subdiscipline in its own right, and most academic papers about research ethics are written from a bioscience perspective. The principles of bioscience now serve, in effect, as a universalized code for researchers in all other disciplines.

The capture of research ethics by the biosciences, where quantitative approaches to investigation dominate, has had a significant impact on qualitative researchers, particularly those working in the arts, humanities and social sciences. This has a number of deleterious effects which may be understood in terms of regulation, principles, practice and language. There is a resulting need to counter the dominance of bioethical principles by developing an alternative way of thinking and writing about research ethics, better suited to the values and aspirations of qualitative researchers.

This chapter will begin by exploring the effects of dominant bioscientific interpretations of research ethics on qualitative researchers. Paternalistic definitions of 'research subjects' and assumptions about the predictability of methodology will be given as illustrations that undermine the values and purposes of qualitative research, institutionalized and policed within the university via research ethics committees. The second part of the chapter will outline an alternative way of conceptualizing research ethics through virtue theory, and demonstrate how qualitative researchers can give voice to an authentic and character-led means of analysing ethical dilemmas in their practice. In exploring the ethics of qualitative research this chapter will complement Chapter 6 by Duncan and Watson.

The capture of 'research ethics'

Most universities now require researchers to seek 'ethical approval' before they start any form of empirical investigation, processes which are well established in universities in the United States, Canada, Australia and the United Kingdom. Similar governance requirements are emerging in many other national contexts, including South Africa and Japan. These structures are mainly about seeking to manage institutional risk, both financial and reputational (Allen, 2008). In a UK context, although research ethics committees (RECs) date back to the mid-1960s, their contemporary growth resulted from government guidance issued in 1991 that all clinical research projects should have ethical approval at a local level.

Aside from the many well-known criticisms of RECs (see Tilley, 2008; Jamrozik, 2004), their operating assumptions about 'research' and 'research ethics' represent a bias against the values and purposes of qualitative research for a number of reasons. First, RECs are part of an approach to research ethics that assumes that ethical issues are essentially predictable and may be 'managed out' of the research process. Qualitative research is often framed as an inductive exploration of a problem or issue rather than a deductive testing of a hypothesis, as in much quantitative research. For a qualitative researcher it is normally important to be adaptable and even spontaneous 'in the field'. This means that research design tends to be more provisional or emergent rather than rigidly defined. Consequently, it is difficult for qualitative researchers to provide as much advanced information about how their research problem will be framed, as they accept the idea that they may not know all the parameters of the problem at the outset.

While a quantitative researcher can provide details about a questionnaire or a series of experiments that will be undertaken, a qualitative researcher may only be able to write in more general terms about their intention, for example, to conduct participant observation or interviews where the course of the conversation can never be entirely predetermined. Conventional mantras concerning confidentiality and informed consent are even less readily accommodated in the context of 'undercover' or 'insider' research. From an audit perspective, this does not provide an REC with as much 'hard' information about what will happen in practice. It wants research to be a predictable, linear process, and as far as possible 'risk' free. Qualitative research can appear to be more risky, as the research design parameters in dealing with human participants tend to be less predictable.

Quantitative researchers tend to operate on the basis of principalism despite the philosophical contradictions between many of these principles. Taken individually, few would object to principles such as 'respect for persons' or that research should only be undertaken where the benefits for society outweigh the costs. In practice, though, principles collide. A cure for Alzheimer's disease, a progressive loss of brain function, would be of enormous benefit to society given that it is estimated to affect over 700,000 people in the United Kingdom alone. The problem for researchers, though, is how to demonstrate compliance with respect for persons as a principle, when the sufferers of this condition are unlikely to be able to give their 'informed' consent to participating in studies. The problem of obtaining consent is similarly problematic for qualitative researchers seeking to understand people with severe intellectual disabilities, including those with little or no spoken language (Hubert and Hollins, 2007). The giving of consent by proxy might appear a practical solution to these problems, but how much real authority should be vested in relatives or parents who may have had little recent contact with a disabled or elderly family member? There is no easy answer to such a question, especially when the criteria are based on conflicting principles.

Qualitative researchers favour a more particularist stance (Hammersley, 2009), a position that moral judgement can only be determined on the basis of a particular set of circumstances rather than following 'absolute' principles. This is because of the more 'messy' and less predictable reality of much qualitative research. However, the capture of research ethics by the medical and biosciences community means that qualitative researchers must conform to a set of bioethical principles, chief among which is confidentiality. This principle derives from medicine, where it is assumed that patients would be less likely to seek out treatment if confidentiality were not maintained (Yu, 2008). It has become a default position that researchers from all disciplines must offer participants confidentiality and anonymity even though in practice this can be problematic to achieve. Confidentiality is also based on the idea that research participants are in some way vulnerable and less powerful than the researcher, and that consequently they need 'protection'.

Yet confidentiality is not always as important for participants as we might think. The notion that participants are vulnerable is a patronising assumption not made in other areas of professional life. In journalism, for example, individuals making comments are normally named, and confidentiality is granted by exception. Many participants in qualitative research studies, such as teachers and lecturers in educational research, are far from 'vulnerable' (Yu, 2008). Sometimes the participant is equal in social status or more powerful than the researcher, or may be keen to be 'quoted' (see, for example, Watson and Amoah, 2007). Research 'subjects' can even be eager to tell their own friends and family about their participation in a piece of research (LaRossa, 1977). There are also practical reasons why trying to maintain confidentiality can be little more than a fig leaf, such as in single-institution case studies. Furthermore, at a practical level, qualitative researchers sometimes find it necessary to break promises of confidentiality when participants are felt to be at risk (Wiles et al., 2008).

Aside from confidentiality, the rigid focus on gaining 'informed consent' from research participants can have the effect of undermining trust of participants in the researcher and the research process. It is now common to ask participants in any kind of social research to sign a consent form. This is a defensive and quasi-legal means of trying to 'protect' the university, and to some extent the researcher, from litigation or other accusations of wrongdoing. But researchers have found that demanding someone reads and signs consent forms can make them suspicious and even sometimes unwilling to participate (Grayson and Myles, 2005).

The basis upon which someone participates in research is rarely connected with whether or not a study has been approved by an REC. It is far more likely to rest on a sympathy with the purpose of the research, and perhaps knowing and/or trusting the researchers (Coggon, 2007). The opposite of this situation is where researchers are operating in developing countries and collecting data from the poor and underprivileged. The requirement to sign consent forms can be more about litigation protection than concern for the needs and interests of the participant (Humphreys, 2007). Consent forms can have negative consequences for quantitative researchers too. Here, the requirement to include elaborate and legalistic statements is said to damage response rates, which in turn can have a deleterious effect on the extent to which tests for statistical significance can be relied on (Grayson and Myles, 2005).

Finally, research ethics is also, crucially, about language. The dominant discourse is premised on the otherness of the research 'subject', and positions the researcher as a neutral scientific investigator. In this chapter I have hitherto, and quite deliberately, used the word 'participant' rather than 'research subject', but more often than not RECs adopt the latter term in their paperwork. This is a symbol of the dominant discourse of quantitative scientific research. Such language can be alienating for qualitative researchers outside the medical sciences, along with other standard questions and terminology contained in ethical approval guidelines, such as whether the researcher will be undertaking any 'invasive procedures' (Hughes, 2005).

Research ethics as political correctness

The use and mis(use) of language is at the heart of political correctness (Lea, 2009). Euphemistic 'uptitling' has converted bin collectors into 'refuse disposal operatives' and shop assistants into 'sales executives'. Political correctness can be about self-censorship, or not saying what you really think in case it might give offence (Loury, 1994). In a higher education teaching context this might take the form of thanking students for a contribution to a discussion rather than telling them that you think they are wrong. It can also be about deliberately adopting language that makes a strategic assessment about the way a sentiment is understood by its audience. The pervasiveness of quality assurance processes in higher education has led some academics to adopt a scripted language that connotes commitment to certain principles (for instance, that students are 'customers' and that teaching is 'student-centred') which they do not necessarily believe in (Cheng, 2009). This scripting of communication is an extension of the deskilling of fast-food employees (Ritzer, 2000) to incorporate the professional academic.

Writing by academics and students about research ethics strongly illustrates scripted communication. This can be found in published research papers and student theses and dissertations. Here, the politically correct language of 'universal' research ethics is strongly in evidence through researchers emphasizing the importance of obtaining informed consent, confidentiality, anonymity, 'safe' storage of data, or noting the right of research 'subjects' to withdraw, among other 'commitments'. Given that ethical issues are defined in terms of the effect or potential impact on the human subject and little else, there is no politically correct need to comment about broader ethical concerns or the messy, real issues faced in the field.

Demonstrating that you have 'covered' research ethics in the language of biomedical science is now a de facto requirement for anyone seeking to pass a masters or doctoral thesis, or get a paper published in a peer-reviewed journal. This is about inauthentic, scripted communication. While the fast-food worker may be required to tell the customer to 'have a nice day!' academic researchers are required to state that they 'kept all data confidential' or that 'the identity of research subjects was anonymized'. Clichéd statements of this type represent little more than sham compliance with the audit of RECs, journal editors and reviewers, and lecturers who assess theses and dissertations. They demonstrate that the researcher understands the strategic 'game' and has chosen the politically correct language to convey the right impression to the reader (Lea, 2009). It is about a demonstration of emotional performativity. Researchers have shown that they 'care' about the impact of their research on others, whether they genuinely do so or not.

In practice, researchers know that once they have overcome the 'hurdle' of the research ethics committee or written about 'ethical issues' in the methodology section of their paper or thesis, then they can carry on 'as normal'. Here, there is an important distinction between 'procedural ethics', which is about satisfying the research ethics process, and 'ethics in practice', where the real challenges lie in making decisions in the field (Guillemin and Gilliam, 2004). Some researchers may have considerable real concern for ethical issues while others may pay little regard to such matters in practice. The focus on principalism and approval processes does not get to the heart of this matter. The regulation of research ethics by research ethics committees results in the classic audit paradox (Hammersley, 2009). Audit processes demonstrate the capacity of academics to play the role of being audited rather than the actual phenomena that are being audited.

Reframing research ethics

The uncertainty and unpredictability of the research process means that real research ethics consist of facing moral challenges in the field. It has nothing to do with seeking ethical approval. It is what happens next that really matters. We need a way of thinking and writing about research ethics that breaks the dominance of principalism. While qualitative researchers are particularly in need of such a new approach, I would argue that it is no less relevant to quantitative researchers.

The alternative to principalism does not have to be its opposite extreme, that of moral particularism. Just as people who do not believe in religion may choose not to be defined by a lack of religious belief (as atheists) but as something more positive (for instance, as humanists), so it is perfectly possible to construct a positive, alternative way of thinking about morality through virtue ethics. This is about a belief in the importance of possessing certain virtues (or excellences of character) that make it possible to lead a 'good' life. Virtues are excellences of character such as courage or (proper) pride. A virtue-based approach to ethics focuses on *being* rather than *doing*. In other words, virtue theory is concerned with defining what we mean by a 'good' person rather than trying to predetermine how someone should act through identifying principles that pay no regard to culture, context or the personality of the actor. In the context of research ethics there are personal values and virtues that are central to being a 'good' researcher. Several writers have sought to identify what these virtues might be in reference to research, such as courage (or bravery), respectfulness, resoluteness (or perseverance), sincerity (or honesty), humility (or modesty) and reflexivity (Pring, 2001; Kiley and Mullins, 2005; Macfarlane, 2009).

To take courage as an example, this virtue is of central relevance to any researcher, and may be applied or interpreted in a variety of ways (Martin and Booth, 2003). The chosen method of research may represent a deviation from standard practice in the discipline, or the researcher may be similarly audacious in challenging received wisdom in the form of a dominant disciplinary ideology or paradigm. The researcher may have decided to tackle an unpopular or taboo subject where the fact that there is little funding or even disapproval from peers must be faced. Such a decision, while courageous, might represent taking a significant career risk. Even more fundamentally, a really courageous researcher is prepared to ask questions that challenge their own previous research findings or assumptions about the world. The results of research can prove to be so controversial that the researcher may, in extreme cases, risk professional and sometimes public vilification. Such a dilemma most famously confronted Charles Darwin (1859) in the much delayed publication of *On the Origin of Species*.

Every virtue is linked to, and comes under pressure from, twin vices which represent the lack or excess of a particular disposition at either extreme. Courage, for example is linked to the twin vices of cowardice and recklessness. Human emotions play a big part in the research process, as in any other life activity. Emotions such as love, ambition, greed, boredom and laziness can have both positive as well as negative consequences. A cowardly researcher might shrink from the challenge of pursuing a difficult or taboo topic which might go against the grain of current academic fashion. A reckless researcher might take on the challenge of a demanding research theme or question without engaging in sufficient preparation through examining the available literature, or simply be wildly overambitious in their aims. What is needed, in other words, is a balance, a means which lends itself toward the middle state of courage. This is what a virtue is.

Other virtues of relevance might demand that a researcher demonstrates respectfulness not just toward research participants but also to wider communities (such as indigenous peoples) and the physical environment. There is a need to be resolute in the pursuit of a research question despite challenges connected with the time-consuming nature of a project, its scope, or difficulties in collecting or interpreting data. It is tempting to cut corners and compromise original intentions. Researchers must then 'convert' hard-won data or other materials and ideas into meaningful 'results'. In practice this is about producing some kind of interpretation, critique, model, theory, design or artefact. There are many temptations to be avoided during this creative phase of research: ways to misrepresent data (both qualitative and quantitative) including 'trimming' results that do not 'fit' the researchers', or even a sponsors', own favoured beliefs or desired outcome. Here, the virtue of sincerity is critical in avoiding the twin vices of concealment and exaggeration. While the results of anyone's research might later be shown to be flawed, what is vital is that researchers only present what they believe to be true at the time. Ultimately, research is about the pursuit of truth, and to do anything other than this is to pervert the entire process. In subsequently presenting what one might believe to be true it is important to be modest and humble, paying due regard to the prior research of others and their possible 'priority' in connection with particular ideas or discoveries. Finally, throughout the research process, or at least at its conclusion, a reflexive state of mind is needed to assess the extent to which the purposes or questions posed at the outset have been answered, and to be self-critical about one's own personal performance as a researcher. This is about epistemological and personal reflexivity.

Virtues are closely connected with human emotions and personalities. Nobody is perfect, and it is important to recognize that a virtue approach is about realizing the importance of trying to improve through practice. In other words, one only becomes courageous by doing courageous things. Some virtues are more about action, such as resoluteness, while others are mainly about empathy, sensitivity and self-awareness, such as respectfulness. Here, a division is made between 'instrumental' virtues, where there is an emphasis on 'getting things done', and those that are essentially 'non-instrumental', like resoluteness (Pincoffs, 1986). Human beings, and thus researchers, have different personalities which makes some of us more empathy-oriented than others, for example (Cawley et al., 2000). Personality differences are also said to be connected with gender, where a 'care' approach to addressing dilemmas is associated with young women as opposed to men (Gilligan et al., 1988).

Finally, virtues are subject to different interpretations according to the discipline. For example, early publication might be the 'right' course of action where data can help other researchers to advance, but in some fields the opposite consideration might apply, when an incomplete picture might mislead as much as inform. A chemist might be frowned on for withholding the results of an experiment, whereas an archaeologist who publishes on the basis of some incomplete analysis of an early civilisation could be accused of being less than circumspect, so potentially misleading academic peers. There is a fine line between informing and misleading. The pressure to publish is, of course, connected to the vice of boastfulness, something which increasing audit of university research in recent years has only served to exacerbate.

Living the virtues – the 'ordinariness' of research ethics

A virtue approach provides a way of thinking about how to live research ethics rather than treating this complex element of our practice as about abiding by a set of static principles. As researchers we are rarely faced by the kind of dramatic 'ethical dilemmas' that tend to attract popular attention. We are all familiar with high-profile scandals where there has been outright falsification of results, research participants have been treated inhumanely, or someone has stolen the work of others and claimed it as their own. Yet real research ethics is rarely about headline-grabbing incidents of scandal and drama. There is an 'ordinariness' about the day-to-day decisions we face which is rarely recognized.

What is this 'ordinariness' about? In practice, we might be tempted to cut the odd corner – say on the extent of data collection, or by excluding an interview transcript that contradicts all the others. This is about making a judgement call where we know that the decision will probably never be exposed. It is about living with oneself rather than worrying about public scandal and exposure. It is about thinking through daily practice and avoiding the little temptations, such as keeping the audio recording going for a few minutes after completing a formal interview in the hope that the interviewee might say something more interesting; promising to send someone a transcript to check and never doing so in the (almost) sure knowledge that there will be no consequences; referencing to sources that we may have found in the bibliographies of others but never actually read ourselves; or taking more authorial credit than we should do when working with other, perhaps less powerful or experienced, researchers.

Few who have worked as researchers could honestly say that they have never succumbed to any of these types of temptations. Hence, being a 'good' researcher demands a vigilant attitude toward oneself. It calls for a kind of extraordinary ordinariness, as the examples in Table 3.1 seek to explain. This is not about being 'good' or 'bad', but about trying to act reasonably according to the dictates of our conscience and experience.

Table 3.1 Living the virtues (some examples)

Courage
- Seeking to challenge one's own presuppositions or conventional wisdom.
- Developing a project that might not necessarily attract funding or represent a 'fashionable' topic.
- Pursuing a line of research without undue regard to career and other financial imperatives.
- Freely admitting when research does not go to plan or when you feel your previous research was factually or conceptually mistaken.

Respectfulness
- Being respectful to others including vulnerable individuals and communities.
- Being aware of the temptation to take advantage of organizational, social or intellectual power over others.
- Taking care not to cede too much power to others who may wish to distort the research process for their own ends.

Resoluteness
- Being transparent about circumstances when the extent of data collection or creative endeavour has been compromised from original intentions.
- Being aware of the temptation to start analysing data or other results before a representative sample or case study has been completed.

Sincerity
- Ensuring that the results of research are based on an accurate representation of all the relevant information collected.
- Resisting overt or covert pressure from a powerful sponsor or stakeholder to skew results to meet their needs or expectations.
- Being aware of the temptation to conceal or exaggerate results in order to gain some advantage, either materially and/or to reputation.

Humility
- Fully acknowledging one's intellectual debt to others.
- Ensuring all research partners are fairly represented in being accorded publication credit corresponding with their relative contribution.
- Inviting others to challenge your own thinking and/or results.
- Reflexivity
- Being self-critical about one's own research findings or personal performance as a researcher.

The examples contained in the table just skim the surface of living out a virtue approach to research ethics, a more complete illustration of which may be found in Macfarlane (2009). What this approach demonstrates is that 'research ethics' may be connected to a much broader range of real issues throughout the lifecycle of a piece of research, rather than simply being confined to conforming to a set of mantras in a formalized and decontextualized front-ended process. Crucially, virtue theory provides a way of connecting 'research ethics' with one's own lived experience as a researcher. Virtue theory provides no formulas or 'step-by-step' recipes. It brings responsibility down to the level of each individual researcher, and demands an authentic rather than formulaic consideration of day-to-day decisions.

Conclusion

What does it mean to be ethical? This is partly about appreciating the dialectical interplay between particularism and principalism (Hammersley, 2009), but it is also potentially about understanding the way that virtue and vice can cause us to do good and bad things. Being 'ethical' is thus about developing a deep, personal understanding of virtue rather than being politically correct enough to espouse bioethical principles. Above all, it is about being authentic rather than slipping into the easy assumptions of principalism and justifying a pre-determined course of action based on whichever principle happens to most conveniently 'fit' with the research design.

Wisdom and uncertainty are key themes in this book, and are interlinked in relation to research ethics for qualitative researchers. In conducting qualitative research, front-ended 'ethical approval' will never capture the uncertainty and unpredictable nature of the research process itself. Here, the researcher must rely on their own personal values and virtues in order to handle ethical issues in the field. This is about practical wisdom (or what Aristotle (1906) termed *phronesis*). Getting better at handling ethical issues only comes with practice, experience and learning from the good (and bad) example of others; learning, in the process, whom to respect and whom to ignore.

Wisdom comes with practice and experience, and understanding the need to respond to unpredictable circumstances. Ethics is a bit like jazz. It is about more than simply following the notes on the page. It demands improvisation and an ability to be an interpreter of moods and situations. No two renditions will ever be exactly the same. In research ethics, a similar ability to think on one's feet is required as researchers need to deal day-to-day with unique challenges. The rigidity of the ethical approval process and the mantras of principalism offer little assistance in facing this reality.

References

Allen, G. (2008) 'Getting beyond form filling: the role of institutional governance in human research ethics', *Journal of Academic Ethics*, 6(2), 105–16.

Aristotle (1906) *The Ethics of Aristotle: The Nicomachean Ethics*, trans. G. H. Lewes, London: Walter Scott.

Cawley, M. J., Martin, J. E. and Johnson, J. A. (2000) 'A virtues approach to personality', *Personality and Individual Differences*, **28**(5), 997–1013.

Cheng, M. (2009) *Changing Academics: Quality audit and its perceived impact*, Saarbrucken, Germany: VDM Verlag.

Coggon, D. (2007) 'Research ethics committees: a personal perspective', *Research Ethics Review*, **3**(4), 118–21.

Darwin, C. R. (1859) *On the Origin of Species by Means of Natural Selection, or the Preservation of Favoured Races in the Struggle for Life*, 1st edn, London: John Murray (online) <http://darwin-online.org.uk/> (accessed 20 November 2009).

Gilligan, C., Ward, J. V. and Bardige, B. (1988) *Mapping the Moral Domain*, Cambridge, MA: Harvard University Press.

Grayson, J. P. and Myles, R. (2005) 'How research ethic boards are undermining survey research on Canadian university students', *Journal of Academic Ethics*, **2**(4), 293–314.

Guillemin, M. and Gilliam, L. (2004) 'Ethics, reflexivity, and "ethically important moments" in research', *Qualitative Inquiry*, **10**(2), 261–80.

Hammersley, M. (2009) 'Against the ethicists: on the evils of ethical regulation', *International Journal of Social Research Methodology*, **12**(3), 211–25.

Hubert, J. and Hollins, S. (2007) 'Ethnographic research in closed institutions: ethical issues', *Research Ethics Review*, **3**(4): 122–6.

Hughes, J. (2005) 'Ethical cleansing? The process of gaining 'ethical approval' for a new research project exploring performance in place of war', *Research in Drama Education*, **10**(2), 229–32.

Humphreys, S. (2007) 'Drip-feeding: how the pharmaceutical industry influences research ethics committees', *Research Ethics Review*, **3**(4), 113–17.

Jamrozik, K. (2004) 'Research ethics paperwork: what is the plot we seem to have lost?' *British Medical Journal*, 329: 286–7.

Kiley, M. and Mullins, G. (2005) 'Supervisors' conceptions of research: what are they?' *Scandinavian Journal of Educational Research*, **49**(3), 245–62.

LaRossa, R. (1977) *Conflict and Power in Marriage: Expecting the first child*, Beverly Hills, CA: Sage.

Lea, J. (2009) *Political Correctness and Higher Education*, London: Routledge.

Loury, G. C. (1994) 'Self-censorship in public discourse', *Rationality and Society*, **6**(4), 428–61.

Macfarlane, B. (2009) *Researching with Integrity: The ethics of academic enquiry*, London: Routledge.

Martin, E. and Booth, J. (eds) (2003) *Courageous Research*, Altona, Australia: Common Ground.

Pincoffs, E. (1986) *Quandaries and Virtues: Against reductivism in ethics*, Lawrence, KS: University Press of Kansas.

Pring, R. (2001) 'The virtues and vices of an educational researcher', *Journal of Philosophy of Education*, **35**(3), 407–21.

Ritzer, G. (2000) *The McDonaldization of Society*, Thousand Oaks, CA: Pine Forge.

Tilley, S. A. (2008) 'A troubled dance: doing the work of research ethics review', *Journal of Academic Ethics*, **6**(2), 91–104.

Watson, D. and Amoah, M. (eds) (2007) *The Dearing Report: Ten years on*, London: Institute of Education.

Wiles, R., Crow, G., Heath, S. and Charles, V. (2008) 'The management of confidentiality and anonymity in social research', *International Journal of Social Research Methodology*, **11**(5), 417–28.

Yu, K. (2008) 'Confidentiality revisited', *Journal of Academic Ethics*, **6**(2), 161–72.

Chapter 4

Relocating truths in the qualitative research paradigm

Lana van Niekerk and Maggi Savin-Baden

Introduction

This chapter explores strategies that might be used in the establishment of truths in qualitative research. The motivation for this article arose from our experiences of managing the complexities of notions of truth and rigour in health research. This chapter argues for the development of strategies that are in keeping with the ontological foundations of work undertaken, the importance of making explicit strategies and stances that are adopted, and recognizing the complex interactions of the sociopolitical agenda at play in the research.

The arguments we present here might be seen to violate many postmodern guidelines for inquiry, which are in themselves insubstantial in terms of potential for application, particularly those aligned with sceptical postmodernism and all with extreme orientations. We suggest a late modern stance would be more appropriate and helpful since it is a position that embraces some of the ideas from the postmodern camp but offers realistic implementation possibilities. The focus here is not to contribute to postmodernism per se, but to give careful consideration to contextually situated influences that might shape research practices in particular ways. Thus we argue here that truths in qualitative research are spaces of mediation, and that our biographies, positions and practices affect how we see and practice truths in qualitative research.

Truths as spaces of mediation

The limitation of truth as a concept is that there is often a perceived and expected moral value which is, in the main, located within the stance of the individual. Thus the production of knowledge is complicated by a number of factors, not least of which is that reality is understood and mediated by the reflective process. To shift from truth to truths moves beyond positivism to interpretivism. Such a position is where we acknowledge that truths are complex and fragile, and need to be seen as places where issues of power, consent and negotiation are mediated by our own values and biographies. While we recognize that the categorization of approaches in particular locales is deeply problematic and does not recognize sufficient difference, particularly in discussions relating to poststructuralism and postmodernism, it is important to recognize that positivism and postpositivism are used as polar opposites, and that this distinction tends to muddy notions of and stances towards truths. The positivist paradigm is organized around a normative epistemology, which contends that 'normal is what is most representative in a larger population, and it is to that "normal" population that generalizations are directed' (Denzin, 1997: 7). Criteria and strategies regularly used within a postpositivist orientation have been problematized by those adopting a postmodern or poststructuralist reading, which rejects both the ontological premise for trustworthiness criteria and the purpose for attempting to establish these. No attempt is made to propose that a stable reality exists around which lasting theories can be developed, hence nullifying attempts to repeat research actions with an expectation that the same results could be obtained. Issues of representation and legitimization nonetheless continue to be at the forefront of researchers' minds.

Mays and Pope (1995) propose that all research is selective and that the researcher cannot capture the literal truth of events in any sense. They believe it depends on collecting particular sorts of evidence through the prism of particular methods, each of which has its strengths and weaknesses. In contrast, Denzin (1997: 9) reiterated the critical-poststructuralist argument that 'an entirely new set of criteria, divorced from the positivist and post positivist traditions, need to be constructed'. Such criteria would have to flow from the qualitative project, and should foreground 'subjectivity, emotionality, feeling and other antifoundational criteria' (Denzin, 1997: 9). Postmodernists believe that validity or authority is determined by the critical understandings produced; in other words, the only expectation should be that situated understandings are produced.

Our stories and stances

The influence of postmodern thinking on the construction of truths in our projects was informed by our reading of the futility of attempts to achieve 'stable', 'valid' and thus generalizable findings. Knowledge constructions that necessarily involve the exclusion of experiences that fall outside 'norm' behaviour, in order to ensure generalizability, do not in our opinion contribute the types of understanding that are required to understand complex phenomena. Furthermore, most research available for reading had been generated in developed countries of the world and with samples that often resemble a small minority in developing countries. We adopted an approach that sought to transform authoritative claims of truth into speculative suggestions that might have application value in complex/multifaceted contexts.

Lana: As a South African who grew up in the apartheid era, and is now experiencing the transition of our society, I appreciate how the powerful influences of government and political party politics penetrate personal domains, such as religion, relationships and work. The traditional rural environment in which I grew up provided a sheltered childhood in a close-knit community that was strongly shaped by paternalistic principles which were used to justify apartheid policies and practices. My father, in his positioning as a critic of both his peers and dominant discourse, created the freedom for me to question taken-for-granted practices; however, my insight and experiences are limited to that of a white, middle-class woman who benefited from social and educational structures created during apartheid. My personal journey to understand the impact of power and privilege as social determinants is ongoing, and has been guided by close working relationships with (especially black) colleagues.

My professional journey led me to become interested in discrimination experienced by people with psychiatric disability, and to recognize how ineffective current services were in promoting equitable participation in work. Health research in South Africa rarely took into account the political and/or social forces that might have influenced the questions asked and the answers constructed. For example, very little research explores why persons with psychiatric disability have remained on the margins of society and, in fact, the disability movement.

The absence of political power and will, required to bring about change, has been ignored – and was something that I found deeply troublesome.

Maggi: Although I grew up in a white middle-class family in the north of England I was always aware of what I was not; not working-class, not from Pakistan and not underprivileged. This awareness was enshrined in our family values largely by my father, who had grown up in a working-class family and as a head teacher in a primary school, which unusually had 80 per cent Pakistani children attending, sought to do all he could to try to improve their lives. After school I moved 200 miles to London to attend college and then to work. The notion of difference always fascinated. Yet I always seemed to be conscious of how unaware I was, and how difficult it was to even begin to understand the impact of stereotyping on people's lives. Visiting South Africa over a number of years has taught me much, not least that my values about what counted as privilege and oppression were distorted by the cultures and spaces in which I grew up. Yet I still struggle to see truths and realize that dialogue can be both ends of dis/empowerment.

Shifts towards truths

In previous research experiences our focus had been on establishing trustworthiness that would fit within a postpositivist orientation. Both of us have at times sought to adopt some or all of the four criteria for the establishment of trustworthiness, namely *credibility, transferability, dependability* and *confirmability*. To achieve these we have used strategies such as member checking, peer debriefing, thick description and the establishment of an audit trail. These strategies were chosen because they were easy to understand, provided structured guidelines and seemed useful. However, their limited application value became clear, and will be illustrated with the use of an example.

We adopted the interpretive biography approach to explore the influences that impact on the work-lives of persons with psychiatric disability in the Western Cape, South Africa. Data construction involved the use of narrative interviews and observation. While the construction of narratives during interviews served as a primary source of data, participants' unfolding life stories made a rich contribution to data construction. Research within this group required recognition of sociopolitical factors and attention to situated experiences. Location of truths became a prominent consideration in the study to counteract generalized societal assumptions about persons with psychiatric disability, some of which had been internalized by participants in the study.

Our researcher stances initially moved toward postmodernism although we believed there might also be shortcomings with it as both a methodology and method. Postmodernism comprises two broad (general) orientations which are divergent, even contradictory: the 'sceptical' postmodernists and the 'affirmative' postmodernists. According to Rosenau (1992), sceptical postmodernists (or merely sceptics) draw their inspiration from Continental European philosophies that include Heidegger and Nietzsche, and are concerned with the dark side of postmodernism, 'the post-modernism of despair, the post-modernism that speaks of the immediacy of death, the demise of the subject, the end of the author, the impossibility of truth, the abrogation of the Order of Representation' (Rosenau, 1992: 15). Conversely, affirmative postmodernists (or affirmatives) agree with the critique of modernity but hold a more hopeful and optimistic view of the postmodern age. They are either open to positive political action or content with recognizing visionary, celebratory, personal non-dogmatic projects across a broad spectrum of social movements; importantly, their intellectual practice remains non-dogmatic, tentative and non-ideological... The issue of representation also seems to be one of the most contentious areas of disagreement between qualitative researchers who hold different perspectives. This for us was unsurprising, since to debate the issue of representation would usually draw into question the very processes with which the voices of participants are believed to be captured and presented. We consider that such opinions are, in turn, strongly influenced by views that are held about the nature of truth.

New strategies and different stances

The combined impact of literature reviewed and our attempt to apply theoretical constructs in practice has led to the development of strategies which we believe will guide all researchers doing health research. These strategies are proposed with an acceptance that no claims can be made of a truth that will remain stable. We suggest three options, namely:

- negotiated honesties
- verisimilitude
- locating power for reconscientization.

Negotiated honesties

Negotiated honesties reflect the idea that there needs to be a sense that what counts as trust-worthiness and truth is a negotiated position in research. It seemed unacceptable to us to talk about collaborative inquiry when there is no evidence of collaboration; to advocate cli-ent-centred practice but leave the client voiceless in the reporting of the study; and to lay claim to an interpretive study but show no evidence of interpretation or, if this is done, not share those interpretations with participants (for further discussion on this see Savin-Baden and Fisher, 2002). We would argue that professional discourse transcends the worlds of research and professional practice. What we mean here is that debates about ethics, conduct and accountability can be distinguished by differences of theory and practical action, but they can never actually be isolated from one another. The difficulties with many of the current arguments and suggestions for validity are that they are generally located in straight-forward assumptions about notions of truth. To accept current perspectives seemed to us to lay claim, through such practices as member checking, to a validity that is often seen as rela-tively unproblematic.

Instead we suggest that honesties should be an instantiation of a new stance. 'Honesties', following Stronach and colleagues (2002), allows the acknowledgement of fragility, messi-ness and supercomplexity. Yet there is a sense that the process of negotiating honesties involves constantly moving in and out of a hermeneutic circle. Hermeneutics holds as a point of departure the interpretation of texts, or exegesis, with the main theme being that *'the meaning of a part can only be understood if it is related to the whole'* (Alvesson and Skoldberg, 2000: 53) (italics in original). Hermeneutics propose solutions to the apparently unsolvable contradiction of the so-called hermeneutic circle (that parts can only be understood from the whole, and the whole only from the parts). Attention is initially focused on some part, insights gained are then tentatively related to the whole upon which new insights are gained; focus is again returned to the part studied (Alvesson and Skoldberg, 2000: 53). The circle of *objective* hermeneutics considers the relationship between the part and the whole as explained above. Alethic hermeneutics advocates a different cycle, one that considers the tension between preunderstanding and understanding: 'The common trait of the hermeneutic circles (and more than two are conceivable) is that they present a processual, dialecting solution, alternating between the poles in a contradiction which at first sight, and regarded statistic- ally, seems unsolvable'(Alvesson and Skoldberg, 2000: 54).

What this seems to point to is liminality. The state of liminality tends to be characterized by a stripping-away of old identities, an oscillation between states and personal transforma- tion. Liminal spaces are thus suspended states, and serve as transformative in function, as someone moves from one state or position to another. The idea of a liminal state is taken from ethnographic studies into rituals, for example rites of passage, such as the initiation of adolescent Xhosa boys into manhood. Turner (1969) adopted the term 'liminality' (from the Latin *limen*, 'boundary or threshold') to characterize the transitional space/time within which the rites were conducted. We suggest the ability to engage and work with notions of honesties is often a space of liminality. There is a sense in much of the literature (see for example Malesevic, 2006) that liminal spaces are ones in which an individual stays for a time, and then emerges into a new place or position. Yet research texts that address liminality (or forms of disjunction and stuck-ness) have rather underplayed its complexity, as both a concept and as a position. Instead we would suggest that in some areas of our lives we tend to remain in liminal spaces for months, possibly years, before the dilemmas and concerns are resolved.

Furthermore, there is also a sense in which it is possible to remain in a liminal space along- side normal life, thus it is as if liminality is occurring at a metalevel where ideas and concepts are merging, and at the same time everyday living occurs on a parallel track. The shift into a liminal space can begin when we seek to represent people through stories, and in so doing fall into an 'honesty trap'. Issues of representation and empowerment fly in our faces. For example, the tendency, when biographies are written, is that the production will start in family history (Denzin, 1989). However, the tendency in this study was for participants to initiate biographies at the point of their first experience of psychiatric impairment. This was an interesting departure from the usual convention, one that might point to the severity of disruption experienced by participants when they first experienced psychiatric impairment. This became for us not only a space of interruption, but also a liminal space. This was evident when participants needed to manage sometimes conflicting notions of identity which required them to balance competing views and beliefs.

Verisimilitude

Denzin proposed deconstructive verisimilitude as a strategy that might be used to provide legitimate answers to the research questions. He argues that it is vital to examine what 'seems to be true', in order to consider if, when and how something might not be true. Here we use data to develop the argument posited by Denzin. A strand of conversation that flowed through three consequent research interviews is presented below:

> *First interview*: Nicolas stopped playing snooker, his favourite leisure activity, because he decided his friends no longer wished him to be a member of their club when they knew of his psychiatric disability. He made this decision when he discovered, after his discharge from a psychiatric hospital, that he was no longer included in the first team. He 'read' rejection into his team members' actions and thus withdrew, thereby losing the activity he loved more than any other as well as social contact with his friends. Other

social contexts were made uncomfortable by the fact that Nicolas, unlike his friends, did not use alcohol.

Second interview: Conversation takes place during which Nicolas is considering the motivations his friends might have had for their rejection of him. He reflects on the situation and considers all possibilities, in the process concluding that they perhaps were being 'over-protective' in that they did not want to expose him to the pressure during matches for the A team. He left the interview without mentioning his intention to discuss the matter with his friends, but returned to the *third interview* weeks later to report that he had been reinstated in the A team, and that he was happy to be involved with the club and his friends again.

The structured interview provided a reflective space in which Nicolas reconsidered the behaviour of his friends and thus his own assumptions. His initial explanation of events was informed by his own anticipation of stigma. However, alternative explanations were generated during deeper reflection, thus leading to a change in his behaviour. It is not clear to what extent Nicolas's initial perception of being stigmatized was informed by an unwelcoming environment, or by anticipated stigma. It could very well be that Nicolas's friends underwent a similar process of mediating their own feelings and decisions. However, by the time of the third interview the situation was different for all concerned, and ideas around stigma were being reconstructed, based on different sets of experiences.

Rather than merely confirming understandings of interviews that preceded the member check, a framework of categories (which was the outcome of early analysis processes) was discussed with the participants. Questions that had come to mind since the interview were discussed with the participant; often such questions highlighted what looked to be contradictions. The process allowed participants to 'revisit' their own shared experiences, often adding depth or specificity. It also allowed them to 'rethink' their own constructions in the light of an emerging framework which included the views of other participants. Verification was not done by asking participants to 'check' interpretations and 'approve' correctness. Instead, discussion was re-entered and participants would further elaborate or clarify their responses. This approach was used successfully with Jessica, a beauty therapist.

First interview: Jessica expressed her shame in sharing her 'fragmented' work history, with a dominant pattern of terminating work after three months. However, she emphasized that she was, in fact, a very good worker and that she would be welcomed back at any of her previous places of work. This initially seemed to be a contradiction, thus calling Jessica's construction of herself as a good worker into question. Jessica's merit as a good worker was confirmed when, at the time of our *second interview* (six months later), she was working as a locum in the salon from which she had resigned two weeks earlier (at almost double her original salary). Jessica's merits as a good worker was confirmed; she arrived for our *fourth interview* having come directly from a breakfast meeting with her former employer. During casual conversation she shared how her former employer referred to her as 'the best investment she had ever made' and also asked Jessica to 'stay in touch'.

The complexity of influences that impacted on Jessica's decisions could only be understood by exploring the verisimilitude of how seemingly contradicting influences as these impacted on her decisions. In fact, this is the only way to reconcile the complexity of influences that shaped her thinking and behaviour. Without a thorough consideration of the verisimilitude of conditions, an oversimplified understanding of Jessica's ability as a worker would have led to judgements that were superficial and unjust.

Prolonged engagement was something we found provided an essential foundation for exploring the verisimilitude of findings, in that behaviour patterns and the nature of relationships formed added to the understandings that were gained during interviews. In the process of data construction, serious attention was given to explore multiple truths at every step of the process, without an expectation that there would be a single or stable answer to complex questions.

Locating power for reconscientization

Special consideration is needed to limit the potentially negative impact of power imbalances at each stage of the research process. Unequal power relationships impact negatively on data construction because they inevitably interfere with open and honest sharing of experiences. A constant awareness of power, its sources and consideration of the potential limitations imposed on the research project could reduce negative consequences. As a point of departure researchers have to recognize that they inevitably operate from a position of power and privilege. Consideration of this position is required to understand the potential negative consequences for the research project.

When the researcher does not 'belong' to the group that is the focus of the research, power imbalances will be more marked. A first step to curb negative consequences of the power imbalance that inevitably exist between researcher and participant is to acknowledge the imbalance and explicate its sources as far as possible. Personal constructions of privilege associated with race, class, gender, sexual orientation, education, religion, health status and employment require consideration. Issues that further magnified the power imbalance in the research example included participants identifying themselves as belonging to a socially disenfranchised group, their experiences and anticipation of stigma, and connotations of previous helper–helped relationships. However, researchers should guard against a tendency to overemphasize difference by juxtaposing contrasting positions, so confirming that the two groups are legitimately different.

Denzin highlighted that biographical texts 'are gendered, class productions, reflecting the biases and values of patriarchy and the middle class' (Denzin, 1989). Many have argued against the notion of identity, suggesting that it delineates people too clearly from a Western stance. Further Malesevic says, 'If the social actors in their every day life operate with the terms such as "identity", "ethnic identity" or "national identity" as something self-evident and unproblematic this does not mean that a researcher should treat these categories in the same manner' (Malesevic 2006:20).

Thus linkages to a group with a reduced social standing could be expected to have an impact on the identity construction of its members. As such, participants' narratives could situate themselves closer or further away from a social disenfranchised or marginalized group. In so doing, the reality of being associated with such a group could influence identity construction to a larger or lesser extent. Freire adopted the term 'conscientization' to describe the process whereby people come to understand that their view of the world and their place in it is shaped by social and historical forces which work against their own interests. He argued that the oppressed lack a critical understanding of their reality. To them the world is something that is fixed, to which they must adapt (Freire, 1974).

Data construction is almost always done with an 'other' in mind. The presence of the 'other' inevitably influences the prominence given to key events, both in the telling of stories and in the interpretation of the meaning of such events. The process of constructing (and interpreting) data, with the 'other' in mind, leads to a reappraisal of key events, foregrounding those aspects in which the 'other' is deemed interested. In the research example participants knew that they were telling their story to a researcher with an interest in promoting equity and the participation of people with psychiatric disability in work. Participants might therefore have favoured positive experiences and stories. In the researcher's mind the 'other' was an intellectual community of policy makers and service providers. The dynamic process of telling a story with an 'other' in mind would inevitably require a reconscientization of what is considered pertinent and relevant. This should be done to limit a natural tendency for data construction to be shaped according to anticipated outcomes.

Recommendations

We suggest that a late modern stance then should move away from positivist and postpositivist notions of validity and instead seek to develop honesties and understand truths through the questions raised in Table 4.1.

Table 4.1 Relocating truths

Stance	Questions
Negotiated honesties	What does collaboration mean in this context and who decides? Which data is privileged and which is not? Whose voices proliferate? How are data managed, interpreted and presented, and who decides? What possible explanations might be offered for what seem to be contradictions? How to foster sharing of uncertainties or probabilities during data collection. Which components of shared experience/narrative seem to be in transition (in other words, aspects of identity/narrative are evolving)?
Verisimilitude	What reality or truths are expressed that seem to be accepted without any scrutiny? Which experiences/opinions initially seem improbable? What conditions might show these to be real? What contradictions are revealed; could these be reconciled in any way?
Locating power for reconscientization	What will contribute to a position of power and privilege, including gender, class, race, religion, employment and health status? In what possible ways could power and privilege impact on questions asked and answers constructed? Who will benefit from the findings obtained and/or knowledge constructed in the research? In what ways will this impact on the research process? Will this contribute to imbalances in terms of power and privilege?

Conclusion and reflections

Criticisms raised against positivism include that in some cases it legitimizes the preference for powerful, normative research, and that fact and results have been used in an ad hoc fashion to '"prove" the value of subjective political policy preferences' (Rosenau 1992: 10). The intention and outcome of research within this framework tends to use a static and predictable view of 'normality' as a point of departure for the development of assessments and classifications that serve to highlight 'abnormality' without consideration of diversity.

It is our view that the extent to which a piece of research succeeds in situating experiences within the broader social and political context should determine the credibility and quality of the study. Since knowledge is socially constructed and research findings are influenced by the social and political situatedness of researchers and participants, key values that shape research outcomes are best made explicit. A late-modern orientation, with strategies proposed in this article, proved useful in health research. We suggest that a new stance, one of postmodern possibilities which embraces negotiated honesties, verisimilitude and locates power for reconscientization, should be a next stage for those undertaking qualitative research in complex spaces.

References

Alvesson, M. and Skoldberg, K. (2000) *Reflexive Methodology: New vistas for qualitative research*, London: Sage.

Denzin, N. K. (1989) *Qualitative Research Methods: Interpretive biography*, Newbury Park, CA: Sage.

Denzin, N. K. (1997) *Interpretive Ethnography*, Newbury Park, CA: Sage.

Freire, P. (1974) *Education: The practice of freedom*, London: Writers and Readers Co-operative.

Malesevic, S. (2006) *Identity as Ideology: Understanding ethnicity and nationalism*, New York: Palgrave Macmillan.

Mays, N. and Pope, C. (1995) 'Rigour in qualitative research', *British Medical Journal*, 311, 109–12.

Rosenau, P. M. (1992) *Post-Modernism and the Social Sciences: Insights, inroads, and intrusions*, Princeton, NJ: Princeton University Press.

Savin-Baden, M. and Fisher, A. (2002) 'Negotiating honesties in the research process', *British Journal of Occupational Therapy*, **65**(4), 191–3.

Stronach, I., Corbin, B., McNamara, O., Stark, S. and Warne, T. (2002) 'Towards an uncertain politics of professionalism: teacher and nurse identities in flux', *Journal of Educational Policy*, **17**(1), 109–38.

Turner, V. (1969) *The Ritual Process: Structure and anti-structure*, London: Routledge.

Chapter 5

Imagining intersectionality and the spaces in between

Theories and processes of socially transformative knowing

Rebecca Ropers-Huilman and Kelly T. Winters

Introduction

Many of our colleagues have argued that there is a need for research that reflects the complexity of contemporary theoretical and paradigmatic understandings. We share this view. We find that our own thinking is often informed by paradigms and theories that call on researchers to question and reject unifying definitions, grand narratives and claims of universal truths. As such, our goal in this chapter is to move in a different direction from the authoritative tone that is sometimes present in the 'overview of theory' portions of books on qualitative research. In place of the list of definitions, categories, charts and graphs that can contribute toward a directive, how-to discourse, we would like to consider what it might mean to listen, engage and communicate with the many voices, stories, identities and positionalities that can compose theory.

In order to illustrate these complex interrelationships we choose to consider intersectionality as one way to imagine the relationship between theorizing, knowing and implicating in qualitative research. Intersectionality argues that unique perspectives, social institutions and identities are created by the ways in which intersecting identities and related social structures create a fluid and complex 'wholeness' in and among individuals and groups. To understand this wholeness is to attempt to make sense of the many and sometimes seemingly contradictory messages, questions and perspectives that researchers and participants engage with in the research process. This engagement is always partial, and grounded in the local and global contexts in which it is based.

Throughout the chapter we explore the use of the theory of intersectionality, as well as its complexities in informing research, education and action. We look to sources both inside and outside academic theory to explore the concept of intersectionality and the ways in which researchers are implicated by multiple ways of knowing and being. We then consider its use for cultural analysis, arguing that the ways we learn about our social world have relevance for the work we do in academic settings. In one example, we explore the new questions that are raised when we use the concept of intersectionality to consider the recent media interpretations of the arrest of Professor Gates, Jr. by Sergeant Crowley in Cambridge, Massachusetts.

In addition to race, class and gender, researchers are positioned in myriad other ways that affect their patterns and desires for knowing. We argue for an acknowledgement of the fluidity of our knowing, and assert that how and what researchers know and do in non-academic settings has implications for academic and scholarly research. We keep at the heart of this chapter our belief that research can be of use in social justice and transformational work, even though justice and change are in and of themselves complex, ambiguous and contested concepts. Throughout, we consider the implications that intersectionality raises for qualitative researchers who are positioned within social institutions.

Intersectionality

Intersectionality is a concept that has developed over several decades, and has been adopted in many different research contexts. Intersectionality draws attention to the ways in which unidimensional analyses based on one meaningful social category tend to privilege and render dominant one identity, while obscuring the relationship between other identities, social contexts, histories and lived experiences (Cole, 2009; Crenshaw, 1993; McCall, 2005). For example, within the higher education research context in the United States, the lives of women of colour (a term broadly signifying those women who do not identify as white) have not received sufficient attention from research focusing on women (which tends to use as a normalizing focus the experiences of white women) and on race (which tends to use as a normalizing focus the experiences of men of colour). Grounded in feminist theory and more specifically critical race feminism, intersectionality points to the ways in which people live 'layered identities and can simultaneously experience oppression and privilege' (Dill *et al.*, 2007: 629). It is interdisciplinary, intellectually transformative and has the capacity to generate new ways of thinking, knowing, and interacting (Cole, 2009; McCall, 2005; Wing, 2003).

While some assert that intersectionality encompasses 'the examination of race, sex, class, national origin, and sexual orientation, and how their combination plays out in various settings' (Delgado and Stefancic, 2001: 51), others consider the specific categories of analysis are not quite as set. Intersectionality also considers how the components and interpretations of identity are interconnected to each other, and made different given particular manifestations of other identities (Parker and Lynn, 2009). How one comes to know these identities is also shaped by interactions with individuals and social institutions. As Taylor suggests, 'In considering intersectionality, it seems urgent to think about what matters and why, given that all junctions are not equally picturesque or dangerous' (2009: 190).

Context and the negotiation of lived experiences may take shape and be interpreted differently because of uniquely intersecting experiences. Such interpretations of difference lead to localized understandings, even as they are rooted in larger social systems. Different people interpret different aspects of their lives as being dominant or less significant in influencing who they are and how they understand their lived experiences (Foster, 1994; Grillo and Wildman, 1997; Naples, 2007; Williams, 1991). Intersectionality urges researchers to consider how individual and social constructions of 'difference' and 'commonality' matter in ways which are intertwined. The local manifestations of those constructions have significant consequences for maintaining or changing social structures.

A focus on the intersections of multiple identities in both individual and larger social circumstances is central to critical race feminism (Wing, 1997, 2003), and of multiracial feminism from North American contexts. Within this context, multiracial feminism, as described by Zinn and Dill (2003), 'asserts that gender is constructed by a range of interlocking inequalities' which work simultaneously and systematically. It 'emphasizes the intersectional nature of hierarchies at all levels of social life,' noting that 'intersecting forms of domination produce both oppression and opportunity.' Multiracial feminism also 'highlights the relational nature of dominance and subordination, insisting that women's differences are connected in systematic ways,' and insists that 'within the constraints of race, class, and gender oppression, women create viable lives for themselves, their families, and their communities'. Further, this thinking in multiracial feminism encompasses multiple methodological approaches to knowing, noting that 'marginalized locations are well suited for grasping social relations that remained obscure from more privileged vantage points.' Finally, it brings together the diverse and ever-changing experiences of women as individuals and groups (Zinn and Dill, 2003: 357–8).

It is important to examine issues of power as manifested in individual relationships, identities and larger social systems which structure interactions and self-constructions. As Delgado and Stefancic articulate, 'Categories and subgroups, then, are not just matters of theoretical interest. How we frame them determines who has power, voice, and representation and who does not' (2001: 55). In research and knowledge construction, then, those who determine which identities should be framed as dominant have the potential to enact a power that could shape both the possibility of social understandings and equitable (or inequitable) social institutions. And, while some people are very aware of their own multiple identities, others are less pressed to consider the resulting intersections and the meanings they might have for their participation in society.

It is important to note that while intersectionality has more often been understood and engaged with as it relates to individual and group identities, it is also a tool for examining social institutions (Dill *et al.*, 2007; McCall, 2005). Specifically, intersectionality is useful for understanding how power in society is manifest in systems of privilege and oppression (Dill, 2009). Approaches to knowing, then, that are based in intersectional understandings are focused on both individual experiences of multiplicative identities, and the social structures that simultaneously give those identities meaning, and perpetuate privilege and oppression on a larger scale. These broad-scale and critical analyses can be understood through lenses of structural intersectionality (wherein lived experiences are qualitatively different for those at a particular intersection), political intersectionality (where political efforts associated with discrete parts of identities can actually further discriminate against members of particular intersectional identity groups), and representational intersectionality (where cultural representations reinforce particular constructions that limit experiences of members of some groups) (Crenshaw, 2009: 214).

Theory and research into change

Theories related to social justice are variously positioned around the concept of change, whether that means changing social structures, changing what we know or changing the allocation of resources. Intersectionality is informed by feminism (Dill, 2009), an approach that uses knowledge and theory 'to inform effective politics' (McCann and Kim, 2003: 1–2). Changes in sociopolitical structures involve changes in both knowledge and what is intelligible within discourses informing those structures. Feminism posits that women's contributions to knowledge 'will not merely widen the canvas, but result in a shift of perspective enabling us to see a very different picture' (Narayan, 2003: 308).

These theories also explicitly and implicitly suggest that the identities of the knowers matter in how knowledge towards change is created. For example, critical race feminism has been formed by women of colour who have contributed to understanding how identities shape experience in educational, legal and other social settings (Cho, 1997; Gilmore, 2003; Montoya, 2000, 2003; Williams, 2003). As Wing (2003) notes, critical race feminism has developed in response to the limitations in legal, critical race and feminist theories. Critical race feminism suggests that no one unidimensional category accurately encompasses all persons for whom that category is a part of their identity. Instead, intersectional identities embed difference within any social group or organization, are always present and shift over time and according to context (Alémán, 2003; Berry and Mizelle, 2006; Harding, 1991; Hartsock, 2003).

Theories of intersectionality can contribute to locally grounded understandings of justice and equity. Such understandings can enable researchers to envision both the possibilities and consequences of change. If qualitative researchers take seriously the tenets of intersectionality in shaping research and knowing – in recognizing that the contexts of ideas and identities matter – what are the implications for their listening and learning?

Transformative possibilities: intersectionality in research/ learning/knowing

In this section, we explore how intersectionality implicates our research stances and roles as scholars. As we have previously noted, intersectionality is one way to disrupt, transgress and deconstruct unified, homogenized categories of identity, and simultaneously bring forth the possibility of changing social structures. What is the role of qualitative research in participating in these possibilities for transformation?

Which identities matter in the context in which I am learning?

Intersectionality suggests that we are composite, whole individuals whose membership in groups matters, but is not definitive. All individuals within a group do not have the same 'essence'. Yet, as Collins (1990) noted in her landmark text, *Black Feminist Thought*, to suggest that all persons from any socially constructed group are different does not imply that they do not share common experiences that affect the ways they experience and live in the world. For black women and other historically oppressed groups in the United States, their positioning has led them to find and develop ways 'to escape from, survive in, and/or oppose prevailing social and economic injustice' (Collins, 2003: 325).

Intersectionality, then, would suggest that qualitative researchers would do well to engage in critical reflection – with participants and focused on systems – on the various configurations of identities that are most salient to given situations, opportunities and outcomes. It would also suggest that the salience of identities be explored in terms of how resistance, power, discrimination and agency were constructed from within unique intersectional places. Given that marginalized people are often able to know differently than those situated at the centre, listening for different forms and outcomes of meaning-making is essential to transformative understanding.

At the same time, paying attention to the larger social institutions that inform the ways people live and are able to name their experiences and situations is critically important. How do the identities of individuals get constructed as part of that larger social system, within both global and local contexts? How does acknowledging the meaningful intersections of social categories that are constructed over time help researchers see social institutions as perpetuating or interrupting those categories? What is 'normal' within a given way of thinking or being? What is unusual or constitutes a rupture? What are the desired and/or unanticipated effects of those norms, ruptures and structured invisibilities?

How do my multiple identities affect my relationships and knowing?

Intersectionality also asks scholars to recognize how their identities, the interpretations of which cannot be controlled, are implicated in knowledge construction and social interactions. As researchers construct their work, seeking an ongoing understanding of the dominant messages and silences that inform their own knowing is a critically important task. If knowledge is partial, complex and intersectional, how can research be conducted that recognizes and honours uncertainty and ambiguity? Can these complexities be informed differently if viewed from a different perspective or with different priorities? What needs to be in place for scholars to see differently, more inclusively and with attention, to working towards authentic collaboration with people from different intersectional places, who may be making different negotiations? Collins emphasizes the difficulty of moving beyond ignorance (or presumed neutrality) towards equitable knowledge and action, in noting that 'Reclaiming black feminist intellectual traditions involves much more than developing black feminist analyses using standard epistemological criteria. It also involves challenging the very terms of intellectual discourse itself' (2003: 331).

The scholarly community is implicated and intertwined with the larger community, and privilege and oppression are part of this enmeshment. Qualitative research methods have certainly called on scholars to bracket their experiences, disclose their perspectives or describe how their identities might affect (or bias) the research. We suggest, though, that those methods are far from complete. Researchers simply cannot know the boundaries of knowledge. Not all research or knowing can be comprehensive. For those reasons, it is important to position oneself and take one's place in a much larger conversation, facilitating the hearing of voices of those with marginalized intersectional identities whenever possible. At the same time, work towards social change and justice requires partnerships with those who can question the silences that are currently structured into our collective knowledge.

How can researchers build transformative partnerships?

Intersectionality, in its calls to recognize multiple identities and move towards equity, recognizes that no one individual or group can make the kinds of far-reaching change that is needed to transform social institutions. As such, part of the implicatedness for scholars who wish to take intersectionality seriously relates to the need to reach across categories of being, to find connection and strength in multiplicity and diversity. The need for collaboration in multiple forms is clear for multiple – if complex – reasons.

First, positions and views of the world are partial, and as such, privileged interpretations of experience may become dominant lenses through which epistemological and ontological meanings are made. If change is a goal within social institutions, and if researchers sincerely want to inform that change, then they should seek out the voices that may be positioned differently relative to the power structures that have produced and reproduced these social structures. As Smith writes:

> from the vantage point of the colonized, a position from which I write, and choose to privilege, the term 'research' is inextricably linked to European imperialism and colonialism. The word itself, 'research,' is probably one of the dirtiest words in the indigenous world's vocabulary.
>
> (Smith, 1999: 1)

Since the research endeavour and the researcher are woven into larger social structures which have used the production of knowledge for colonizing practices, it is important to consider how formulations of social change that come from research perspectives are similarly problematic. Social change is not an innocent practice, as change is grounded in intention toward a different way of being, the effects of which are not neutral. In order to limit the potential negative effects of researchers' attempts to engage in social change, we emphasize here the importance of coalition building as an important part of intersectional theorizing.

As researchers interested in understanding the ways in which identities have effects on individual interactions and social systems, it is important to think about how learning is continuous and always present in research. Working in collaboration with others is a critical source of that learning. This collaboration can take many forms, even when those involved are seemingly working toward the same ends. As Molina articulates:

> I have learned that coalitions and alliances are different. Coalitions are intellectual/ political exercises where individual needs are sacrificed for the cause.... Coalitions are necessary as long as we keep in mind that they are temporary, formed with specific goals in mind, and they need to be disbanded as soon as the objective is achieved. Alliances, on the other hand, are about individuals, they are about love, they are about commitment and they are about responsibility. They are about concrete manifestations of our rebellious spirits and our sense of justice. They are about shared visions of a better society for all of us.
>
> (Molina, 1990: 329)

This repositioning does not require one to take on another person's identities, or to 'walk in their shoes'. Coalitions may be all that is possible for researchers, and as Molina points out, they may be effective in reaching common goals. Such coalitions benefit from explicit and purposeful understandings about the relationships formed, and could inform understandings that help researchers move beyond their own intersectional knowledge, while also ideally providing additional resources to respond to questions that are generated within that coalitional space.

Working together in alliance requires an awareness of the partial nature of knowledge, and of how relationships between contexts and systems of power have constructed identities differently. These complexities are negotiated through a commitment to learning and listening, imagining how to better hear the melodies played by others, and recognizing the social structures that might make only some songs appear to be 'natural,' 'real,' or 'true'. It is this ongoing process of learning that:

> shifts the base of social movement such that movement itself must change. Alliance formation is never a completed project; neither is democratic contestation. The work of producing new norms that can materialize diverse relationships in all of their complexity remains constitutive of on-going moral and political life.
>
> (Jakobsen, 1998: 27)

Alliances can be part of the ongoing work of researchers, framing who they want to be as social knowers who often have institutional power to enact ideas.

The work of constant revision destabilizes the ways of knowing that are normalized within social institutions:

Alliances shift locations and interests, and these shifts produce complicated and boundary-blurring relationships. Thus, alliances can do the work of pulling persons and groups out of their specific interests and identities and into newly articulated meanings and positions, while simultaneously maintaining commitments to and materializations of diversity and complexity.

(Jakobsen, 1998: 164)

Since all research and researchers are shaped by social institutions, intersectional approaches provide a framework in which it is possible to imagine openness and situational knowing rather than closure and timeless truth.

Which stories can I/you/we hear? Gates, Crowley, Obama and the public

In this section, we first introduce a story drawn from national print, online and televised media sources, recognizing that each version of it is constructed. We consider what was both 'ever-present' and obscured for those involved, including the many public commentators. As Collins points out, 'Within U.S. culture, racist and sexist ideologies permeate the social structure to such a degree that they become hegemonic, names, seen as natural, normal and inevitable' (2003: 321). In trying to make sense of incidents, we consider how cultural understandings of race, class, employment status and gender influence what is normal, acceptable and inappropriate, and what constitutes evidence in 'the field'.

In July 2009 Professor Henry Louis Gates, Jr. of Harvard University was arrested at his home after police were alerted by an emergency telephone call of a possible break-in. While the details of this situation were much debated, the arresting officer Sergeant James Crowley claims that Gates was disorderly, and Gates claims that Crowley profiled him because of his race. US President Barack Obama initially made his own judgement on the events of that day, and then after public concern about his comments, invited those involved to the White House to discuss the situation over beer and pretzels.

While the 'primary' stories of this incident were from Gates and Crowley, public interpretation of the experience and Obama's subsequent involvement raised many questions about the complexity and limitations of the public's ability to engage with intersectional knowing and learning. Gates' official statement, released from his legal counsel, states that he was returning from a trip to China, only to find that his front door did not open because it had been damaged. Gates and the taxi driver who had driven him home from the airport successfully forced open the front door. An officer arrived shortly thereafter and asked Gates to step outside. When Gates eventually complied, he was placed under arrest.

The incident entered into the public discourse a few days later. From the beginning, media reports made the identities of both individuals, as well as those who spoke about them, contextual factors that were used to explain the 'story'. In his efforts to contribute to these stories, Gates identified himself as a Black man who is a Harvard professor. He also stated that he is 5 ft 7 in and 150 pounds (Olopade, 2009) and should not be perceived as 'tumultuous'. He noted that he is both partially white and has white family members, and 'handicapped' because he uses a cane. On the second and third days of the news story, Crowley was identified by name as the arresting officer and was described as an upstanding white man who has a strong record as a police officer. He has also taught classes on racial profiling to the Lowell Police Academy, and several of his black colleagues characterized him as a 'good man', arguing that there had been a 'tremendous rush to judgment' and that 'race had nothing to do with [the incident]' (Turner Broadcasting System, 'Cambridge cops', 2009).

The charges were dropped shortly after Gates' arrest, but the case continued to draw national and international attention. Notably, after delivering a press conference on health care reform, President Obama took questions from the press. A reporter asked his thoughts on the arrest of Professor Gates, and Obama commented that while he didn't know all the details, he believed that the police force had 'acted stupidly' in the arrest (Obama, 2009). Obama's comment, and not the content of his policy speech, made the news and late-night satire rounds for a few days. Obama expressed regret over the 'acted stupidly' comment, and invited Crowley and Gates to have a beer with him and Vice President Joe Biden on one of the White House lawns. This invitation resulted in a gathering of men in suits to discuss racism over beer and pretzels in the backyard of the White House, one of the most culturally recognizable symbols of power.

As members of the public who are aware of and invested in interrupting racial injustices in this country, we watched this story with apprehension and frustration. This situation demonstrated how identities are constructed both internally (our constructions of ourselves) as well as externally (others' constructions of our identities), and of how those identities and constructions can bring to light larger social systems. 'Who we are' as manifest in relationships with others and with cultural structures and institutions is not necessarily who we think we are, since these external narratives about what constitutes intelligibility affect how we can be known and understood in the world (Loseke, 2007). The selves and identities that we might believe to be the most authentic and comfortable to perform are not unitary (Montoya, 2003). Yet the call for research to ferret out the unitary 'truth' of a given situation urges researchers to find and define authenticity and ultimately offer closure. The desire is to get the story right.

So how do we know 'what happened' in the situation with Gates and Crowley in July? In an effort to learn from this situation, which of the stories can I/you/we hear? In the aftermath of the White House Beer Summit, Crowley said that one outcome was that those involved 'agreed to disagree' (Williams, 2009). But how does that improve race relations in our country, or even in Cambridge? How does it help us move towards greater understandings of how identities take shape in both palpable and subtle ways, ways that affect how we know and learn our many environments? Can researchers look beyond words to listen and learn about the ways in which identities affect the social institutions that many of us are invested in and produced by? How do intersectional understandings move towards and away from truth, change or justice in and through social organizations?

Intersectionality asks scholars to recognize how their identities, the interpretations of which cannot be controlled, are implicated in knowledge construction and social interactions. In the example above, Crowley claims that he was not racist. The suggestion that others know and would vouch for him – both professionally and personally – substantiates that claim. Gates claimed that Crowley's actions were motivated by race, and that racial profiling is what happens to black men in the United States. As researchers construct their own work, seeking an ongoing understanding of the dominant messages and silences that inform their own knowing is a critically important task.

Recognizing danger: some caveats

Taking intersectional endeavours seriously asks that researchers sit with and reflect upon what it might mean to have an awareness of the unintended consequences of research, and the limitations of making meaning when that meaning is intended to promote positive social change. The complexities can be overwhelming. As a part of the global research community, we fear that we won't be able to make a difference, because we learn how much there is to do. We are not certain that we will 'do no harm' as we attempt to understand others' experiences through our own identities. We fear that by instituting change, we may create new, unintended barriers. While coalitions and alliances will help to address these challenges, danger and fear are still present in this work. What if the truths put forth – tentative as they may be – do harm to those whose positions were not considered? What if research endeavours fail to construct meaningful knowledge that is useful, now or in the future? What if scholarship and scholarly positions in academic settings serve primarily to continue personal privilege, while failing to disrupt the hierarchies of intersectional identities that drive various social structures? What if research becomes a vehicle through which researchers 'become voyeurs, passive onlookers who do not relate to the less powerful, but who are interested in seeing how the "different" live' (Collins, 2000: 458)? What if qualitative research fails to interrupt dominant knowledge structures and ways of knowing?

Opening and foreclosing change through qualitative research

I do not want you to ignore my identity, nor do I want you to make it an insurmountable barrier between our sharing of strengths.

(Lorde, 1990: 321)

Our aim as researcher-storytellers is not to seek certainty about correct perspectives on educational phenomena but to raise significant questions about prevailing policy and practice that enrich an ongoing conversation.

(Barone, 2007: 466)

As researchers, our own professional careers have been focused on educational processes and institutions. While the concepts explored in this chapter can certainly be considered in other social settings, our articulation of them is grounded in our beliefs that education can be a social good. Qualitative research can facilitate re-examinations of policies and practices that enabled unjust situations to occur in the past and that maintain their effects to this day. And, as Lorde suggests above, that re-examination can be forged in partnership with others whose intersectional identities are not like our own. Researchers can work across differences to examine how we all are implicated by the intersections of various identities, social institutions and ways of living, being and engaging power. As Tatum writes, 'Our ongoing examination of who we are in our full humanity, embracing all of our identities, creates the possibility of building alliances that may ultimately free us all' (2000: 14).

How do our own identities and positionalities make certain paradigmatic and theoretical lenses possible and desirable? As qualitative researchers, what do we bring to our coalitional places? What is simply not in our understanding or experience, such that we need to rely on allies or partners? As Dillard (2006) has noted, debates about paradigms and theories are often conducted by academics with identities that are situated in socially privileged locations, and have resulted in practices that have excluded the epistemologies and research interests of a broad range of identities. We want to remember that we are always implicated both by what perspectives are represented in a given situation and by those that are not represented.

Conclusion

Intersectionality invites a deconstruction of how academic identities work to perpetuate the very knowledge regimes that researchers interested in social change wish to transform. The complexities and ambiguities of such work require ongoing praxis, and the willingness to both contribute to and question the knowledge gained from the places of intersection. This chapter takes seriously how researchers are implicated by intersectional understandings, because in feminist research, 'We can see ourselves in others, see others in ourselves' (Richardson, 2007: 465). Through listening carefully and critically, examining and re-examining positionalities, desires and sense-making practices, and also working to develop coalitions and alliances, researchers, research and scholarly engagement can come closer to a world that simultaneously honours differences and nurtures communities.

References

Alemán, A. M. (2003) 'Gender, race, and millennial curiosity', pp. 179–98 in B. Ropers-Huilman (ed.), *Gendered Futures in Higher Education: Critical perspectives for change*, Albany, NY: SUNY Press.

Barone, T. (2007) 'A return to the gold standard? Questioning the future of narrative construction as educational research', *Qualitative Inquiry*, **13**, 454–70.

Berry, T. and Mizelle, N. D. (2006) *From Oppression to Grace: Women of color and their dilemmas within the academy*, Sterling, VA: Stylus.

Cho, S. K. (1997) 'Converging stereotypes in racialized sexual harassment: where the model minority meets Suzie Wong', pp. 203–20 in A. K. Wing (ed.), *Critical Race Feminism: A reader*, New York: Routledge.

Cole, E. R. (2009) 'Intersectionality and research in psychology', *American Psychological Association*, **64**(3), 170–80.

Collins, P. H. (1990) *Black Feminist Thought: Knowledge, consciousness, and the politics of empowerment*, Sydney: Allen & Unwin.

Collins, P. H. (2000) 'Toward a new vision: race, class, and gender as categories of analysis and connection', pp. 457–62 in M. Adams, W. J. Blumenfeld, R. Castaneda, H. W. Hackman, M. L. Peters, and X. Zuniga (eds), *Readings for Diversity in Social Justice: An anthology on racism, anti-semitism, sexism, heterosexism, ableism, and classism*, New York: Routledge.

Collins, P. H. (2003) 'The politics of black feminist thought', pp. 318–33 in C. R. McCann and S. Kim (eds), *Feminist Theory Reader: Local and global perspectives*, New York: Routledge.

Crenshaw, K. (1993) 'Demarginalizing the intersection of race and sex: a Black feminist critique of antidiscrimination doctrine, feminist theory and antiracist politics', pp. 383–95 in D. K. Weisbert (ed.), *Feminist Legal Theory: foundations*, Philadelphia, PA: Temple University Press.

Crenshaw, K. (2009) 'Mapping the margins: intersectionality, identity politics, and violence against women of color', pp. 213–46 in E. Taylor, D. Gillborn, and G. Ladson-Billings (eds), *Foundations of Critical Race Theory in Education*, New York: Routledge.

Delgado, R. and Stefancic, J. (2001) *Critical Race Theory: An introduction*, New York: New York University Press.

Dill, B. T. (2009) 'Intersections', *Ms.*, **19**(2), 65–6.

Dill, B. T., McLaughlin, A. E. and Nieves, A. D. (2007) 'Future directions of feminist research: intersectionality', pp. 629–37 in S. N. Hesse-Biber (ed.), *Handbook of Feminist Research: Theory and praxis*, Thousand Oaks, CA: Sage.

Dillard, C. (2006) 'When the music changes, so should the dance: cultural and spiritual considerations in paradigm 'proliferation', *International Journal of Qualitative Studies in Education*, **19**(1), 59–76.

Foster, M. (1994) 'The power to know one thing is never the power to know all things: methodological notes on two studies of Black American teachers', pp. 129–46 in A. Gitlin (ed.), *Power and Method*, New York: Routledge.

Gilmore, A. D. (2003) 'It is better to speak', pp. 114–19 in A. K. Wing (ed.), Critical Race Feminism: A reader, 2nd edn, New York: New York University Press.

Grillo, T. and Wildman, S. (1997) 'Obscuring the importance of race: the implication of making comparisons between racism and sexism (or other isms)', pp. 44–6 in A. K. Wing (ed.), *Critical Race Feminism: A reader*, New York: New York University Press.

Harding, S. (1991) *Whose Science? Whose Knowledge? Thinking from women's lives*, Ithaca, NY: Cornell University Press.

Hartsock, N. C. M. (2003) 'The feminist standpoint', pp. 292–307 in C. R. McCann and S. Kim (eds), *Feminist Theory Reader: Local and global perspectives*, New York: Routledge.

Jakobsen, J. R. (1998) *Working Alliances and the Politics of Difference: Diversity and feminist ethics*, Bloomington, IN: Indiana University Press.

Lorde, A. (1990) 'I am your sister: Black women organizing across sexualities', pp. 321–5 in G. Anzaldúa (ed.), *Making Face, Making Soul: Hacienda Caras*, San Francisco, CA: Aunt Lute.

Loseke, D. R. (2007) 'The study of narrative identity', *Sociological Quarterly*, 48: 661–88.

McCall, L. (2005) 'The complexity of intersectionality', *Signs*, **30**(3), 1771–800.

McCann, C. R. and Kim, S. (2003) *Feminist Theory Reader: Local and global perspectives*, New York: Routledge.

Molina, P. (1990) 'Recognizing, accepting and celebrating our differences', pp. 326–31 in G. Anzaldúa (ed.), *Making Face, Making Soul: Hacienda Caras*, San Francisco, CA: Aunt Lute.

Montoya, M. E. (2000) 'Silence and silencing: their centripetal and centrifugal forces in legal communication, pedagogy and discourse', *University of Michigan Journal of Law Reform*, **33**(3), 263–327.

Montoya, M. E. (2003) 'Máscaras, Trenzas, y Grenas', pp. 70–7 in A. K. Wing (ed.), *Critical Race Feminism: A reader*, 2nd edn, New York: New York University Press.

Naples, N. (2007) 'Standpoint epistemology and beyond', pp. 579–90 in S. N. Hesse-Biber (ed.), *Handbook of Feminist Research: Theory and praxis*, Thousand Oaks, CA: Sage.

Narayan, U. (2003) 'The project of feminist epistemology', pp. 308–17 in C. R. McCann and S. Kim (eds), *Feminist Theory Reader: Local and global perspectives*, New York: Routledge.

Obama, B. (2009) 'Statement from the President following his conversation with the Vice President, Professor Gates and Sergeant Crowley', July 30, (online) <http://www.whitehouse. gov/the_press_office/Statement-from-the-President-following-his-conversation-with-the-Vice-President-Professor-Gates-and-Sergeant-Crowley/> (accessed 19 November 2009).

Ogletree, C. (2009, July 20) 'Statement on behalf of Henry Louis Gates, Jr.', *The Root* (online) <http://www.theroot.com/views/lawyers-statement-arrest-henry-louis-gates-jr> (accessed 19 November 2009).

Olopade, D. (2009, July 21) 'Professor Henry Louis Gates, Jr. speaks out on racial profiling after his arrest by Cambridge Police', *The Root* (online) <http://www.theroot.com/views/skip-gates-speaks> (accessed 19 November 2009).

Parker, L. and Lynn, M. (2009) 'What's race got to do with it? Critical race theory's conflicts with and connections to qualitative research methodology and epistemology', pp. 148–62 in E. Taylor, D. Gillborn, and G. Ladson-Billings (eds), *Foundations of Critical Race Theory in Education*, New York: Routledge.

Richardson, L. (2007) 'Reading for another: a method for addressing some feminist research dilemmas', pp. 459–67 in S. N. Hesse-Biber (ed.), *Handbook of Feminist Research: Theory and praxis*, Thousand Oaks, CA: Sage.

Smith, L. T. (1999) *Decolonizing Methodologies: Research and indigenous peoples*, New York: Zed Books.

Tatum, B. D. (2000) 'The complexity of identity: 'Who am I?'' pp. 9–14 in M. Adams, W. J. Blumenfeld, R. Castaneda, H. W. Hackman, M. L. Peters, and X. Zuniga (eds), *Readings for Diversity in Social Justice: An Anthology on racism, anti-semitism, sexism, heterosexism, ableism, and classism*, New York: Routledge.

Taylor, Y. (2009) 'Complexities and complications: intersections of class and sexuality', *Journal of Lesbian Studies*, **13**: 189–203.

Turner Broadcasting System (producer) (2009) Cambridge cops support Crowley. August 24 (video clip) (online) <http://www.cnn.com/video/#/video/us/2009/07/26/nr.comrade.in.arms.cnn?iref=videosearch> (accessed 19 November 2009).

Williams, J. (2009) 'Over beers, a taste of what's to come: Gates, Crowley vow to meet again', *Boston Globe*, 31 July (online) <http://www.boston.com/news/nation/washington/articles/2009/07/31/over_beers_a_taste_of_whats_to_come/> (accessed 30 December 2009).

Williams, P. J. (1991) *The Alchemy of Race and Rights*, Cambridge, MA: Harvard University Press.

Williams, P. J. (2003) 'Spare parts, family values, old children, cheap', pp. 159–66 in A. K. Wing (ed.), *Critical Race Feminism: A reader*, 2nd edn, New York: New York University Press.

Wing, A. K. (1997) *Critical Race Feminism: A reader*, 1st edn, New York: New York University Press.

Wing, A. K. (2003) *Critical Race Feminism: A reader*, 2nd edn, New York: New York University Press.

Zinn, M. B. and Dill, B. T. (2003) 'Theorizing difference from multiracial feminism', pp. 353–61 in C. R. McCann and S. Kim (eds), *Feminist Theory Reader: Local and global perspectives*, New York: Routledge.

Chapter 6

Taking a stance
Socially responsible ethics and informed consent

Madeleine Duncan and Ruth Watson

Introduction

> It is midday and hot outside. We (Ruth, Madeleine and Xakathile, our Xhosa-speaking translator/research assistant) enter a cool, thatch-roofed mud hut in a remote rural African village. There's not space for everyone on the one available bench so we sit on the dried dung floor. A few chickens peck in the ashes around the fire in the middle of the hut, on which a pot of food is gently simmering. Our eyes adjust to the smoke and the darkness inside the dwelling as we watch household members enter, greet us and settle down. Everyone in this household is interested, and implicated, in what is about to transpire. We listen as Xakathile explains in isiXhosa (an indigenous African language) our presence and purpose. When this has been done, and if identified (sampled) household members agree to talk to us, we discuss their rights as research participants. This is never easy to do because people are generally hospitable, polite and accepting, but we can't help wondering what they really think, feel and understand about what is being requested.

This vignette unfolded during the data collection phase of a longitudinal mixed-method study undertaken by the authors in a rural area of the Eastern Cape Province, South Africa. For the past five years we have been exploring the dynamic relationship between chronic poverty, disability and occupation in households living on the margins of South African society in peri-urban informal settlements and deep rural villages (Duncan, 2009; Duncan and Watson, 2009; Watson, 2004, 2007). The aim of the study was to understand these three dimensions (poverty, disability and occupation) individually and intersectionally, with the purpose of fulfilling professional obligations towards the country's development goals (Watson and Swartz, 2004). As researchers we could only gain an understanding of people's occupations through participant observation and respondents' voluntary accounts of the everyday things they do in dealing with their life circumstances. A naturalistic, participatory research approach was indicated, but in order for people to consent to participation they needed to be familiar with, and have personal experience of, their fundamental citizen rights. People who are not used to exercising their rights are especially vulnerable, and attention therefore needed to be given to the participant–researcher relationship and the way in which informed consent was applied.

This chapter argues for transparency, representivity and reflexivity as normative stances towards emergent ethical dilemmas in social inquiry. It suggests that the essential human processes that inevitably confound the research journey should become a secondary focus of the investigation and should, as such, be embedded in its oral and written accounts. Three ethical orientations are briefly reviewed, the combined and iterative use of which, it is suggested, enables socially responsible ethicizing to occur. Ethicizing involves being ethically and morally present in each participatory moment of the research process. Informed consent is examined in the latter section of the chapter, emphasizing the need for contextually and culturally relevant ethical practices.

Adopting a stance

According to Parker (2005) social inquirers can be blithely unaware, simply uncaring or reflectively deliberate in thinking through the ways in which their everyday treatment of and attitude towards research participants is intimately linked to their own socialization and the wider social forces operating in people's sociopolitical and cultural contexts. Care should be taken not to override what Wells (2005) calls an 'ethic on diversity'. Race, gender, culture and other social forces, so central to people's identity, need to be considered throughout the inquiry to ensure the benefit of the research, not only to science and society but to individual subjects as well. We came to realize that socially responsible research ethics involves consciously adopting stances that would enable us to systematically think through why and how we participated in the world of those we engaged as informants. What counted as real in the relationships implicated by the research process depended, in part, on where we positioned ourselves in relation to the politics of power. As cultural and historical 'outsiders' we had to remain vigilant about our assumptions, open to learning from people about the impact that the research process had on their lives, and sensitive to the moral-political dimensions of relationships that developed as the inquiry unfolded (Watson, 2009). Transparency, representivity and reflexivity proved to be useful stances for thinking through the many ethical and moral dilemmas we faced in the field.

At this point a distinction between moral and ethical thinking is indicated, although clearly it is not easy to separate these types of reasoning. Morality is a personal set of values and beliefs which guide self-discipline (including respect for others) and may be expressed through sensitivity (an ability to interpret a situation), judgement (the discernment of whether an action is morally right or wrong), motivation (prioritizing values) and character (having courage to act on convictions) (Rest and Narvaez, 1994). Ethics is an attempt to codify and regulate morality by stipulating norms and principles for behaviour. Ethical thinking is concerned with core values, both general and specific to a profession, the latter underlying its goals. Moral thinking is about the morally justifiable means of achieving these goals. Both are central to ethicizing, and helpful in dealing with the process and relational dilemmas that arise during social inquiry.

Transparency

Transparent ethicizing deals overtly with what happens between the means (methodology and methods) and ends (impacts and outcomes) of the research process. Research participants may not fully appreciate the issues at stake, while researchers are not necessarily open and honest in detailing the research purpose, methods and process because disclosure may jeopardize the validity of the findings. Nevertheless, ethical and moral integrity demands that researchers find ways to be open about their research practices. We found a middle path involved spending time helping participants to understand the study problem and being honest about our struggles to do 'the right thing'. Adopting a transparent stance meant that we acknowledged our limitations in addressing troubling ethical dilemmas. Staying with the discomfort of uncertainty and opening subjectivities up for clarification made the research more appreciative of local cultural, social and moral issues. Points of impossibility in the research process sometimes revealed the reality of the situation for participants. When contradiction, conflict and discomfort were acknowledged and processed as points of learning about and from research participants, the possibilities for research as social change started to open up.

Knowing and understanding are however not the same thing. Unconscious motivations, ignorance and arrogance may operate on the dark side of transparency. Despite attempts to be transparent, our intentions, emotions and interiority were not always accessible to ourselves, and even less so to informants and readers of this research account. Parker's (2005) advice to avoid the tendency to dichotomize people into 'good' or 'bad' proved helpful. He suggests that since neither essential goodness nor badness lies inside human beings, questions for research ethics should rather focus on thinking through how perceptions about good and bad emerge, and how they are judged as such. This is not easy, but may be managed by 'fidelity to the commitments made during a research event, staying true to what happened and reflexively attending to the institutional location of historical and personal aspects of the research relationship' (Parker, 2005: 25).

Reflexivity

According to Doucet and Mauthner (2002: 134), a 'wide and robust concept of reflexivity should include reflecting on, and being accountable about personal, interpersonal, institutional, pragmatic, emotional, theoretical, epistemological and ontological influences on our research and specifically about our data analysis processes'. Reflexivity lies at the heart of critical research. It involves 'working with subjectivity in such a way that we are able to break out of the self-referential circle that characterizes most academic work' (Parker, 2005: 25). Self-referential circles perpetuate particular notions of reality. We often felt out of our depth in understanding the local cultural practices and prevailing political, historical and institutional structures that influenced peoples' lives. Smith (1999: 47), writing about colonizing research and its impact on indigenous peoples, calls the mind trained by Western notions of reality a 'force-field that unconsciously screens out competing and oppositional discourses'. She argues that Western theories and rules of research 'are underpinned by a cultural system of classification and representation, by views of human nature, human morality and virtue, by conceptions of time and space, by conceptions of gender and race. Ideas about these things help determine what counts as real' (Smith, 1999: 44). It was difficult to deconstruct some entrenched professional assumptions about humans as occupational beings originating from our Eurocentric training in occupational therapy. Reading relevant Afrocentric literature, consulting people who held local wisdom, debating contentious influences and being aware of the limits of our worldviews went a long way in helping us make sense of a cultural territory fraught with ethical ambiguities and epistemological uncertainties.

Representivity

Representative ethicizing requires conscious engagement with the power of the word as voice. Parker (2005) suggests that engaging this power may mean making first-person confessions (for example, articulating assumptions and biases); clarifying second-person social positions (indicating where diversity issues may confound voice, for example, gender, race and disability); being aware of third-person theorizing (for example, adopting a critical perspective towards taken-for-granted ideas) and crafting a report that foregrounds instances of disjunction (for example, being explicit about the impact of subjective dissonance on objective reporting). Representivity is also concerned with capturing authentic versions of people's lives. It requires vigilance about the ways in which language is used to describe their realities, especially when researchers and research participants do not share the same first language. The role of interpreters, translators and transcribers is critical in cross-cultural research to ensure that the meaning of words and gestures is accurately conveyed. We were fortunate to have an interpreter/ translator as a member of the research team. Since learning to speak or understand isiXhosa was not possible in the study timeframe, we developed a nosology of frequently used words, idioms and proverbs which helped us make sense of people's stories, and went to great lengths to clarify, through lengthy discussions with our translator, exactly what the nuanced meanings were behind what they said. These discussions also served as a platform for discerning how to respond, using a range of ethical orientations, to the ethical dilemmas that emerged when we engaged with people's responses to our presence in their lives.

Ethical orientations

While bioethics continues to guide the development of study protocols and to inform research practice, a growing body of social inquirers argue for alternative ethical guidelines that will enable researchers to deal in normative ways with the uncertainties that inevitably arise amidst the 'messiness' of inquiry in everyday life (Marshall, 2007; Olweny, 2009; Tolich and Fitzgerald, 2006; van den Hoonaard, 2002). Research ethics involves much more than an academic exercise which can be neatly compartmentalized and ticked off as a once-off consideration to meet the requirements of an ethics review board. This approach to ethics can obscure the need to continually reflect on the ethical implications of researching people's lives.

Table 6.1 summarizes the core features of three orientations that we have found useful in our work. There are other combinations; the point is that the adoption of a single frame may screen out other ways of viewing the world, and in so doing, lead to oppressive research practices.

Table 6.1 Ethical orientations

Orientation	Bioethics (Beauchamp and Childress,1994)	Ethics of care (Sevenhuijsen, 2003)	Participatory ethics (Kotze and Myburg, 2004)
Approach	Positivist Rational Prescriptive	Feminist Relational Responsive	Interpretivist Praxis Reflexive
Principles	Autonomy Beneficence Non-maleficence Justice	Trust Attachment Interdependence	Solidarity Participation Power sharing

The differences between the three orientations are evident in approach and principles, their combined application at different stages and for different purposes throughout the research process ensuring that ethicizing remains grounded in theory. Diverse and contradictory interpretations of socially constructed knowledge are a reality of life, which implies the need for flexibility when selecting theoretical orientations for research ethics in contexts character-ized by historical disadvantage, marginalization and structural inequity. While the bioethical orientation alerts the social researcher to the demands of ethics review boards and ensures compliance with universal standards for the protection of human research subjects, the ethics of care and participatory ethics present flexible and contributory orientations that affirm a partnership between researcher and researched with due consideration of the social dis-courses operating within the research context and relationships.

Bioethics

Bioethics sets out guidelines for 'doing things right', and has become regularized as the benchmark for social inquiry used by ethics review boards (van den Hoonaard, 2002). Seminal publications such as the Belmont Report (National Commission for the Protection of Human Subjects of Biomedical and Behavioural Research, 1979) describe principles such as beneficence, justice and autonomy for minimizing risk to participants. Informed consent, confidentiality and anonymity are based on simple edicts: do no harm, do not cheat, respect difference and withhold judgement. Despite helpful guidelines such as these, the 'messiness' of social inquiry is often situated in relational uncertainties between researcher and inform-ant. Here the ethics of care provides some direction for action.

Care ethics

While bioethics is individualistic, the ethics of care sees 'interdependency, care and solidarity as basic moral phenomena' (Sevenhuijsen, 2003: 395). In this orientation moral dilemmas are not necessarily a collision between different ethical principles but can be understood as conflicts of responsibilities. Care ethicists value a personalized, relational and responsive approach in research that pays attention to the responsibilities associated with trust, attach-ment and interdependence between researcher and participants. It is used by those who seek to understand both their professional practice and research from a relational perspective, and is a good match for the requirements of qualitative research, where mutuality and reciprocity between participant and researcher are crucial for research effectiveness. The notion of care in research may however be seen as potentially paternalistic and unequal, with the researcher inadvertently acting as care giver and the participant as a care receiver. A participatory orien-tation seeks to equalize the interactive field.

Participatory ethics

Writing from a social development perspective, Kotze and Myburg (2004) propose partici-patory ethics as 'the right things to do' by making the 'researched' equal partners in a lib-eratory social inquiry. They view ethicizing as a dynamic process in which ethics is 'located in the discourse and praxis with the disempowered and marginalized – those who seldom benefit from the ethics of discourses created and entertained by the powerful or knowledge-able' (2004: 14). By challenging oppressive attitudes, the researcher seeks to promote trans-formation through respect for particularity and diversity. The dynamic relationship between researcher and participants is constantly negotiated to deconstruct power, achieve and main-tain trust, promote equality and ensure reciprocity. A participatory solidarity with partici-pants is emphasized here, where participation is not a step in the research process, but a description of the process. The researchers' obligation becomes the use of their knowledge and power to ensure that participation in research is beneficial to everyone involved. Participatory ethics argues that prescribed research systems, such as filling in consent forms, may inadvertently be oppressive because people are often excluded from the process of shaping the content of documents pertaining to their participation. In the next section we focus on informed consent, drawing on examples from our fieldwork to illustrate the limitations of a procedural, documented approach at the start of a study.

Informed consent revisited

On some days, when we were the only white people for miles around, people willingly agreed to be interviewed. There appeared to be a certain news value and prestige attached to being visited by a stranger in a remote place. Introducing written consent forms under such circumstances was potentially gratuitous and even exploitative. We could not assume that research participants were able to make reasoned choices about voluntary participation once they had been informed about the risks and potential benefits of their involvement. Initially some participants did not fully appreciate the issues at stake, while others appeared motivated to become involved, in anticipation of some material benefit. For example this happened when, after the purpose of data collection had been explained twice, a consent form signed and questions invited and answered throughout, including participant expectations, a participant still asked as we left his dwelling, 'But what are you going to do for us? We are very poor and struggling.'

Informed consent has been defined as 'the knowing consent of an individual, or a legally authorized representative, able to exercise free power of choice without undue inducement or any element of force, deceit, duress, or other form of constraint or coercion' (Fluehr-Lobban, 2003: 166). It assumes moral standards such as truthfulness, openness, confidentiality and fidelity on the part of the researcher. Informed consent was originally articulated as a formal legal-ethical construct in biomedical practice and research. It was intended to protect human subjects from potential harm by alerting them to the risks associated with various medical and research procedures, and advancing their autonomy by giving them choice and control over their participation. An ethics proposal usually defines anticipated harm in the context of the research; discerns whether it is potentially physical and/or psychological, and whether any danger might extend to an individual, group or even future generations. The identified risks are then summarized in a suitable written and/or verbal format for presenting to envisaged respondents/subjects to secure their 'informed' consent.

The fulfilment of the requirements for informed consent can be much more complex than anticipated. Before our study commenced we summarized preliminary research information in a consent form translated into isiXhosa. This covered the purpose and scope of the study, including the type of questions that were likely to be asked; the use to which the results would be put; and the method in which participant's utterances would be reported including confidentiality and anonymity. While we realized that consent should be treated as a process rather than a one-off event, we were yet to learn that different stages and issues within the research process are fraught with ambiguity, conflicting interest, fine lines, judgement calls and awkward decisions. We struggled with questions such as: could consent to participate be predicated by the respondent's anticipation of some perceived benefit? Will certain information about the risks of the research threaten the trustworthiness of the findings? Could the power dynamics between researcher and subject override voluntary agreement to participate? And what about cultural perspectives on who has the right, authority and independence to grant consent? We came to understand that members of particular communities were not in a position to claim the individual autonomy that is assumed by a bioethical orientation. At the start of the study we had to broker verbal community and household consent before proceeding to individual written consent.

Brokering community consent

Particular groups and communities – women, the economically oppressed, ethnic minorities, disabled and indigenous peoples – may be deeply suspicious of the researcher's motives. Smith (1999: 10), in discussing the politics of colonizing research, suggests that the questions to be asked by communities and activists who are approached by social researchers should include:

> 'Whose research is it?
> Who owns it?
> Whose interests does it serve?
> Who will benefit from it?
> Who has designed its questions and framed its scope?
> Who will carry it out?
> Who will write it up?
> How will its results be disseminated?'

Before entering the study area, we sought permission to proceed from community 'gate-keepers' (Tindana *et al.*, 2006). In the rural areas we met with the 'imbiza' (tribal authority), chaired by the local chief, and attended by the village headmen and councillors. We explained the project purpose and methods, and they gave permission for us to visit their villages once they felt adequately informed, particularly with regard to who would be participating and the ways in which the broader community stood to gain from the encounter. We made sure not to raise any expectations of material benefit, but did promise to return at the end of the first phase to give a report and where possible, to direct people to relevant service resources. When we subsequently arrived at various villages and homes, people already knew who we were and what we were doing in their community, thereby facilitating the process of informed consent in households.

Consideration of the questions that community elders may pose can be viewed as a test of political correctness. The most desirable answers can still be judged incorrect because they are, according to Smith (1999: 10), part of a larger set of judgements on criteria a researcher cannot prepare for, such as:

> Is her spirit clear?
> Does he have a good heart?
> What other baggage are they carrying?
> Are they useful to us?
> Can they fix our generator?
> Can they actually do anything?

These questions are relational, pointing to the ethics of care in securing participant engagement with the study problem and process. The middle path is an informed consent process shared with participants from the planning through to the termination stage of a study. This can be very demanding, and is not always possible given the many constraints faced by researchers. Despite explanations desperate people still hoped that we would be able to change their dire situation. It was imperative to admit that this was not possible. The agreement we reached translated into a dynamic relationship of giving and receiving information, renegotiating 'consent' when changes occurred, and sharing the findings and outcomes of the research with all concerned with due consideration of prevailing limitations.

Obtaining individual consent

The moral imperative of informed consent is full disclosure through discussion in advance using appropriate channels. However, we could not predict the vulnerabilities to which participants were subjected as a consequence of participating in the study, or how the need for different forms of consent would unfold once fieldwork commenced. Commitments made at the start of the study became redundant or impossible to meet because of factors beyond our control. Participants' impairments such as thought disorder, lack of insight or hearing loss also posed particular challenges for obtaining consent. Informants who were not accustomed to being considered or asked for permission found the concept of signing a written consent form or giving verbal consent at odds with their perceived social position. Communication had to be clear and understandable. It could not be hurried. This proved difficult when we were pressured for time or when a participant was illiterate or did not speak a language that we understood. Ethicizing facilitated our ability to navigate these and other uncertainties, as the following example illustrates:

> Although Dorcas was psychiatrically disabled and the sole breadwinner of a household of five, she did not view herself as independent from the social structures within which she functioned, nor did she see herself as entitled to making autonomous decisions about her participation in the study. She deferred to her elder brother as the appropriate person to grant informed consent on her behalf. While we stood in solidarity with her spirit of independence and against her social marginalization as a disabled person on the one hand, we were uncertain how to curtail her vulnerability on the other hand. We were torn between the ethical imperative of gaining informed consent from her and caring about the socioeconomic consequences if we acknowledged her brother's authority. If he knew that Dorcas would gain materially in the form of food parcels (tokens of appreciation for participation and to compensate for potential loss of income), her creditworthiness and bargaining power within the extended household would be increased, but paradoxically, so would her vulnerability. First, she would be expected to share whatever scarce staple foods she received (either to repay debts already incurred or to build a buffer of credit against future hard times) and second, by receiving attention and food from us she opened herself up to jealousy and suspicion which could impact negatively on her social capital ('maybe she is also receiving money and hiding it from us').

Talking and thinking through the likely outcomes for Dorcas with our translator/cultural broker helped us identify ways of enabling her to digest information that respected her rights and dignity. He advised getting someone known and trusted to help Dorcas decide on the best way forward. After consulting a neighbour and her brother, she agreed to participate in the study. We revisited this agreement throughout the study in response to her fluctuating mental health and her brother's insistence on being kept informed about our visits within the boundaries of confidentiality. The unpredictable nature of qualitative interviewing methods also required the availability of additional support and debriefing for informants. Interviews were sometimes emotionally painful and the questions potentially intrusive. Despite the standard methods used to avoid compromising the interviewee, the possibility remained that an effective interview might lead the respondent into the discovery of new insights, which they may have preferred to leave unexplored. Regular checking with our trusted interpreter was helpful in discerning the ethical limits of probing. We also made sure to refer (and followed up) participants to locally relevant and accessible services when indicated.

Conclusion

In this chapter we have argued for a transparent, reflexive and representative research stance that recognizes the strengths and limitations of prescriptive ethical guidelines and seeks to remain as vigilant as possible about the tacit infringements on research participants' dignity, cultural values and worldviews. By tracing the basic tenets of bioethics, the ethics of care and participatory ethics, we have illustrated how the iterative and flexible use of a range of ethical orientations may promote socially responsible research ethics. A focus on informed consent highlighted ways of honouring the individual and the communities' dignity and rights by building a platform for reciprocal gain through a negotiated and inclusive research relationship. Given the development of diverse ways of doing research, we suggest that a deeper understanding of contested spaces could prove to be a profitable direction to follow, for social researchers and the people that we serve.

References

Beauchamp, T. and Childress, J. (1994) *Principles of Biomedical Ethics*, New York: Oxford University Press.

Doucet, A. and Mauthner, N. (2002) 'Knowing responsibly: linking ethics, research practice and epistemology', pp.123–145 in M. Mauthner, M. Birch, J. Jessop and T. Miller (eds), *Ethics in Qualitative Research*, London: Sage.

Duncan, E. M. (2009) 'Human occupation in the context of chronic poverty and psychiatric disability', unpublished doctoral dissertation, University of Stellenbosch, South Africa.

Duncan, M. and Watson, R. (2009) 'The occupational dimensions of chronic poverty', Working Paper 14, Bellville, South Africa: Institute for Land and Agrarian Studies. University of the Western Cape.

Fluehr-Lobban, C. (ed.) (2003) *Ethics and the Profession of Anthropology: Dialogue for ethically conscious practice*, Oxford: Altamira Press.

Kotze, D. and Myburg, J. (2004) *Ethical Ways of Being*, Pretoria: Ethics Alive.

Marshall, P. A. (2007) 'Ethical challenges in study design and informed consent for health research in resource-poor settings', Special Topics in Social, Economic and Behavioural (SEB) Research report series, no. 5. Geneva: World Health Organization on behalf of the Special Programme for Research and Training in Tropical Diseases (TDR) (online) <http://www.who.int/tdr/publications/publications/seb_topic5.htm> (accessed 18 November 2009).

National Commission for the Protection of Human Subjects of Biomedical and Behavioural Research (1979) *The Belmont Report: Ethical Principles and Guidelines for the Protection of Human Subjects of Research*, US Department of Health, Education and Welfare.

Olweny, C. (2009) 'The ethics and conduct of cross cultural research in developing countries', *Psycho-Oncology*, **3**(1), 11–20 (online) <http://www.wiley.com/journal/5807/home> (accessed 22 August 2009).

Parker, I. (2005) *Qualitative Psychology: Introducing radical research*, Maidenhead: Open University Press.

Rest, J. R. and Narvaez, D. (1994) *Moral Development in the Professions*, Hillsdale, NJ: Lawrence Erlbaum.

Sevenhuijsen, S. (2003) 'Principle ethics and the ethics of care: can they go together?' *Social Work*, 39, 393–9.

Smith, L. (1999) *Decolonising Methodologies: Research and indigenous peoples*, London: Zed.

Tindana, P. O., Kass, N. and Akweongo, P. (2006) 'The informed consent process in a rural African setting: a case study of the Kassena-Nankana district of Northern Ghana', *IRB: Ethics and Human Research*, **28**(3), 1–6.

Tolich, M. and Fitzgerald, M. H. (2006) 'If ethics committees were designed for ethnography', *Journal of Empirical Research on Human Research Ethics*, 71–8. (online) <www.ucpress.edu/journal/rights,htm> (accessed August 2009).

Van den Hoonaard, W. (ed.) (2002) *Walking the Tightrope: Ethical issues for qualitative researchers*, Toronto: University of Toronto Press.

Watson, R. (2004) 'Poverty, disability and occupation: Khayelitsha', unpublished final report, Saldru: University of Cape Town.

Watson, R. (2007) *Poverty, Disability and Occupation: Mpoza District, Mount Frere, Eastern Cape, South Africa*, Unpublished monograph, SANPAD.

Watson, R. (2009) 'Diversity matters: guiding principles on diversity and culture', in A. Kinébanian and M. Stomph (eds), *Diversity Matters: Guiding principles on diversity and culture*, Forrestfield, Western Australia: World Federation of Occupational Therapists.

Watson, R. and Swartz, L. (eds) (2004) *Transformation through Occupation*, London: Whurr.

Wells, S. A. (2005) 'An ethic of diversity', pp. 31–41 in E. B. Purtilo, G. M. Jensen, and C. B. Royeen (eds), Educating for Moral Action: A sourcebook in health and rehabilitation ethics, Philadelphia, PA: F.A. Davis.

Part II

Methodologies and methods

Chapter 7

Writing ethnodrama

A sampler from educational research

Johnny Saldaña

Introduction

The purpose of this chapter is to describe basic methods of adapting qualitative educational research (and by extension, social science research) into scripted and performed work for the stage. The written representation of this genre is labelled ethnodrama, a compound word drawn from 'ethnography' and 'drama', coined by the anthropologist Turner (1982: 100). Turner wisely understood that embodied reenactment of other people's practices would better inform students of rich cultural meanings:

> I've long thought that teaching and learning anthropology should be more fun than they often are. Perhaps we should not merely read and comment on ethnographies, but actually perform them.... How, then, may this be done? One possibility may be to turn the more interesting portions of ethnographies into play scripts, then to act them out in class, and finally to turn back to ethnographies armed with the understanding that comes from 'getting inside the skin' of members of other cultures.
>
> (Turner, 1982: 89–90)

In addition to classroom studio exercises, ethnodramatic play scripts also function as progressive, arts-based qualitative research representation and presentation. The dramatic modality is purposefully chosen over other research genres, such as grounded theory or narrative inquiry, when the dramatic art form will most credibly, vividly and persuasively exhibit for readers and audiences the investigated social world. If a shared goal of theatre and qualitative inquiry is to explore and learn more about the human condition, then the outcomes are doubly if not exponentially increased when the two disciplines merge, bringing with them their best representational and presentational modes of expression through dramatic text.

Definitions and context

As working definitions for this chapter, an ethnodrama or ethnodramatic play script 'consists of dramatized, significant selections of narrative collected through interviews, participant observation, field notes, journal entries and/or print and media artifacts' (Saldaña, 2005: 2), which may also include or consist solely of the playwright's autoethnographic reflections. Ethnodrama is groundwork for ethnotheatre, which 'employs the traditional craft and artistic techniques of theatre production to mount for an audience a live [or mediated] performance event of research participants' experiences and/or the researcher's interpretations of data' (Saldaña, 2005: 1). I have located over sixty related and synonymous terms (such as performance ethnography, verbatim theatre, docudrama, non-fiction playwriting) in the literature across several academic disciplines. In this chapter, ethnodrama and ethnotheatre will be the terms employed.

Adapting ethnographic fieldwork data, published ethnographies and autoethnographic reflections effectively for the stage does not require but is certainly enhanced by the skills of an experienced theatre scholar and artist. Play scripts written by non-theatre academics with minimal or no play production background are little more than 'collages' of verbatim interview transcript excerpts interspersed with dramatically incompatible devices such as footnotes or citations of the related research literature. The conventions and grammar of scholarly research reporting do not transfer into ethnodramatic writing for the stage. Play scripts written by those with theatrical experience tend to include lengthier storylines with more impactful, emotion-evoking monologue and dialogue in a variety of styles and genres.

Ethnodramatic representations and presentations of educational life bring the field's pedagogical, sociological and political issues to heightened prominence. Perhaps more than the academic journal article, the ethnotheatrical performance – if well done for a receptive audience – holds potential to increase awareness, deepen understanding, and provide experiences that generate sympathetic and empathetic responses and memories for future applications, and transfer into classroom practice and possibly educational policy making.

In this chapter, I share a methods overview of writing ethnodramatic monologue and dialogue, and include selected excerpts of exemplars from the field of educational research, hoping that these may serve as illustrations and models for the reader's own ethnodramatic writing. These works were written by those with and without theatrical production experience, and range in content from stories of exemplary educators to the ethos of students in inner-city schools. Ethnodramatic plays about teachers most often appear as a presentational genre colloquially labelled 'stand-up storytelling'. When students become part of the cast of character-participants, however, the play scripts tend to venture more toward conversational realism.

Writing monologue

A stage monologue is the one-actor delivery of an extended narrative, which in performance can range anywhere in length from one minute to a two-hour solo presentation. Monologues can be spoken to other characters on stage, as 'direct address' to an audience and/or as 'soliloquy', a rumination in which the audience witnesses the character's internal thoughts spoken out loud. Briefer, self-standing monologues are colloquially called 'portraits in miniature' by theatre practitioners, because the character presents an inclusive story or coherent assembly of reflections that provide for an audience an impressionistic rendering of an individual's life. The teacher and student, as 'stand-up storytellers', are social roles with rich bodies of experiences to share with audiences.

Writing an original one-to-three-minute monologue is an effective exercise for beginning playwrights to develop their craft because the task focuses on composing plotted (in other words, structured) text for just one character. For qualitative researchers who feel that a sole participant through interviews has presented intriguing material that lends itself to live stage performance, rather than lengthy indented quotation in a written article, the task is to edit and adapt verbatim transcript into an elegant and artistically shaped monologue.

Ethnodramas about teachers (which in this case generally refers to an educator as the single case and by default, protagonist in the play script) include character-participants ranging from pre-service to in-service, from novice to veteran, from preschool educator to university professor, and from the typical day at school to the critical turning point in one's career. Students do not generally appear in these one-person or small-group plays as individual characters – they are most often referred to and talked about. In a few exceptional cases, the solo actor portraying the teacher also embodies the student character-participants on stage.

All of these ethnodramas portray teachers describing their instructional, management or personal dilemmas in the classroom which, appropriate to the genre, generate *conflict and tension* – essential dramatic qualities to drive character action and enhance audience engagement. The primary subcategory of this genre, much like commercial film plots and a substantial body of educational research, is the novice teacher struggling with their practice. The teacher-as-storyteller relates vignettes about challenges with students, parents, other teaching colleagues and administrators.

As an example, in the verbatim, unedited transcript excerpt below, an interviewer asked a veteran female secondary school teacher, 'How you do you deal with conflict and discipline in the classroom?' The teacher responded:

> I laugh because this last week has been a big discipline week for me. And, a couple of teachers on campus are talking about it. Why is it our freshman are so unruly and disrespectful? And so I pulled out a really good book, and I'm gonna tell you this, *55 Essentials*, by – it's a teacher on the West Coast and he wrote this book and they just had a big CNN thing on him. He's great. If you want to know the name, e-mail me, and I'll get that for you. Anyways, how do I deal with discipline? I am very forward, straight, and up front. So, I don't take crap from anybody. And I call kids on their behavior. And this happened today in class, as a kid sat there and rolled his eyes at me, again. And I just stopped him and I said, 'When you roll your eyes, you are basically saying 'F.U.' to the person you're talking to and that is disrespectful and not acceptable in my room. So you either be gone and get written up for disrespect and dis-, insubordination.'. Here on campus it's two days off campus. So, here at school, we are very, um, disciplined on the basis of respect as a number one issue. And so, I enforce that and I teach that in my classroom every day by being honest, and calling kids. Now, some kids get freaked out because that's the way they learned at home. But eventually they get used to my style and they appreciate it, and they always come back and say, 'Wow. I never looked at it that way.'. So, it's a cool thing, but it's funny you bring it up because this week has just been a nightmare week and I don't know why. Isn't that weird?
>
> (adapted from Saldaña, 2009: 103–4)

Once an intriguing passage of data has been selected, the next step for the ethnodramatist is to envision its performance and recraft the text into a more aesthetic form by deleting unnecessary or irrelevant passages, rearranging sentences as necessary for enhancing the structure and flow of the story, and recommending appropriate physical and vocal action through italicized stage directions. The 304-word verbatim transcript above has been transformed into a 121-word monologue below for an actor to portray in front of an audience:

(to the audience, as she cleans up her classroom after a long day)

DIANNE: Why are freshman so unruly and disrespectful? One of my students today rolled his eyes at me – *again.* I stopped him and said,

(as if talking to the student)

'When you roll your eyes at me, you are basically saying 'fuck you' to the person you're talking to. And that is disrespectful and not acceptable in my room.'

(to the audience)

I don't take crap from anybody. At this school, *respect* is the number one issue. I enforce that and I teach that in my classroom every day by being *honest.* Now, some kids get freaked out by that, but they eventually get used to my style and they appreciate it. They always come back to me and say,

(as if portraying a dense student)

'Wow, I never looked at it that way.'

(as herself, shakes her head, laughs)

Isn't that weird?

Notice how this monologue excerpt, adapted from extensive interviews with the actual teacher, captures and expresses the participant's values system and identity, two of the distinguishing functions of monologue.

Ethnodramas about students and teacher–student interactions include character-participants learning more about life than the academic curriculum. Rarely is the gifted or ideal child or the pastoral school site portrayed. Most students are characterized as those in conflict with self and others. Ranging from preschool through to university, most plays focus on school students aged 11–18 years.

The black and gay adolescents dealing with racism and homophobia, respectively, are two major themes in this category of plays. Students speak out about the various injustices they encounter in educational settings. A reader's theatre script composed by West-Olatunji and Baker (2006) about male African American youth features this poignant and true monologue. This excerpt is near-verbatim and illustrates two other distinguishing functions of monologue: *the conflict-laden vignette as story* and *characterization through speech and language*:

ADAM: I used to be on the Honor Roll until third grade and then it stopped. I used to have a lot of fights and I didn't get my work done. I was barely passing. When I got to eighth grade, I had a chance to pass and go to the ninth grade, but me and my teacher got into it. I didn't like her. She used to call ya dumb. You know, instead of trying to help the child, she used to call you dumb. One day ... I got tired of it and I told her about herself and she said she could change my grade. I didn't know that she could do that, but she did. She got very upset, then she called my Mama and had a conference. My Mama talked to me and told me to apologize. The next day I did, but she didn't want to listen to me. I did what I was supposed to do. I apologized. She failed me. That's why I got kept back in the eighth grade. And she had no part of me for the next year. The next year, I didn't tell her nothing. I just did my work and got out of there.

(West-Olatunji and Baker, 2006: 7)

An interesting observation about educational ethnodramas is that most works fall into categories of plays about teachers or about students. Only a handful of these works represent both key players on stage interacting with each other in equal measure. Perhaps popular film is the medium that has more accessible capabilities of showing this complex interplay. Nevertheless, I would like to read more play scripts that include students as character-participants. Though problematic to cast and stage for actual ethnotheatrical production, the student themself, more than the teacher as sole protagonist, holds potential to provide more insightful monologue and dialogue about the current state of education. In my own interactions with young people from kindergarten through to high school, I have been awestruck (and sometimes dumbstruck) by some of their revelatory comments.

To recap, some of the functions of ethnodramatic monologue are to profile, in first person, one or more participant's values system and identity, most often through conflict-laden vignettes as story, expressed in naturalistic/verbatim language, yet edited and restructured for dramatic economy and aesthetic purpose. Qualitative researchers can explore monologic construction as practical exercises by taking verbatim interview transcripts and crafting 'portraits in miniature' of participants' experiences.

Writing dialogue

Stage dialogue, consisting of exchanges between two or more people, is more than an academic conversation over ideas, or a series of question–answer–question–answer–question–answer between an interviewer and a participant. Good dramatic dialogue moves a storyline forward by exhibiting characters in tension or conflict, with each one working to achieve their objectives through strategically chosen tactics. The goal is to compose character-participant talk through action, reaction and interaction. Unless participant observation of social life has been conducted, or focus group exchanges have been documented, most dialogic exchanges in ethnodramas are 'creative non-fiction' or plausibly truthful constructions, based on stories culled from interviews and fieldnotes of social action between multiple participants, similar to the short story or novel-length renderings of narrative inquiry.

As a first example, Goldstein (2004, 2006, 2008) explores gay and lesbian issues in the secondary school setting, ranging from young people coming to terms with their sexual identities, to teachers coming to terms with their own homophobic attitudes. In Goldstein's *Alliance* (2006), Roberto, a gay teacher, wrestles with personal disclosure to a gay-questioning student, Jeffrey, in order to help him cope with the homophobic taunts he receives from peers. One scene begins with two teachers patrolling the hallways, discussing the professional and ethical tensions of supporting gay students. The dialogue below is not a verbatim capture of what was actually spoken between two educators at a school, but an imaginative yet reality-based reconstruction of participants' concerns:

> ROBERTO: So around three in morning, instead of sleeping, I was thinking.
> RAHIMA: (*Smiling*) Oh, yeah. Thinking again, were you? About what?
> ROBERTO: Talking to Jeffrey.
> RAHIMA: Talking to Jeffrey about what?
> ROBERTO: Being gay.
> RAHIMA: (*Surprised*) Oh. (*Concerned*) I don't think that's a good idea.
> ROBERTO: Why not?
> RAHIMA: You don't even know if he's gay. Just because he's being called names, doesn't mean he's gay.
> ROBERTO: I think he's gay.
> RAHIMA: How do you know?
> ROBERTO: Gaydar.

RAHIMA: Seriously.

ROBERTO: Seriously. I think he's questioning his sexuality. Don't forget. I was Jeffrey not too long ago.

RAHIMA: What if you're wrong?

ROBERTO: What if I'm right? He needs support.

RAHIMA: But that's not your job. We're not social workers. Maybe you could send him to Guidance.

ROBERTO: None of the people in Guidance is gay. None of them has gone through what he's going through. I have …

RAHIMA: There are still lots of parents who don't like the idea of gay teachers in their kids' school. And you're still on probation. Ask the Guidance people to talk to him.

ROBERTO: (*Soft*) The kind of homophobic bullying Jeffrey is facing?

RAHIMA: Yeah?

ROBERTO: It leads to self-hatred.

(Goldstein, 2006: 157–60)

In the remainder of the scene, Roberto shares his coming-out story to Jeffrey. Though the student does not reveal his own sexual identity, it is inferred by the end of the play that Jeffrey has indeed been helped by his teacher's honest disclosure.

When more than two character-participants are involved in social action on stage, the complexity of dialogue construction increases exponentially with the addition of each person. Thus, portrayals of classrooms filled with students are rare in the ethnodramatic literature. But an interesting subcategory of ethnodramas about teachers is the actor-turned-educator performing their experiences with youth in the classroom. The solo performer with theatrical production experience has a slight advantage over the traditionally trained educational researcher. The actor most often has the ability to take on not just one but several roles involved with school life.

Sun (2008) solves the dilemma of staging the student-filled classroom by portraying not only herself as the teacher but, in her one-woman show, *No Child …*, portraying a principal, a janitor, three classroom teachers, a security guard, a grandparent and eight different students, sometimes in rapid-fire dialogic exchanges with each other.[1] Sun maintains truthfulness by composing scenes of chaotic classroom interactions, such as the one below when she tries to convince a new teacher that she is a visiting theatre artist and not a student:

COCA: Miss, did you hear? Someone stole Ms. Tam's bag and she quit for good. We got some Russian teacher now.

MRS. PROJENSKY: Quiet Quiet Quiet Quiet Quiet Quiet Quiet. Quiet!

MS. SUN: Miss, Miss, Miss. I'm the teaching artist for …

MRS. PROJENSKY: Sit down, you.

SHONDRIKA: Aw, snap, she told her.

MRS. PROJENSKY: Sit down, quiet. Quiet, sit down.

MS. SUN: No, I'm the teaching artist for this period. Maybe Miss Tam or Mrs. Kennedy told you something about me?

JEROME: (*shadowboxes*) Ah, hah, you being replaced, Russian lady.

MS. SUN: Jerome, you're not helping right now.

JEROME: What?! You don't gotta tell me jack. We ain't got a teacher no more or haven't you heard? (*he flings a chair*) We are the worst class in the school.

MRS. PROJENSKY: Sit down! Sit down!

MS. SUN: Guys, quiet down and focus. We have a show to do in a few weeks.

COCA: Ooee, I don't wanna do this no more. It's stupid.

CHRIS: I still want to do it.

JEROME: Shut the fuck up, Chris.

JOSE: Yo man, she's right. This shit is mad fucking boring yo.

COCA: Yeah!

XIOMARA: Yeah!

BRIAN: Yeah!

SHONDRIKA: Yeah!

COCA: Mad boring.

JEROME: Fuckin' stupid.

MRS. PROJENSKY: Quiet! Quiet! Quiet!

(Sun, 2008: 18–19)

Some of the representations in *No Child …* may have been exaggerated for comic effect, but a truthful sense of 'being there' is evident in the script, enhancing the credibility and trustworthiness of this staged representation of classroom life.

To recap, some of the functions of ethnodramatic dialogue are to profile exchanges between two or more participants in social action, reaction and interaction. The participants as characters exhibit conflict or tension as they talk and work toward achieving their individual objectives. The text is, more often than not, reconstructed from self-contained stories found within interviews, or from imaginative yet plausible encounters suggested by participant observation fieldnotes. Qualitative researchers can explore dialogic construction as practical exercises by taking naturalistic data and crafting 'what if' two-person conversational scenarios occurring in real time for the stage.

Recommendations for writing

Ethnodrama provides opportunities for participants with marginalized 'offstage' status in everyday life to stand centre stage and tell their stories. A body of character-participants missing from the ethnodramatic library is the administrative and service staff members of a school system. Imagine a play script told exclusively from the school office receptionist's point of view, from a bus driver's or cafeteria worker's perspective, or from the perspective of a principal describing her first year in the position. More ethnodramas that include the full range of individuals who work at a school would be intriguing, as would the inclusion of parents and their stakes in their children's education.

I also encourage exploration of the scripted adaptation and dramatization of some of the field's best qualitative studies. In my ethnotheatre course at Arizona State University for theatre majors, we were inspired by Victor Turner's charge to mount a culture on stage and experimented with improvising scenes from such works as Michael Angrosino's (1994) classic case study, 'On the bus with Vonnie Lee', and Rebekah Nathan's (2005) ethnography of university student culture, *My Freshman Year*. Is there ethnodramatic potential in dramatizing scenes from books like Tracy Kidder's (1989) *Among Schoolchildren*? Is there someone out there who can write and/or perform an engaging one-man show about Paolo Freire or Rafe Esquith, or a one-woman show about bell hooks, and their educational practices and theories?

Finally, I stated in an article of my own autoethnodrama about my high-school band years (Saldaña, 2008) that you can't learn how to tell someone else's story until you first learn how to tell your own. The reflective practitioner, the autobiographical and autoethnographic examination of one's own career and practice, or even your own history and experiences about your role as a student, is rich material for experimental writing of an original monologue or brief one-act play about your own educational stories (see Chang, 2008 for expert guidance).

Closure

In theatre, the term for a play written to be read but not performed is a 'closet drama'. Researchers can certainly compose a fieldnote-based script as a closet ethnodrama, but the next step and true test of a play's effectiveness come from its production mounting on stage. I encourage all researchers not only to develop written scripts, but to explore their realization through a staged reading or performance (see Knowles and Cole, 2008; Leavy, 2009; Saldaña, 2005 for guidance with arts-based research).

Regardless of your academic discipline, I also encourage you to explore the varieties of genres in qualitative inquiry, including ethnodramatic writing and performance. Each one of us tells monologic vignettes of one kind or another, and we exchange improvised dialogue with others virtually every day of our lives. Theatre simply gives aesthetic shape and magnitude to what we already know how to do. Humans are theatre.

Note

1   To me, Sun's *No Child* ... (2008) is perhaps *the* best ethnodrama about education available in print today, and is highly recommended reading by educational researchers. Clips from Ms Sun's one-woman show are also available on YouTube. Go to www.youtube. com, enter 'Nilaja Sun' in the Search field, press Enter, and click to view the most relevant results.

References

Angrosino, M. V. (1994) 'On the bus with Vonnie Lee: explorations in life history and metaphor', *Journal of Contemporary Ethnography*, 23, 14–28.

Chang, H. (2008) *Autoethnography as Method*, Walnut Creek, CA: Left Coast Press.

Goldstein, T. (2004) 'Performed ethnography for anti-homophobia teacher education: linking research to teaching', *Canadian On-Line Journal of Queer Studies in Education*, 1 (online) <jps.library.utoronto.ca/index.php/jqstudies/article/view/3280/1409> (accessed 24 June 2009).

Goldstein, T. (2006) 'Toward a future of equitable pedagogy and schooling', *Pedagogies*, 1, 151–69.

Goldstein, T. (2008) 'Multiple commitments and ethical dilemmas in performed ethnography', *Educational Insights*, 12 (online) <www.ccfi.educ.ubc.ca/publication/insights/v12n02/articles/goldstein/index.html> (accessed 24 June 2009).

Kidder, T. (1989) *Among Schoolchildren*, New York: Avon.

Knowles, J. G. and Cole A. L. (eds) (2008) *Handbook of the Arts in Qualitative Research: Perspectives, methodologies, examples, and issues*, Thousand Oaks, CA: Sage.

Leavy, P. (ed.) (2009) *Method Meets Art: Arts-based research practice*, New York: Guilford.

Nathan, R. (2005) *My Freshman Year: What a professor learned by becoming a student*, New York: Penguin.

Saldaña, J. (ed.) (2005) *Ethnodrama: An anthology of reality theatre*, Walnut Creek, CA: AltaMiras.

Saldaña, J. (2008) 'Second chair: an autoethnodrama', *Research Studies in Music Education*, 30: 177–91.

Saldaña, J. (2009) *The Coding Manual for Qualitative Researchers*, London: Sage.

Sun, N. (2008) *No Child …*, New York: Dramatists Play Service.

Turner, V. (1982) *From Ritual to Theatre*, New York: PAJ.

West-Olatunji, C. A. and Baker, J. C. (2006) 'African American adolescent males: giving voice to their educational experiences', *Multicultural Perspectives*, 8: 3–9.

Chapter 8

Narrative theory and the construction of qualitative texts

Julia Colyar and Karri Holley

Introduction: rethinking qualitative texts

Qualitative researchers have long struggled with the question of how to represent social reality through the academic text. While researchers historically have been bound by a limited template in terms of scholarly writing, recent decades have seen a challenge to the accepted format of academic manuscripts. Such challenges offer new research outcomes, but also expand the ways in which data are conceived and pursued (Richardson, 1997). Debates across the field have led to the development of innovative textual structures and alternative forms of representation, including a wide variety of presentation styles and strategies (Fine and Weiss, 1996; Lather, 1992; Tierney, 1997). Many of the chapters in this volume offer non-traditional ways of imagining the research process and its products. At the centre of these discussions is the text itself, a document that reflects the many choices researchers make, as well as the findings they seek to articulate.

Positioning the expanded array of writing strategies within postmodern sensibilities, Lincoln noted, 'As the world and our views of it have changed, so, too, have changed the kinds of texts we hope to have represent us to ourselves' (1997: 36). Toward these altered understandings, she continued, scholars should be more deliberate in their writing choices. Lincoln posed these questions to consider: In what voice will I speak? What character am I in the story? Who are my readers? We continue the conversation about forms of writing and qualitative choices in this chapter. In particular, we argue that narrative theory can be used to inform the decisions researchers make about their texts (Holley and Colyar, forthcoming). Narrative theory also offers specific tools and terms that researchers can use to consider the writing of qualitative texts, including the elements of story, character, focalization and plot. Although a qualitative project is more than these individual elements, narrative theory provides a framework for understanding both the research process and its products in new ways.

Narrative theory: evolution and distinction

Narrative theory historically has been used to describe completed products (narrative texts) and to articulate the meaning-making tools which underlie human experience in the world (Czarniawska, 2004). We offer a brief review of narrative as a concept and strategy. Many scholars identify Aristotle's *Poetics* as the first work of narrative theory, in which Aristotle describes the elements of dramatic texts. For Czarniawska (2004), narrative analysis of texts can be traced to hermeneutic studies of the Bible, Talmud and Koran. Contemporary studies of narrative were shaped by theoretical movements such as New Criticism, which emerged following the Second World War (Polkinghorne, 1988). New Critical Studies focused on individual texts and the elements which contributed to a work's coherence. Northrop Frye's work during the late 1950s sought to describe literary and mythological systems, creating conceptual maps for understanding texts and textual production. Further, Frye (1957) asserted that narratives were not the invention of isolated artists; rather, authors unconsciously draw upon the long tradition of stories across generations and genres. In this way, Frye's work privileges the narrative construct and offers a connection across writers, texts and genres (Polkinghorne, 1988). French structuralism and Russian formalism are also considered important antecedents of narrative theory. From scholars such as Levi-Strauss (1968), Saussure (1966) and Propp (1968), narratology took shape, a methodology still popular in such fields as semantics and linguistics.

Narratology is characterized by the analysis of texts through formalized, structured categories (Bal, 1985). The goal of early narratology was to decode the universal grammar that underscored every possible narrative, creating a means of describing and understanding all texts. According to this approach, a shared narrative structure highlights all human interaction. Propp (1968) outlined this perspective through his definition of the basic narratological functions that occur in Russian folk tales. He argued that, despite the content or setting of the tale, despite even the characters themselves, all Russian folk stories exhibit at least some of the same functions. These elements will be familiar to readers of fairytales or more contemporary stories. The hero leaves home at the beginning of the tale, only to encounter challenges that test their courage along the journey. After defeating the villain in combat, the hero returns home to great celebration. These features are not intended to explain a story's meanings, but rather to describe the essential building blocks of folktales.

The influence of Propp's analysis is seen in the work of later scholars such as Labov (1972) and van Dijk (1983). Their work highlighted the role of macrostructures in texts, and acknowledged specific schematic forms of discourse. Readers expect newspaper articles to exhibit similar features regardless of their content; these features are different from those of folktales or novels. Academic research manuscripts share common characteristics as well, independent of their topic or discipline. These taxonomical features include abstracts, a literature review and a discussion of research methodology. Reissman defined these categorical structures as the 'weight bearing walls' that hold texts together (1993: 18). These structures are not the central focus of an argument. They simply provide foundation and stability. Without these essential structures, texts do not have the recognizable components that signify their membership in a particular genre such as scholarship. Macrostructures allow the author not only to be responsive to the demands of the textual field, but also to order the components of the story.

Contemporary work in narrative has moved away from the structuralist approach with an emphasis on categorizing basic elements, yet still recognizes that textual characteristics provide some foundation for narrative understanding. Recent scholars have considered both the process and product, or the act of storytelling and the text itself (Franzosi, 1998). In this body of research, the significance of narrative is also located in cultural expression, and scholars seek to understand the influence of narrative on the text, the reader and the author (Potter, 1996). 'Texts do not just index a relation between words and between texts, but between text and social reality', argued Franzosi (1998: 547). In other words, narrative studies examine text and context rather than focusing simply on cataloguing internal features or elements. The sequence of the text, for example, provides a pattern by which readers shape a social reality in regards to a specific event. Culture, Reissman offered, 'speaks itself through an individual's story' (1993: 5). Over the last generation, a narrative approach to understanding individuals and culture has been embraced by a variety of disciplines including history, anthropology, psychology, sociology, law, medicine and education (Reissman, 1993).

Narrative has also been used as a research methodology, perhaps most notably described in the works of Polkinghorne (1988) and Bruner (1986). Bruner's work offered narrative knowing as an important meaning-making schema, a fundamental cognitive process that explains human perception. Polkinghorne further advocated for the use of narrative inquiry in the study of the human sciences. He argued:

> The narrative scheme serves as a lens through which the apparently independent and disconnected elements of existence are seen as related parts of a whole. At the level of a single life, the autobiographical narrative shows life as unified and whole. In stories about other lives and in histories of social groups, narrative shows the interconnectedness and significance of seemingly random activities.
>
> (Polkinghorne, 1988: 36)

Like the efforts of Frye and other structuralists, Polkinghorne's vision of narrative is connective, bringing together individual experiences and communities. More recently, Clandinin and Connelly's (2000) work on narrative inquiry provided important definitions and context for qualitative research. Narrative as a research method can be seen in contemporary methodologies such as portraiture (Lawrence-Lightfoot and Davis, 1997) and ethnodrama (Saldaña, 2005).

We draw most directly on the structural properties of narrative as well as the ways in which narratives can provide cultural understandings. These two aspects of narrative are inextricably linked: the structural elements of narratives help readers understand cultural meanings, while cultural meanings inform structural properties. Qualitative researchers can use the narrative elements outlined in this chapter as blueprints towards building texts.

Defining narrative

Narrative is highlighted in separate definitions as both product and process. For Frye, narrative is a text that can be described using a set of categories or constructs; for Polkinghorne and Bruner, narrative is a human meaning-making tool, the process by which individuals explore and later explain their experiences. Narrative indeed has been defined in a great variety of ways and sometimes with considerable disagreement. Barthes (1977: 251), for example, famously defined narrative as having infinitely diverse forms: 'Narrative is present in myth, legend, fable, tale, novella, epic, history ... stained glass windows, cinema, comics, news items, conversations.... Narrative is present in every age, in every place, in every society.' Linguist William Labov (1972: 359) highlighted the importance of sequence. He defined narrative as 'one method of recapitulating past experience by matching a verbal sequence of clauses to the sequence of events which (it is inferred) actually occurred'. Ricoeur used a more succinct definition, again emphasizing sequence. Narrative is 'the temporal character of the human experience,' he concluded (1984: 52). For Abbott, the essence of narrative is action. 'Simply put,' Abbott noted, 'narrative is the representation of an event or a series of events' (2002: 12).

We favour a simplified definition combining the importance of sequence and action: narrative is the telling (or retelling) of a story or set of events in a specific time sequence. The elements of story, character, focalization and plot shape how the narrative is organized and presented to the reader. For Bal (1985: 4), these elements are tools which are 'useful in that they enable us to formulate a textual description in such a way that is accessible to others'.

Story and character

Perhaps the most basic element of a narrative is its story as told through a range of characters. For Abbott (2002: 13), a story is 'the event or sequence of events'. The story is the same, regardless of whether it is told in first or third person, past or present tense, chronological or non-chronological order, and the intended audience. For example, the story of Little Red Riding Hood and her encounter with the deceptive wolf is recognizable to many readers. The young girl sets out through the forest to visit her grandmother and is stalked by the wolf. Though its form and audience might vary (for example, some versions are appropriate for children, while others are adapted for adult audiences), the basic story is the same. In this way, the story is a stable component, unaffected by other narrative elements. At the same time, Abbott (2002) points out that a story is rarely apprehended directly. We most often understand stories as mediated through other constructions, which include characters and their actions, point of view and the organization of a text. Story and the other narrative elements are interconnected; we understand story in relation to character, focalization and plot.

For Bal (1985), the most relevant elements in the story are events/actions and actors/characters. Characters are significant narratological constructs because they cause or undergo the events of a story. The wolf, for example, is an important character in Little Red's tale; without him, the story would be very different. Bal also noted that characters in stories can have intentions or be the objects of intentions; this distinction is one way of differentiating between central and non-central characters. Little Red may be considered a central character because she acts with intention, while her grandmother may be considered non-central because she is the object of Little Red's intention. Both characters are important, but serve different roles in the story. Characters are not necessarily human (Bal, 1985: 27). The forest and Little Red's basket also serve as characters. Like the wolf, they are important in the development of the story. Characters ultimately serve as a means for the story to progress through various episodes to its conclusion.

Focalization

The development of a story also depends on focalization, or the point of view from which events unfold. Focalization is an active element of narrative, resulting from an author's choice with regard to character perspective. Bal described focalization as the vision of a text, the location from which the characters and actors are viewed (1985: 100). As a narrative device, focalization provides a lens through which the story is told. Such a device not only impacts on the perspective highlighted in the text, but can also be used to identify those perspectives excluded from the narrative telling. Focalization is an element that may be redirected without changing the basic components of the story. For example, the story of Little Red may be told from Red's perspective, using the girl as the focalizer, or from her grandmother's perspective. In the traditional tale, a narrator serves as the focalizer and stands anonymously outside the text. This approach is common in research texts, where the author frequently assumes the role of an anonymous, omniscient narrator removed from the events. This type of focalization, Bal noted, is external, while focalization provided by characters in the story is internal. The meanings communicated via these various focalizations are different, though the story remains consistent.

Plot

The difference between story and plot often is unclear, and has been variously described. Indeed, Abbott lamented that plot is a term so often misused that it has become disabled. English speakers, he noted, commonly conflate plot and story to mean the same thing (2002: 16). Cobley (2001: 239) described plot as 'the chain of causation which dictates that story events are somehow linked and that they are therefore to be depicted in relation to each other'. The plot also serves to prioritize those events and characters crucial to the story development. The narrative plot responds to the question, why? (Czarniawska, 2004). In Cobley's definition, plot drives the story events. Little Red is well loved by her grandmother, who makes her the red cap she so often wears; she is urged by her mother to visit her grandmother because she is ill and some cake and wine will do the older woman good; Little Red sets out into the woods cautiously but is lured off the path to pick flowers; the wolf, after waylaying Red, runs ahead to grandmother's house and devours her, then disguises himself and waits for Red's arrival. These complications are not simply details that flush out the story. They provide reasons for the story to move forward. In this way, plot serves as the logic for a text.

Application of narrative theory to qualitative research

Though scholarly works differ from fairy tales in content, form, purpose and audience, these narrative elements are useful in understanding the construction of texts, and in particular qualitative research texts. Story, plot, character and focalization serve as constructs that can be used as weight-bearing walls for organizing qualitative research texts. Scholarly texts are, of course, not strangers to organizing constructs (Brew, 2001). Researchers construct knowledge through the systematic use of language, organized in a manner that is recognized by others within the community. The evaluation of research by a scholarly community is dependent on the structure of rules used to organize academic writing. Indeed, writing is frequently held to be the single activity that unites all members of the academic community (Rose and McClafferty, 2001). Brew's rules speak to the role of the researcher and the importance of audience; narrative constructs also invoke these issues, though from within a different framework.

Narrative components can also provide different perspectives from which to address Lincoln's (1997) questions for qualitative researchers: In what voice will I speak? What character am I in the story? Who are my readers? When researchers attend to questions of focalization, they address questions of voice – theirs and those of participants. Thinking about character brings researchers to think about their roles in the inquiry and writing process, but also the roles of various participants, and whether or not they are central or noncentral to the telling. Questions of plot (as well as focalization) can assist researchers as they deliberate over audience. Different audiences will likely resonate with different points of view and textual organization. These terms, then, can provide a framework of rules for qualitative projects.

Establishing story and character

One of the most significant writing challenges for qualitative researchers is to determine the range of actors present in the research narrative. These choices do not necessarily influence the research story, but rather provide a framework through which readers can comprehend the narrative events. The story is about the central characters, but those characters interact with a range of other actors through the text. Who (or what) contributes to the narrative episode?

Early in his book *In Search of Respect*, Philippe Bourgois (2003: 21–2) identified one of his participants, Primo, as his 'closest friend on the streets' and 'the central character of [the] book'. The book opens as Primo helps Bourgois navigate through one of the researcher's many social faux pas. Primo serves as the researcher's guide to the El Barrio area, the Spanish-speaking district in Harlem, New York City, USA, in terms of both the geography and the political, economic and racial terrain of the neighbourhood. The details of Primo's experience provide important examples of the larger social phenomena Bourgois exposes and critiques. At the same time, however, Bourgois is himself a central character. When Bourgois describes the challenges of gaining entry into the social and economic world of the neighbourhood, he admits:

> Everyone began scattering in front of me as if I had the plague; all of a sudden the block was desolate. I felt as if I was infested with vermin, as if my white skin signaled the terminal stage of some kind of contagious disease sowing havoc in its path.
>
> (Bourgois, 2003: 29)

Bourgois's presence in the text, his character in the telling, is ultimately important as the author describes the ways in which El Barrio residents are marginalized. The differences between Bourgois and Primo (in terms of education, class and race) provide context for the research process as well as Bourgois's findings.

Often the narrative is shaped not solely by the introduction of the primary research participants, but also by the locales in which they reside. These locales are articulated in a character role, influencing the thoughts and actions of the human narrative agents. For example, Mario Small (2004) made narrative decisions in his analysis of Villa Victoria, a predominantly Puerto Rican community located in the South End of Boston, USA. The author questions how neighbourhood poverty impacts social capital, and traces the history of a subsidized public housing project. He opens the book's preface by outlining the character of the housing project: 'What first struck me about Villa Victoria … was the landscape. Several rows of three-story concrete houses with high front stoops, pitched roofs and Spanish ironwork abutted a small brick-layered plaza' (Small, 2004: xi). Small continues by describing the neighborhood's deterioration, noting '[the complex] had seen better times – paint had peeled off the walls, garbage was strewn about. But the structure's underlying dignity … was evident to anyone willing to pay attention' (2004: xi).

By immediately positioning the neighbourhood as a primary character within the text, Small prepares the reader for the interaction between the residents and the physical community. Later in the text, the concept of place furthers the story of an isolated, urban neighborhood. The ecological emphasis underscores the outside community as hostile and negative towards the Villa Victoria residents, and adds to the comforting nature of the housing project as an influential character in the lives of its residents. Ultimately, the alignment of the multiple locales reinforces that the underlying dignity of the neighbourhood is reflected in the people who live within its confines. The long-time residents of Villa Victoria note that the fabric of the community binds them to the neighbourhood, just as it excludes them from the upscale surrounding neighbourhoods. Small's approach allows readers to better understand the story of the human characters through their interactions with the community in which they reside.

Defining focalization

Establishing focalization requires the researcher to determine what elements matter in the story. More significantly, focalization requires the researcher to determine through which character, actor or event the story will be told. Bourgois's (2003) study of East Harlem, for example, could emphasize endless points of view: the residents', the researcher's, local police and politicians', business owners' or adjacent community members'. Focalization may also shift between internal or external points of view, where the researcher allows participants to voice their own experiences or serves as the omniscient narrator of the tale.

The author may also structure the text in a manner that highlights shifting points of view. Each chapter of Valerie Hey's analysis of friendship among young women, *The Company She Keeps* (1997), reveals the insights of key character groups, including middle-class and white working-class girls as well as those social institutions with which the girls interact, including school and popular media. Hey opens her narrative by reviewing the vast extant literature related to gender dynamics and social engagement. The reader is informed of what others say about relationships and gender. The text then shifts to a focus on the experiences of young women themselves, each expressing cultural forms of friendship. For example, Hey notes:

> I first encountered one of the most prestigious groups at Eastford School in the fifth form … their star status was confirmed when a teacher, assuming that this was the only group involved in the study, asked me why I had chosen to study this group rather than 'ordinary' girls.
>
> (Hey, 1997: 105)

She contrasts their experience with other girls, including Carol, who 'survived as a truanting working-class girl with little or no money of her own through being street wise' (Hey, 1997: 94). The focalization of the research narrative represents the unique nature of her individual respondents. Just as female friendships manifest in various forms, no single individual in Hey's story solely represents the challenge of friendship among young women. Each girl represents a different perspective on what it means to engage in female friendships. The text is structured to allow for various perspectives which together form the text's story.

Constructing the plot

Researchers organize qualitative data to reveal a specific plot, which tells a story to the reader. Through the plot, authors provide a sequence of time and order to the story. The plot begins with a question or unresolved issue; the author then structures the text to bring some resolution to the question. The textual structure and sequence serve to reveal the plot as the reader progresses. For example, research questions within the text not only orient the reader to main ideas, but also provide a key indication of the narrative plot. Angela Valenzuela takes such an approach in *Subtractive Schooling*, where she writes:

When teenagers lament that 'Nobody cares,' few adults listen ... but what if it were not hyperbole? What if each weekday, for eight hours a day, teenagers inhabited a world populated by adults who did not care – or at least did not care for them sufficiently?

(Valenzuela, 1999: 3)

Her plot unfolds through stories of teachers, students and immigrants, each perspective providing insight into what happens to teenagers who live in such an environment. After summarizing the historical influences on the high school and community featured in her research, Valenzuela then focuses on the crisis within her text: 'The school's obvious systematic problems ... are brushed aside and the burden of responsibility ... is understood as rightfully residing first with the students, their families, and the community' (Valenzuela, 1999: 65). Rather than a joint effort to ensure success and achievement, the plot is structured to reveal how a lack of authentic caring and engagement on behalf of teachers fosters resentment and anger from students. Valenzuela provides a solution to the plot in the latter pages of her work when she writes, 'If a culturally biased premise is built into the school's definition of success, then the well-being of the community will remain in constant jeopardy' (1999: 265). The plot of the research text is not restricted to chronological order, but reflects a logical understanding of the events under consideration. The plot mirrors the story, not simply the data or the role of the researcher. The plot of the research narrative, then, reveals the message the researcher intends to convey to the audience. The message results from the active decision making of the researcher.

Using narrative constructs

In the preceding section, we offered the narrative elements of story, character, focalization and plot as tools that can be used in reading qualitative texts. Though a qualitative project is more than these essential elements, an analysis can begin with these foci. For example, Bourgois's (2003) account of life in El Barrio is enhanced when both the researcher and the central participant are identified as essential characters. The tensions inherent in their differences serve as markers for larger social differences based on class, race and educational opportunity; Bourgois's outsider status works to highlight and critique the ways in which some communities are marginalized and oppressed. Readers understand difference – and its implications – in new ways because of the presentation of characters.

These narrative elements can also be useful as scholars work towards qualitative representations. The questions that arise from applying narrative elements require researchers to confront many of the thorny issues embedded in all qualitative representations, including the role of the researcher and the presentations of participants and events. Examining these questions in concert allows scholars to see the connections between presentation and argument, or the ways in which how a story is told is part of the story itself. Of course, not all authors will use each of the narrative elements in the same ways, or at all. Qualitative texts are shaped by a series of decisions, including the decision to utilize narrative constructs as part of a writing process.

A narrative framework offers a useful strategy for novice and experienced researchers alike. Using these constructs, researchers can identify central characters, connect them to the story, and think through the plot elements that shape a study's findings. Perhaps even more importantly, focusing on story requires the researcher to establish what the project has helped them understand more completely. Considering focalization may remind researchers that the author's is not the only perspective that may be used. Thinking about focalization inspires a consideration of whose voice or perspective should be prioritized in the story, and what it means when one perspective is chosen over another. Different audiences may call for different focalization strategies, and scholars may consider where and to whom their writing is presented. In the end, these decisions are central to the production of a completed study and also respond to Lincoln's (1997) calls for more deliberate textual construction.

Conclusion

Narrative theory and inquiry have had broad appeal in qualitative research for more than a generation. A number of important texts have helped researchers imagine new ways of using narratives as data (see Czarniawska, 2004; Reissman, 1993; Polkinghorne, 1988). In this chapter, we considered how the elements of narrative theory can assist researchers in making sense of data. Narrative constructs serve to mediate how scholars, and later readers, understand the research text. Outlining the story to be told through the research enables the author to determine the range of actors within the narrative. These actors serve to propel the plot. Through the process of focalization, the author provides well-defined lenses through which the narrative episodes unfold. An awareness of narrative constructs also highlights the role of the researcher as a storyteller. Ultimately, however, the approach offered here is not intended as the answer for constructing qualitative texts. The question or representation should continue beyond these pages and this volume. Instead, this chapter suggests a set of guiding constructs that assist our reading and our writing practices.

This approach, as it draws from and reflects a variety of other disciplines, also points researchers towards readers outside their own fields. For Czarniawska (2004: 136), this fact is an essential point; she argued that such interdisciplinarity allows social science to 'matter more in the life of contemporary societies'. Social science texts, she further noted, must be skillfully crafted, respond to questions of validity, and also speak to questions of readability. Indeed, these are no small matters. But representing social reality has never been a small matter. In this chapter, we offer the use of narrative constructs (story, character, plot and focalization) as one approach in creating trustworthy, interesting, relevant and beautifully crafted texts.

References

Abbott, H. P. (2002) *The Cambridge Introduction to Narrative*, Cambridge: Cambridge University Press.

Aristotle (1997) *Poetics*, trans., M. Heath, London: Penguin.

Bal, M. (1985) *Narratology: Introduction to the theory of narrative*, Toronto: University of Toronto Press.

Barthes, R. (1977) 'Introduction to the structural analysis of narrative', trans., S. Heath, in S. Sontag (ed.), *A Roland Barthes Reader*, London: Vintage.

Bourgois, P. (2003) *In Search of Respect: Selling crack in El Barrio*, 2nd edn, New York: Cambridge University Press.

Brew, A. (2001) *The Nature of Research: Inquiry into academic contexts*, New York: Routledge.

Bruner, J. (1986) *Actual Minds, Possible Worlds*, Cambridge, MA: Harvard University Press.

Clandinin, D. J. and Connelly, F. M. (2000) *Narrative Inquiry*, San Francisco: Jossey-Bass.

Cobley, P. (2001) *Narrative*, London: Routledge.

Czarniawska, B. (2004) *Narratives in Social Science Research*, Thousand Oaks, CA: Sage.

Fine, M. and Weiss, L. (1996) 'Writing the 'wrongs' of fieldwork: confronting our own research writing dilemmas in urban ethnographies', *Qualitative Inquiry*, 2(3): 251–74.

Franzosi, R. (1998) 'Narrative analysis-or why (and how) sociologists should be interested in narrative', *Annual Review of Sociology*, 24: 517–54.

Frye, N. (1957) *The Anatomy of Criticism*, Princeton: Princeton University Press.

Hey, V. (1997) *The Company She Keeps: An ethnography of girls' friendship*, Buckingham: Open University Press.

Holley, K. and Colyar, J. (forthcoming) 'Re-thinking texts: narrative and the construction of qualitative research', *Educational Researcher*.

Labov, W. (1972) *Language in the Inner City*, Philadelphia, PA: University of Pennsylvania Press.

Lather, P. (1992) 'Critical frames in educational research: feminist and post-structuralist perspectives', *Theory into Practice*, 31(2), 87–99.

Lawrence-Lightfoot, S. and Davis, J. (1997) *The Art and Science of Portraiture*, San Francisco, CA: Jossey-Bass.

Lévi-Strauss, C. (1968) *Structural Anthropology*, London: Allen Lane.

Lincoln, Y. (1997) 'Self, subject audience, text: living at the edge, writing at the margins', in W. Tierney and Y. Lincoln (eds), *Representation and the Text: Re-framing the narrative voice*, Albany, NY: State University of New York Press.

Polkinghorne, D. E. (1988) *Narrative Knowing and the Human Sciences*, Albany, NY: State University of New York Press.

Potter, J. (1996) *Representing Reality: Discourse, rhetoric, and social construction*, Thousand Oaks, CA: Sage.

Propp, V. (1968) *Morphology of the Folktale*, Austin, TX: University of Texas Press.

Reissman, C. K. (1993) *Narrative Analysis*, Newbury Park, CA: Sage.

Richardson, L. (1997) *Fields of Play: Constructing an academic life*, New Brunswick, NJ: Rutgers University Press.

Ricoeur, P. (1984) *Time and Narrative*, Chicago: University of Chicago Press.

Rose, M., and McClafferty, K. A. (2001) 'A call for the teaching of writing in graduate education', *Educational Researcher*, 30(2), 27–33.

Saldaña, J. (ed.) (2005) *Ethnodrama: An anthology of reality theater*, Walnut Creek, CA: Altamira.

Saussure, F. de (1966) *Course in General Linguistics*, trans. W. Baskin, New York: McGraw Hill.

Small, M. (2004) *Villa Victoria: The transformation of social capital in a Boston Barrio*, Chicago: University of Chicago Press.

Tierney, W. (1997) 'Lost in translation: time and voice in qualitative research', in W. Tierney and Y. Lincoln (eds), *Representation and the Text: Re-framing the narrative voice*, Albany, NY: State University of New York Press.

Valenzuela, A. (1999) *Subtractive Schooling: U.S.-Mexican youth and the politics of caring*, Albany, NY: State University of New York Press.

Van Dijk, T. (1983) 'Discourse analysis: its development and application to the structure of news', *Journal of Communication*, 33(2), 20–43.

Chapter 9

Multimodality, visual methodologies and higher education

Lesley Gourlay

Introduction

In postindustrial urbanized 'developed' nations and beyond, many people inhabit an increasingly visually mediated world. They are increasingly bombarded by a multiplicity of images, and engaged in a range of visual practices in their day-to-day lives via online social networking, use of camera and videophones, and video-sharing sites such as YouTube™. Partly as a result, the presentation of the self is increasingly mediated via visual means, as we document and construct ourselves both textually and visually on sites such as Facebook™ and Flickr™, via a visual avatar in immersive worlds such as Second Life™, or in online games such as World of Warcraft™. This chapter will investigate the implications of this social turn towards a mixture of modes of communication – or multimodality – for research, looking at the features and roles of visual methodologies in the particular context of higher education (HE). It will argue that these new contexts can be better explored by utilizing the potential of the visual in research processes. Additionally, it will look at how visual methodologies might be used more broadly, often in combination with other methodologies such as material and textual, to offer new ways of understanding the experiences of participants in educational contexts.

Multimodality, the visual and research

Kress and van Leeuwen (2001) have pointed to a recent shift away from monomodality in 'Western' culture. In the past, there was a cultural emphasis on textual practices, with more value placed on text-based genres than on visual images. They argue that this dominance has begun to shift, with a move towards multimodality in documents and other types of social practices. By multimodality, they mean a more mixed set of semiotic resources – or modes used for meaning making. One important element in this process has been the gradual ascendancy of the screen over the book as the predominant mode of representation in many spheres of life, bringing with it a greater emphasis on non-textual images and visual layout. As Kress argues, 'what is fundamental is that the screen is the site of the image, and the logic of the image dominates the semiotic organisation of the screen' (2003: 65). The nature and placement of images carry meaning and may render text subsidiary; text is no longer the default dominant means of creating and communicating meaning.

This shift towards multimodality can also be seen in the practices of higher education, with increased use of digital technologies and visual modes in educational process and engagement. Students and academic staff are engaging with higher education in increasingly complex ways, via a more multimodal set of social and communicative practices both face-to-face and online (Kress, 2003). This often includes an increased role for the visual, as may be seen in the increased use of PowerPoint™, which tends to encourage the use of visual images such as photographs, illustrations and video in the face-to-face classroom. Although research has been inconclusive regarding whether PowerPoint™ leads to more effective learning (Szabo and Hastings, 2000), and has found that images used in PowerPoint™ slide-shows may not always be perceived as relevant to students (Bartsch and Cobern, 2003), these images are now a common feature of university provision. Students also routinely use the internet as their primary research tool – an environment that uses text in combination with sound, image and video. The layout and features of virtual learning environments (VLEs), (and increasingly textbooks) draw on a more multimodal – and particularly visual – set of resources, as participants increasingly engage with what Mirzoeff calls 'visual events in which the user seeks information, meaning or pleasure in an interface with visual technology' (2002: 5). This may be reflected in the types of practices often required of today's students, who are not only asked to write essays, but also to produce slide shows, posters and other types of visual/multimodal representations, which are becoming increasingly mainstream as both educational activities and assessment strategies.

However, despite these shifts in dominant communicative modes in wider society and in educational practices, qualitative research in higher education continues to be dominated by textual research approaches, and in particular those which 'textualize' lived experience, such as the prototypical research interview, in which an embodied face-to-face social encounter is mediated into a textual format via subsequent transcription. Although visual representation is already an established part of reporting research in the form of diagrams and charts (Stanczak, 2007), textual modes of conducting research still predominate – using verbal/textual means alone, whether on paper or on the screen. This approach tends not to use visual imagery at all, or may occasionally include visual images as illustration. Interviewing, recording speech and employing transcription is rightly a central research technique in the social sciences, and is a powerful technique to collaboratively investigate themes and create an accurate record for subsequent analysis, or to analyse features of speech and interaction in detail via discourse analysis. However, the overwhelming dominance of textual practices in qualitative research may unnecessarily restrict the potential richness of qualitative enquiry, might flatten participant engagement, and could be underutilizing the potential of other modes in research processes.

Focusing on visual modes of expression, the following sections will provide an overview of two elements of this issue; first, how research in higher education might treat the visual aspects of educational practice as objects of analysis; and second, how visual methodologies might be used more generally to explore student and staff experiences of higher education.

The visual as object of analysis

As argued above, the day-to-day processes of higher education have moved away to some extent from predominantly textual to utilize a wider set of resources for communication, drawing more on visual resources than in the past. Analysis of these visual features may provide researchers with a powerful means by which to understand processes, deconstructing underlying ideologies of pedagogy and powerful cultural ideas about the nature of learning and the subject positioning of participants. An example of this can be seen in Bayne (2008), who analyses how visual semiotic resources are mobilized in the iconography, framing and structure of a VLE. In her analysis she argues that the VLE utilizes imagery associated with traditional authority, emphasizes divisions between 'material' and 'skills', and in general serves to perpetuate assumptions about the nature of learning common in analogue formats. She refers to Cousin's analysis of the WebCT logo of the academic in a gown and mortar board. Cousin points out that this image draws on elitist and exclusionary notions of higher education in its depiction of a white male professor in traditional academic dress, holding a rolled sheaf of paper which appears to be a diploma. Bayne extends Cousin's analysis, describing the image as 'also symbolic in that the gowned pedagogue signifies particular, historicised values of tradition, authority and didacticism' (2008: 402).

Drawing on a strand of critical work around 'multiliteracies' (such as Kress, 2003), she continues, using a close reading of visual semiotic features to argue that the framing of elements within the VLE perpetuate a conservative and essentially hierarchical vision of education. She contrasts this with 'web 2.0' applications, using the example of a wiki (a collaborative website which may be used for a range of activities, in this case to enable the creation of a text with multiple authors online). She argues that this type of application disrupts these hierarchies, allowing for more emergent and interactive forms of engagement. In doing so she provides an example of how the visual features may be 'read' as primary carriers of meaning (as opposed to mere illustration), functioning discursively on several levels to perpetuate power and maintain traditional subject positions. Another emergent area of visual practice in higher education is the use of immersive virtual worlds such as Second Life™, which also demand more use of visual approaches to analysis of educational practice and participation in these visual environments (see Chapter 17 in this volume by Savin-Baden, Gourlay and Tombs).

Approaches like these which consider the visual as an object of analysis are relatively marginal in HE research, but represent an increasingly valuable form of analysis of how visual features are deployed in educational process, in an increasingly visual cultural context. The next section will consider how visual research methodologies may not only be used to investigate these visual practices, but may also be deployed in higher education to open up practices and experiences that are not in themselves visual, but are challenging to investigate.

The visual in research methodologies

The previous section focused on the analysis of visual features of HE process. This section will focus on ways in which visual research methodologies might be used more broadly to explore aspects of participants' experiences, as staff or students in higher education. It will use two studies to illustrate this.

One of the more established uses of visuals in qualitative research generally is as part of ethnographic fieldwork. Pink (2007) describes how the visual, in the form of photography, video and hypermedia, is becoming increasingly incorporated into this field, emphasizing the dimensions and roles images may play 'as cultural texts, as representations of ethnographic knowledge and as sites of cultural production, social interaction and individual experience that themselves constitute ethnographic fieldwork locales' (2007: 1). Pink traces her own work in visuals to the 'new ethnography' of the 1980s, with its challenge to positivism/ realism and resultant emphasis on the central role of subjectivity in knowledge production. Rejecting a scientific/realist sociological framing, she advocates a reflexive approach to the visual and how it might be related to sensory, material and discursive elements of situated practice, going on to discuss developments in visual sociology and an emergent postpositivist notion of the visual not as 'data', but as a collaborative medium for the generation of knowledge and critique (see also Chaplin, 1994).

The use of visual data may be a powerful mode for the reflexive investigation of identities or subjectivities. This data may consist of existing images, or images produced by the participants themselves. These may be analysed within the context of ethnographic research, or may be used in conjunction with other qualitative approaches such as interviewing. A focus on images may provide research participants with a means by which to express complex experiences in an indirect, metaphorical or less threatening manner. If producing the image themselves – unlike in the interactive interview – the participants can take as long as they need to produce the image in their own time.

As Loads (2009) points out, participant artwork has been used to investigate aspects of student experience, for instance in the work of Spouse (2000), which looks at the personal knowledge of student nurses, and Clarke (2004), who investigated the notion of 'flexibility' in further education. The approach has also been used in a similar way to explore the experiences of educators, looking at teacher identity (Leitch, 2006) and teacher development (Ryan, 2005). However, it has been little used in higher education. In her own study, Loads used art to investigate the experiences of nursing lecturers. A series of workshops were held in which participants were encouraged to use artwork to explore experiences of dissonance, ambiguity and uncertainty associated with their roles and their teaching selves. The participants were asked to produce a collage of 'what teaching means to me', an approach that Loads employed in order to 'slow down' the meaning-making process and aim to uncover 'hidden' aspects of their experiences. She followed this up a month later with interviews, using the collages as 'trigger' material for interviews exploring the notion of 'authenticity'.

An approach such as this offers researchers a means to facilitate the exploration of subtle, abstract and difficult themes in a creative way, which may reveal more depth than traditional interviewing techniques. Another advantage of the image is in the representation of metaphor, and the relative ease with which a visual representation can be made to stand for an important concept or difficult-to-express aspect of experience. Loads reports extensive use of metaphor in her collage-making activity, with one participant for example using an image of a lamp: 'Hannah included in her collage part of an advertisement for a lamp that was described as "bright, powerful, flexible" and applied those words to her own aspirations for her teaching' (Loads, 2009: 63). Metaphors were also used extensively in the study reported in Gourlay (2009a). In Figure 9.1, a first-year university student constructs a tableau and photographs a neatly stacked pile of books and a messy pile of open books. In his interview, he explained that he had created these images to express his initial feelings of chaos and lack of control when embarking on a writing task and undertaking the initial reading:

Figure 9.1 Robbie's images interview

Visual methodologies may also be used in narrative or longitudinal approaches, such as via journaling or in combination with interviews or focus groups. Photography and drawing may be used as an alternative to or in addition to text-based formats, providing the research participants with a more multimodal set of semiotic resources, which the researcher can encourage them to interpret collaboratively. Taking photos or producing drawn images may be perceived as less onerous than writing by participants, and may be less influenced by the cultural scripts associated with the text-based journal, which encourages well-known 'dear diary' conventions which might in fact get in the way of a full exploration of the research questions. The written format also tends to be associated with a text which is held privately, and not normally shared and discussed. In contrast, there is already a cultural precedent in place for the sharing and discussion of images such as holiday photos or art works, which may lead to an easier transition from recording to collaborative interpretation, as the researcher may 'naturally' ask the participant for the meaning and significance of images.

Furthermore, images are arguably more abstract and open to multiple interpretations and readings than written texts. Visual methodologies may therefore lead to a deeper and more personalized form of engagement and sense of control of self-representation over time. In Gourlay (2009a), students were asked to keep a multimodal journal documenting and reflecting on their experience of the transition into the first year of higher education. Using a combination of text, drawings and photographs, the participants produced journals in their own time. Figure 9.2 (along with five similar images) was produced by a student who was reticent in the first research interview, and who struggled to express her experiences verbally. However, she spent a great deal of time and effort on the production of these intricate images and brief accompanying notes which illustrated her experience of first year at university.

This is a good example of how visual methodologies may encourage reticent research participants to express themselves in an alternative format, which is highly relevant in HE research as some students may find interviews intimidating, and might find it difficult to talk about the more abstract or personal aspects of their experiences in that context.

As Cousin (2008) points out, exploring an archive of existing visual images can also be used to open up meanings and provide triggers for discussion. She gives the example of how a graduation photo might be used to explore the 'collective messages' inherent in iconic educational imagery. Equally, participants' own photos from school or university days might be used to provide structure and depth to a discussion of educational background. In addition, if the definition of the multimodal is broadened to include artefacts from material cultures, then symbolic objects may also be used to investigate research themes.

An example of this can be seen in Archer (2008), who reports on a first-year Communication course within an Engineering foundation programme in a South African university. Drawing on cultural studies, Archer asked students to select everyday objects which had significance for them, then used them in interviews to open up and explore underlying cultural meanings for the participants and how they related to their experience of participation in higher education, in a similar way to the use of art and photography described above. She emphasized the importance of place, and recontextualization of objects from the students' homes or other environments in the university. An example is given of the object 'wood', where a student talks about the central importance of wood in his community for fires, contrasting it with the lack of importance of wood in the university environment. Drawing on Kress and van Leeuwen's (1996) emphasis on the multimodal nature of 'the semiotic landscape', Archer asked the students to produce multimodal commentary on the significance of the object in their community. This project raised awareness of tensions, shifts and contested values within cultural practice. One of the strengths of this approach is its deployment and critical interrogation of semiotic resources that are meaningful to participants from within their own cultural contexts. Archer advocates this approach for exploration of identities, meanings and material cultures. This could also perhaps be used in research into the experiences of other students traditionally marginalized by the higher education system.

Figure 9.2 Louise's image and notes

Main image: Sometimes life is a bit of a blur to me. I'm not sure what will happen to me after I graduate, whether I'll stay within the publishing industry or whatever.
Picture of silly sandwiches: I'm laughing a lot more now. =D
Picture next to silly sandwiches: Now that I'm older I feel that I can see myself more clearly than when I was in high school. I notice more of my strengths and weaknesses.
Umbrella: One of my weaknesses is that I need someone to be a 'protector' for me, who is around my age and won't be judgemental. Feeling isolated still exists.
Chair: I feel lazy and tired sometimes which affects my learning.
Bus sign: I feel more independent.

Practicalities and ethics

A focus on the visual has much to offer research, as outlined above, but also presents particular demands in terms of planning, ethics and research practicalities. Although the approaches described above can be engaging and creative, they may also meet with resistance from some potential participants, for whom the seemingly playful nature of the research may be perceived as 'non-scientific'. Also, if used to explore experiences and identities, they may be perceived as inappropriately 'therapeutic' and personal. It is vital that participants are provided with a clear rationale for the use of visuals, judicious initial use of more 'traditional' research techniques, or a choice, which may help participants to become comfortable with more unfamiliar practices. Mature adults in particular may feel self-conscious about activities such as drawing or even photography, which they might feel are 'silly', or they might worry that they cannot do them 'well enough' in artistic terms. It is important to emphasize repeatedly that displaying artistic merit is not the object of the exercise.

If cameras or other equipment are being provided, it is helpful to participants to be given clear guidance about their use and the labelling of images. It may be preferable to encourage use of participants' own digital cameras or phones to allow them to use familiar equipment, especially as there are also practical pitfalls in terms of errors or failing technologies, and flexibility is advised in terms of numbers of images required and deadlines for submission.

In terms of ethics, care is needed over explicit informed consent, particularly regarding anonymity where video journaling or filming of others is undertaken. The fact that participants and other individuals can be identified on film may limit how video can be displayed and to whom. For this reason, participants may be more drawn to abstract images, a focus on inanimate objects and scenes, or drawings.

Challenges also exist in terms of the analysis and visual images, regarding the placement and relative importance of the images in relation to textual data, and the need for collaborative interpretation and member checking. Additionally, outside the established practices of visual disciplines, barriers may be encountered when seeking to publish visual representations in formats that have developed over time to accommodate a predominantly textual mode, such as the journal article. Editors may be resistant to accept visual images as 'data', and may prefer to view them as illustration. However, despite these challenges, the potential benefits of expanding the qualitative repertoire towards a more visual orientation are considerable, in terms of both the research process and objects of analysis.

Conclusions and future directions

As Goldstein (2007) argues, the photo does not form part of a 'realist' account in a scientific paradigm. Although this is meant as a note of caution, in the context of this volume the fact that visual and multimodal representations are socially situated forms of meaning-making should be seen as a positive strength.

The examples given in this chapter should be viewed as a flavour of this type of work rather than an attempt to provide a comprehensive review, as projects continue to develop across the sector. As suggested above, different modes of communicative engagement generate different types of research participation and data, addressing different types of research questions. There is synergy in the use of visual methodologies in the investigation of educational practices and processes that are themselves visual, such as in the contexts described above. At a disciplinary level, the more obvious contexts for visual methodologies might include art, design, architecture or digital media – subject areas already steeped in multimodality and processes of reflection around the visual – where participants may respond to educational research that seeks to privilege this mode. Similarly, video may be a powerful means by which to investigate educational experiences that are inherently kinetic and spatial in their orientation. In the creative industries, this may work well with dance or drama, and could also provide a means of expression to students or lecturers in subjects such as sports science, engineering, geography, transport studies or other spatially orientated forms of learning.

However, non-textual research practices also lend themselves to studies that are emotional, personal and/or biographical in their orientation. As discussed above, visuals may be used as metaphorical means of creatively explaining subtle or challenging aspects of personal experience. Exploring another mode, audio-journaling may also be used as an alternative to text journals, maximizing a sense of both intimacy and also participant control over what is disclosed, used in another journaling study with new academic staff by Gourlay (2009b). These participant-generated reflective/autoethnographic approaches seem inherently collaborative and creatively disruptive to the 'traditional' subject positions of researcher and researched. The use of non-textual means of expression may serve to undermine these divisions, as the traditionally power-freighted medium of academic expression is circumvented for modes that may be more emotionally immediate – or at least less mediated by 'social scientific' written discourses. In this regard, they could also present an alternative or supplement to the often problematic format of the written 'reflective portfolio' in HE assessment (Macfarlane and Gourlay, 2009), perhaps reducing the sense of 'written reflection' genre-based mediation which can render these pieces formulaic and perfunctory.

The challenge will be to continue to develop visual research approaches and to bring them into the mainstream. However, there are signs that this process is underway, such as the current ESRC seminar series 'New forms of the doctorate', directed by Andrews (2009/10), which provides a forum for the exploration of new ways to construct and assess doctoral knowledge in multimodal formats, and the 'Building Capacity in Visual Methods' ESRC Researcher Development Initiative based at Leeds (Prosser, 2006–09). These developments, among others, suggest a growing recognition of the importance of the visual/multimodal as research focus, process and outcome.

References

Andrews, R. (2009–10) *New Forms of the Doctorate: The influence of multimodality and elearning on doctoral theses in education and the social sciences*, Economic and Social Research Council Seminar Series (online) <http://newdoctorates.blogspot.com/> (accessed 4 September 2009).

Archer, A. (2008) 'Cultural studies meets academic literacies: exploring students resources through symbolic objects', *Teaching in Higher Education*, 13(4), 383–94.

Bartsch, R. and Cobern, K. (2003) 'Effectiveness of PowerPoint presentations in lectures', *Computers and Education*, 41, 77–86.

Bayne, S. (2008) 'Higher education as a visual practice: seeing through the virtual learning environment', *Teaching in Higher Education*, 13(4): 395–410.

Chaplin, E. (1994) *Sociology and Visual Representations*, London: Routledge.

Clarke, J. (2004) 'Picturing places in the assemblage of flexibility in further education', pp. 139–56 in R. Edwards and R. Usher (eds), *Space, Curriculum and Learning*, Greenwich, CT: Information Age.

Cousin, G. (2008) *Researching Learning in Higher Education*, London: Routledge.

Goldstein, B. (2007) 'All photos lie: images as data', in G. Stanczak (ed.), *Visual Research Methods: Image, society and representation*, London: Sage.

Gourlay, L. (2009a) 'Threshold practices: becoming a student through academic literacies', *London Review of Education*, 7(2), 181–92.

Gourlay, L. (2009b) 'Peripheral practitioners and troubled transitions: challenging "communities of practice"', paper presented at the Annual Conference of the Society for Research into Higher Education. Cardiff, UK.

Kress, G. (2003) *Literacy in the New Media Age*, London: Routledge.

Kress, G. and van Leeuwen, T. (1996) *Reading Images: The grammar of visual design*, London: Routledge.

Kress, G. and van Leeuwen, T. (2001) *Multimodal Discourse: The modes and media of contemporary communication*, London: Hodder Arnold.

Leitch, R. (2006) 'Limitations of language: developing arts-based creative narrative in stories of teachers' identities', *Teachers and Teaching: Theory and Practice*, 12(5), 549–69.

Loads, D. (2009) 'Putting ourselves in the picture: art workshops in the professional development of university teachers', *International Journal for Academic Development*, 14(1), 59–67.

Macfarlane, B. and Gourlay, L. (2009) 'The reflection game: Enacting the penitent self', *Teaching in Higher Education*, 14(4), 455–9.

Mirzoeff, N. (ed.) (2002) *The Visual Culture Reader*, 2nd edn, London: Routledge.

Pink, S. (2007) *Doing Visual Ethnography*, 2nd edn, London: Sage.

Prosser, J. (2006–09) *Building capacity in visual methods researcher development initiative*, Leeds: Economic and Social Research Council (online) <http://www.education.leeds.ac.uk/research/visual-methods> (accessed 4 September 2009).

Ryan, A. (2005) 'Teacher development and educational change: empowerment through structured reflection', *Irish Educational Studies*. 24(2–3), 179–98.

Spouse, J. (2000) 'Talking pictures: investigating personal knowledge through illuminative artwork', *NTResearch*, 5(4), 253–61.

Stanczak, G. (2007) *Visual Research Methods: Image, society and representation*, London: Sage.

Szabo, A. and Hastings, N. (2000) 'Using IT in the undergraduate classroom: should we replace the blackboard with PowerPoint?' *Computers and Education*, 35, 175–87.

Chapter 10

Participatory action research

An integrated approach towards practice development

Katherine Wimpenny

> Those who wish to take the path of collaborative research be warned: this is no easy way forward. There will be doubt and mistrust, there will be disagreement and conflict, and there will be failures as well as success. For the birth of an integrated consciousness means the death of the old. It means learning to trust the wisdom of the unknown other.
>
> (Reason, 1994: 56)

Introduction

This chapter aims to provide an overview of participatory action research (PAR) and its uses for practice development. It begins by discussing the basic ideas that underpin PAR to illustrate why this method is a complex, challenging yet essentially illuminating approach to adopt in conducting human inquiry. It presents how one might navigate a path through a PAR process (including what obstacles may be encountered along the way). The aim of this chapter is to provide a perspective on PAR methods currently advocated within the literature, and to relate theoretical and experiential observations on the application of PAR within a recent professional practice development project, to highlight what is currently either missing or not well articulated in the literature. In particular, focus is directed to researcher relationships and what can be meant by authentic participation.

Throughout the chapter I draw upon my experience as a primary researcher recently involved in PAR within a practice development initiative. As an occupational therapy educator in the UK, interested in practice epistemology and in establishing closer links with practice, I was approached to work with an occupational therapy service based in a mental health National Health Service trust. The project aimed to improve the therapists' profile in light of multidisciplinary team working and their specific contribution to client care. It included focus on reviewing the evidence base and theoretical knowledge underpinning their practice. The importance of collaboration and participation in social practices led to the selection of a participatory action research strategy.

What is participatory action research?

As the name suggests, PAR involves participation and action. As an evolving approach to human inquiry, a fundamental premise of PAR is that it embraces the concerns experienced by a group, community or organization (McTaggart, 1997; Stringer, 1999, 2007; Taylor *et al.*, 2004). Put simply, this method of research is about a group of people who are affected by some problem or issue and decide to get together to work out how they want to tackle the problem. As a collaborative research methodology it offers significant benefits in that it can contribute to the discovery and development of the conditions and actions for change that are sustainable, and thereafter the PAR element disappears.

PAR has an explicit set of social values: it should be democratic, equitable and liberating for those involved. As Cockburn and Trentham (2002: 29) claim, PAR provides a framework 'for new ways of conceptualising relationships with our clients and others with whom we work'. This recognizes that the primary researcher and those involved come together in a more 'communitarian way' (Lincoln, 2001: 127), breaking down the old borders between knowledge-producing and knowledge-consuming elites. Yet negotiating ways forward that embrace a range of opinions is challenging. While there is room for creativity, uncertainty and messiness prevail. Nonetheless, the aims of PAR remain consistent: increasing participant awareness of external forces affecting decisions in their lives, including the self-confidence and capacity to develop decisions that enable a new level of awareness and competence.

Situating participatory action research

PAR could be situated within a social constructivist paradigm (Guba, 1990; Lincoln, 2001) in its focus on how participants come together to co-create their understandings of the issues under investigation (Crotty, 1998; Heron and Reason, 1997). Within this relativist ontology, social constructivism offers an extended epistemology, embracing the contribution of propositional knowledge, practical knowing and experiential knowing or knowing by encounter (Heron, 1981; Reason, 1988). Yet while constructivism and PAR are both concerned with socially constructed meaning amongst participants, the influence of culture and tradition requires acknowledgement, and such issues bring into focus the structures of the wider political context. As such, meaning making is not solely a product of the individual mind influenced by social process (Crotty, 1998: 58), but encompasses interaction with other objects, spaces and political structures (Gergen, 1999). Thus PAR could also be situated within social constructionism (Crotty, 1998; Gergen, 1999, 2003). From this theoretical perspective, while individuals are seen as engaging in their world and making sense of it, this is viewed in the context of social perspective, ritual and history.

Furthermore, in its focus upon the social, economic and political needs and opinions of ordinary people (Kemmis and McTaggart, 2005), PAR principles link with Habermas's (1996) work concerned with 'communicative action', in which people find a communicative space where they may find solidarity as understandings of their situation are jointly considered. In conceptualizing the generation of knowledge as that which enables human beings to emancipate themselves from forms of domination through processes of self-reflection and action, a critical theory paradigm (Fals-Borda, 1991; Habermas, 1996) might also present an appropriate theoretical perspective to adopt. Through communicative action individuals are enabled, in the context of mutual participation, to consider such issues as what is comprehensible to them, what is acceptable in the light of knowledge, what joint commitment to understanding may offer, and what can be judged prudent and appropriate to do considering the circumstances in which people find themselves (Habermas, 1996). Here a key role of the primary researcher is to heighten the participants' awareness of how external forces affect their decision making. The PAR process then focuses upon how work with the participants can consider action built upon new levels of awareness.

In summary, my experience has led me to the perspective that PAR does not sit neatly within one paradigm, but may be appropriately situated at the boundary of a number of theories. Whatever the decision, those theories that apply need to adequately account for and embrace the reframing and reconstructing of individual practices within a social and political meaning-making process.

The underlying intention of participatory action research

Historically PAR has been associated with social transformation in the third world and human rights activism (Fals-Borda, 2001) (as distinct from purely political activism), yet in recent years its uses have broadened (Kemmis and McTaggart, 2005). PAR processes can be used to improve local situations across business, education, health, social care and community settings. The underlying intention is to value discourses from a range of intellectual origins (Savin-Baden and Wimpenny, 2007).

PAR methodology challenges the notion that legitimate knowledge lies only with the privileged experts, and supports the premise that knowledge should be developed in collaboration with local experts; the voices of the 'knowers'. PAR offers practical problem-posing and problem-solving approaches at grassroots level, the intention being that such action can lead to meaningful social change for those directly involved, to the system of which they are a part, and to wider cultural practices. Indeed Stringer (1999) argues that if a [participatory] action research project does not make a difference in a specific way for the participants, it has failed to achieve its objectives. Honouring such aims places considerable pressure on the primary researcher, but can be an important driver for seeing a PAR process through. Moreover, I believe it provides a powerful message about who can learn from research.

As PAR methodology is premised on research conducted *with* people as opposed to *on* people (Heron and Reason, 2001), the participants within PAR are encouraged to consider themselves as co-researchers, driving the study forwards as a group of individuals with shared objectives and decision-making powers. However, the development of the individual's sense of empowerment within research relationships requires significant consideration, and this key theme will be discussed as the chapter progresses.

The practice of participatory action research

PAR can be undertaken using a diverse range of methods, and it is important to adopt an approach that is appropriate to the research context. Although quantitative research is not ruled out within a PAR inquiry, a qualitative perspective is more usual, in particular where the intention is to travel along with participants in their natural social settings.

Getting going

Fals-Borda (1991), Reason (1994) and Kidd and Kral (2005) all suggest that PAR is usually adopted because the participants request the chance to engage in a PAR project in the first instance. In reality a community of participants are normally aware of problems to be addressed, and then are more likely to be advised that PAR is an appropriate way forward. A PAR project may therefore arise through a coincidental meeting between a researcher and a group of individuals, or a group may approach a researcher known to possess some experience and support to offer them in addressing their problem. Whatever the reason, from the onset a PAR process should strive to be collaborative in nature, as it is vital that participants have some level of investment in the study. Lewin (1946) argued that people are more likely to test out new practices when they participate actively in developing agreed strategies. It follows that 'getting going' with PAR requires an important amount of groundwork, and early sessions should focus on exploring the PAR method, encouraging the development of collective decision making, and a commitment to improvement, and with that, consideration of researcher roles.

Researcher/participant roles

Kidd and Kral (2005) identify the importance of creating opportunities between participants to initiate dialogue and share understandings of the issues at hand. This includes the discussion of roles within the inquiry and the sharing of power in terms of joint responsibility for the research process. Yet, as Rahman (1991) and McTaggart (1997) highlight, most groups who engage in PAR are accustomed to traditional research hierarchies and may resist the sharing of power that is offered. PAR processes are indeed complex. They make visible individual values, characteristics, limitations and abilities. Moreover, while a primary researcher does not assume expertise, they are nonetheless required to be skilled, supportive and resourceful. Considering issues of power amongst individuals in light of their different visions of the inquiry, its aims, methods and actions, and making this process amenable to all, is a task not to be underestimated. Equally, it is important to appreciate that participants will not hold static positions. I suggest the development of 'co-researcher' roles needs to be nurtured within a culture of participation which recognizes power imbalance. Nonetheless, from the outset all participants need to feel that they have a valued role in being a co-inquirer/co-researcher and member of the community, and in this role they may legitimately be more or less engaged (Lave and Wenger, 1991).

The use of self-reflective cycles

Strategies employed within a PAR process to achieve meaningful social change involve engaging with a group or groups of participants in a series of self-reflective cycles, which include planning a change with the 'community'; acting and observing the process and consequences of change; reflecting on these processes and consequences; and then further cycles of planning, acting and reflecting (Heron and Reason, 2001; Kemmis and McTaggart, 2005) (See Figure 10.1). In reality, the process is not a straightforward set of neat self-contained spirals of planning, acting and observing. Stages overlap; initial plans require review in the light of experience and learning. Yet PAR is not about following a set of prescribed steps, rather, the reflection and action cycles provide a space within which critical dialectic discourse can be developed and meaningful change considered (a form of consciousness raising) (Friere, 1970).

My involvement with PAR provided an appreciation of how the cycles of reflection and action become 'operationalized' within a range of learning spaces which move from a predominant anchor point outwards. For example, our predominant learning space and anchor point was a monthly community meeting, in which the occupational therapists examined their current practice repertoires to explore what was working well and what was not. The monthly meeting remained a key space throughout the inquiry process, but over time and as participants chose to act, this reflection and action space also moved outwards into the therapists' work-based settings, where alternatives for action were considered. In addition, individuals were seen to use their own personal space for reading and or reflection. Back in monthly group meetings, amongst other peers, dialectic discourse was encouraged and meaningful change considered in terms of creative ways to move the research agenda forward (Wimpenny *et al.*, 2006). The point here is that a combined use of learning spaces provides

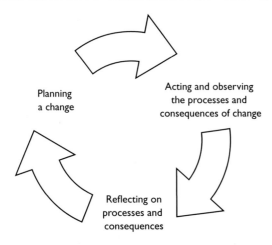

Planning
a change

Acting and observing
the processes and
consequences of change

Reflecting on
processes and
consequences

Figure 10.1 Representation of the action and reflection cycle

the means by which consciousness raising can be achieved, enabling participants to gain a sense of how their actions and the understanding of their actions can develop. Yet disjunction is visible within these 'learning spaces', not least through the requirement that the participants be open to others' views while potentially feeling vulnerable and challenged regarding their own perspectives.

Negotiating authentic participation

Fundamentally, a PAR methodology needs to get on with the job in hand. PAR is after all situated within the everyday working practices of those involved. A distinctive feature of PAR is the commitment that participants engage in research for themselves, yet the idea of participation within this is problematic and requires some teasing out. I suggest a number of key elements require attention during PAR processes to continually question the level of participation achieved:

- relocation of power: primary researcher responsibilities
- development of a sound dialectic
- generation of knowledge and understanding
- development of shared quality criteria to ensure validity.

Relocating power: primary researcher responsibilities

Authentic participation in research requires sharing the way in which research is conceptualized, practised and brought to bear in light of the person's situation (McTaggart, 1997). It involves focusing on the production and generation of knowledge as a shared task. The primary researcher, in taking responsibility for seeing a PAR process through and seeking to effect meaningful change with those involved, can inadvertently 'silence voices and undermine the entire process' (Kidd and Kral, 2005: 190). Ownership of the agenda amongst participants requires that the PAR facilitator engage in an ongoing examination of their own voices and actions, and the effects of these on the research process. Expressed as 'inner and outer arcs of attention' (Wadsworth, 2001; Marshall, 2001), this self-reflexive process provides an opportunity for PAR facilitators to embrace critical subjectivity (Reason, 1994).

Critical subjectivity involves a self-reflexive attention to the ground on which one is standing. In simple terms this means developing awareness that we do not come into an inquiry with a 'clean slate', and that the issues of power and privilege prevailing need to be reduced initially, then levelled amongst participants as far as possible. PAR requires significant reflexive capacity in order for the primary researcher to continually question their response toward situations as they arise, and to acknowledge that people think differently from one another, and importantly that they themselves do not always know what is best.

Development of a sound dialectic

PAR is a social process; it requires a deliberate method of discovering, investigating and attaining mutual understanding. It requires a degree of willingness of participants to engage in dialogue in order to uncover social practices. PAR is concerned with a collaborative sense of agency (Kemmis and McTaggart, 2005), and the facilitator needs to consider how to encourage development of such social practices. McNiff *et al.* (2003) identify that when people engage in action research for the first time it may appear that the techniques are nothing new. Yet PAR is more than reflection upon practice and problem solving. It involves problem posing, examining values and questioning motives. It involves committed action in which a range of views and feelings are taken into account. However, while PAR processes aim to open up space for participants to communicate and share their understandings of the situation, such spaces can only be used when people want to and feel able to share their views. A significant challenge to the process is therefore participants' readiness to engage, including the required investment of time and energy. As experienced within our inquiry process, despite commitment at the outset, participants may well meet personal and environmental barriers which impact upon their intentions to act (Armitage and Conner, 2001).

Heron (1992) identifies how learning is best achieved by self-generated interest, but attempts by teachers to impose or instil particular conditions often negate or distort such opportunities. Yet learning in itself creates disjunction as individuals oscillate between old and emergent forms of understanding (Savin-Baden, 2008). The disruption that PAR can create for participants' working lives is not to be underestimated. Participants can express feelings of confusion, which can surface as anger and resentment. Such challenges highlight how learning is never just a cognitive task; rather, learning is linked to individual biography and involves participation in social practices. Feelings and dynamics aroused in group settings are complex where there are multiple layers of relationships. PAR requires participants to make new choices and take risks, and raising emotion is part of this process. Yet equally the disruption created can set the agenda for change. Nonetheless the impact of change needs to be taken into account, and strategies are required throughout to enable participants to feel supported and respected (Guba and Lincoln, 1989). Such strategies should include:

- consideration of the participants' sense of pride
- recognition of the importance of validating individuals' social identities and efforts
- affirmation of the participants' feelings of autonomy and competence and with that, their ability to be accountable for their actions.

Developing a sound dialectic within PAR involves using strategies whereby the rethinking of individual knowledge construction is enabled in light of complex group dynamics. PAR facilitators can find themselves swaying between didactic and participatory approaches in attempts to support new learning as it emerges in the context of group practices. They can feel the need to step in, to advise and coach. Attaining the right balance between incorporating rather than imposing knowledge is a significant challenge (Wimpenny *et al.*, 2006). Participants may not always pull in the same direction. Yet being with participants and navigating a path through periods of disharmony links with Lave and Wenger's (1991) assertion that learning, thinking and knowing result in enhanced relationships between people in, with and arising from the socially and culturally constructed world. Periods of 'storming' can also lead on to greater 'performing', since the bonding between participants grows stronger through adversity. However, even within a more mature group of people, the experience of being within a PAR inquiry process can remain exciting yet upsetting. Participants may express the emotional distress of trying out new actions which do not go as planned, coupled with the joy and sense of breakthrough experienced as new methods are realized (Reason, 1988).

Generation of knowledge and understanding

In terms of how knowledge is created and/or understood, knowing is expressed via the participants' 'thought-worlds' or unique interpretative repertoires (Dougherty, 1992). In social settings this can be evidenced via the participants' practical knowledge, their individual skills, competencies and their ability to solve problems they face. Through the continued application of skills, competencies and capabilities, experiential knowledge is gained by the participants (Heron, 1981; Kakabadse and Kakabadse, 2003). However, knowledge development of this kind is often 'underground' or tacit and so seldom surfaces. Guba (1990) highlights the importance, within the inquiry process, of democratic dialogue and the use of time and sustained effort to identify and share experiential knowledge. Such dialectic discourse can then unearth assumptions leading to intellectual discovery and new presentational knowledge, that emerges through the sharing of individual experiences.

Meaning-making involves the ongoing process of sharing knowledge, discussion, reflection, action and the consequences of action; for participants to revisit shared experiences which challenge previous ways of thinking and participating. As openness amongst participants develops, group members may become more able to express their feelings, review their work, hear alternative views and try out newly reviewed practices (Howie *et al.*, 1995).

Importantly, while participants may join forces to enhance understandings and generate alternate practices, the focus of knowledge production remains linked to whatever is useful for the individual within their own work context. Thus the common project which may change the culture or systems of a group or community must also provide knowledge that is useful at a personal level.

Developing shared quality criteria to ensure validity

Under a relativist ontology, where multiple realities are co-constructed, establishing what benefits emerge from a PAR inquiry needs to be considered from each individual's perspective. Through sustained contact, participants have more opportunity to develop ownership of the study and reveal what is important to share through open discussion. Thus the development of shared criteria requires that participatory action research:

- Pledges a high degree of personal involvement from the primary researcher to support the process of learning. This can expose the researcher to potential risks as well as positive experiences that are often not evident within more traditional paradigms. As such, the researcher needs to maintain a critical awareness during the inquiry process.

● Provides genuine opportunity for the shared interpretation of themes amongst all participants, in order to revisit shared experiences and to adequately contextualize the outcomes generated.

● Acknowledges that all participants have been involved as reflexive individuals, with the ability to disseminate their own experience of the inquiry process with others as it occurs relative to context.

McTaggart (1997) appropriately identifies that validity procedures should be considered carefully, not purely to satisfy academic processes, but importantly to highlight the challenge of implementing PAR successfully. As Lewin (1946) recognized, given the complexity of social situations, it is not possible to anticipate everything that needs to be done. In questioning if PAR processes are sufficiently valid I argue attention should be focused at the participatory level, and whether those involved have taken an active part, including their perception of whether their situation has improved or not. At a more fundamental level questions need to focus on whether the inquiry has achieved as much as it might.

The primary researcher needs to recognize how they might be operating from a position of power and privilege, which can become a dominant discourse and has potential to undermine participants' stated views. This tension can be evident during decision-making procedures, for while PAR encourages democratic and inclusive forms of knowledge creation, the approach of using PAR for altering boundaries of knowledge is complex. McTaggart's (1997) perspective regarding the roles groups of people who engage in PAR may hold, offers a means of exploring validity issues in collaborative inquiry. McTaggart makes a distinction between the worker and researcher roles to illustrate that as well as distinctive tasks each group or individual takes in relation to their own institutional and cultural contexts, all parties are joined in a commitment to inform and improve a particular practice. McTaggart's perspective links to my experience of PAR, in that as participants we were involved in different ways. The achievement of joint ownership is often a complex process, certainly in terms of achieving this from start to finish. Participants may not readily assume co-researcher roles, at least initially; indeed certain participants may well wish to remain at the periphery of the inquiry, which is an equally valid place to be. Nonetheless, progress is seen in negotiating a way through difference of opinion, in engaging in 'authentic negotiation and confrontation' (Reason, 1988: 20). As this quote suggests, while it is not necessarily a comfortable process, the journey remains worth the effort.

On a final note, while authentic participation encourages collective agency, I believe an important element of PAR inquiry requires 'recognition of the person-in-the-world as a valid member of the socio-cultural community' (Lave and Wenger, 1991: 52). Developing a shared repertoire with participants during PAR requires an ability to connect with the individual therein. PAR involves individuals in a process of confronting self-understandings, and regular checks are required to ensure those who do not appear to have a voice remain an important focus of the group's work. A key strategy, which kept our venture alive at critical periods of the inquiry, was the use of individual meetings. These provided a different platform from which relationships with team members could be nurtured, and dynamics regarding the 'ongoing business' of the group could be addressed. Fals-Borda (2001: 31) states how PAR can 'convert those who engage in its processes to become thinking feeling persons'. Certainly in my experience, the value of human connectedness between participants and myself proved to have potency in terms of setting a more caring tone within sessions, from which commitment to the venture grew.

Conclusion

Participatory action research importantly provides a framework which allows room for individual response to a research agenda, and a genuine sharing of interests which appropriately recognizes community need and community interest (Lincoln, 2001). Yet PAR is not solely about interaction with other people, it involves examination of the processes by which people come to describe, explain or otherwise account for their situation in the world (Gergen, 2003). Through PAR the interrelationship between personal agency and the influence of the participants' wider social world is appreciated.

This chapter has outlined some of the approaches and strategies that may be used when engaging in PAR. The importance of action that needs to be flexible and responsive given the complexity of social situations has been considered. The nurturing of research relationships has been argued for and the practice of authentic participation has been explored, in terms of recognizing the need for participants to be involved in different ways yet still with the control for setting the agenda for change.

Importantly, the writing-up and dissemination of the findings of PAR should not detract from what is also relevant, and often more difficult to account for, and this relates to the ongoing impact of the inquiry on the individuals' lives and practices. A key aim embraced within PAR is the commitment to inform and improve a particular practice. However, the practical and dialectical processes necessary for achieving such aims are not to be underestimated, and the primary researcher's role can be considerable in holding the inquiry process together. Nonetheless PAR is a powerful and evolving learning process which changes the researcher, the participants and the situations in which the research takes place. Reason's (1994) foreboding at the start of this chapter sets a tone for the research methodology which requires careful examination by those considering its use, yet equally, it should not detract from the satisfying opportunities PAR can provide to change practice through collective wisdom.

References

Armitage, C. J. and Conner, M. (2001) 'Efficacy of the theory of planned behaviour: a meta-analytic review', *British Journal of Social Psychology*, 40, 471–99.

Cockburn, L. and Trentham, B. (2002) 'Participatory action research: integrating community occupational therapy practice and research', *Canadian Journal of Occupational Therapy*, 69(1), 20–30.

Crotty, M. (1998) *The Foundations of Social Research: Meaning and perspective in the research process*, London: Sage.

Dougherty, D. (1992) 'Interpretive barriers to successful product innovation in large firms', *Organization Science*, 3, 179–202.

Fals-Borda, O. (1991) 'Some basic ingredients', in O. Fals-Borda and A. Rahman (eds), *Action and Knowledge: Breaking the monopoly with participatory action research*, New York: Apex Press.

Fals-Borda, O. (2001) 'Participatory (action) research in social theory: origins and challenges', in P. Reason and H. Bradbury (eds), *Handbook of Action Research*, Thousand Oaks, CA: Sage.

Friere, P. (1970) *Pedagogy of the Oppressed*, New York: Continuum.

Gergen, K. J. (1999) *An Invitation to Social Construction*, London: Sage.

Gergen, K. J. (2003) 'Knowledge as socially constructed', in M. Gergen and K. J. Gergen (eds), *Social Construction: A reader*, London: Sage.

Guba, E. (1990) *The Paradigm Dialogue*, Newbury Park, CA: Sage.

Guba, E. and Lincoln, Y. S. (1989) *Fourth Generation Evaluation*, London: Sage.

Habermas, J. (1996) *Between Facts and Norms: Contributions to a discourse theory of law and democracy*, Cambridge, MA: MIT Press.

Heron, J. (1981) 'Philosophical basis for a new paradigm', in P. Reason and J. Rowan (eds), *Human Inquiry: A source book of new paradigm research*, Chichester: Wiley.

Heron, J. (1992) 'The politics of facilitation: balancing facilitator authority and learner autonomy', in J. Mulligan and C. Griffin (eds), *Empowerment through Experiential Learning Explorations of Good Practice*, London: Kogan Page.

Heron, J. and Reason, P. (1997) 'A participatory inquiry paradigm', *Qualitative Inquiry*, **3**(3), 274–94.

Heron, J. and Reason, P. (2001) 'The practice of co-operative inquiry: research "with" rather than "on" people', in P. Reason and H. Bradbury (eds), *Handbook of Action Research: Participative inquiry and practice*, London: Sage.

Howie, L. M., Kennedy-Jones, M., Lentin, P., MacDonald, E. M. and Giffin, J. (1995) 'Supervision in a group training curriculum: reflections on experiential learning', *Australian Occupational Therapy Journal*, **42**(4), 167–71.

Kakabadse, N. K. and Kakabadse, A. (2003) 'Developing reflexive practitioners through collaborative inquiry: a case study of the UK civil service', *International Review of Administrative Sciences*, 69: 365–83.

Kemmis, S. and McTaggart, R. (2005) 'Participatory action research: communicative action and the public sphere', pp. 559–604 in N. Denzin and Y. Lincoln (eds), *Handbook of Qualitative Research*, 3rd edn, Thousand Oaks, CA: Sage.

Kidd, S. A. and Kral, M. J. (2005) 'Practicing participatory action research special issue: participatory action research', *American Psychological Association*, **52**(2), 187–95.

Lave, J. and Wenger, E. (1991) *Situated Learning: Legitimate peripheral participation*, Cambridge: Cambridge University Press.

Lewin, K. (1946) *Action Research and Minority Groups: Resolving social conflicts*, New York: Harper & Row.

Lincoln, Y. (2001) 'Engaging sympathies: relationships between action research and social constructivism', in P. Reason and H. Bradbury (eds), *Handbook of Action Research: Participative inquiry and practice*, London: Sage.

Marshall, J. (2001) 'Self reflective inquiry practices', in P. Reason and H. Bradbury (eds), *Handbook of Action Research: Participative inquiry and practice*, London: Sage.

McNiff, J., Lomax, P. and Whitehead, J. (2003) *You and Your Action Research Project*, 2nd edn, London: RoutledgeFalmer.

McTaggart, R. (1997) 'Guiding principles for participatory action research', in R. McTaggart (ed.), *Participatory Action Research: International contexts and consequences*, New York: State University of New York.

Rahman, A. (1991) 'The theoretical standpoint of PAR', in O. Fals-Borda and A. Rahman (eds), *Action and Knowledge: Breaking the monopoly with participatory action research*, New York: Apex Press.

Reason, P. (1988) 'The co-operative inquiry group', in P. Reason (ed.), *Human Inquiry in Action: Developments in new paradigm research*, London: Sage.

Reason, P. (1994) 'Human inquiry as discipline and practice', in P. Reason (ed.), *Participation in Human Inquiry*, Thousand Oaks, CA: Sage.

Savin-Baden, M. (2008) *Learning Spaces: Creating opportunities for knowledge creation in academic life*, London: Society for Research into Higher Education and Open University Press.

Savin-Baden, M. and Wimpenny, K. (2007) 'Exploring and implementing Participatory Action Research', *Journal of Geography in Higher Education*, **31**(2), 331–43.

Stringer, E. T. (1999) *Action Research: A handbook for practitioners*, 2nd edn, London: Sage.

Stringer, E. T. (2007) *Action Research: A handbook for practitioners*, 3rd edn, London: Sage.

Taylor, R. T., Braveman, B. and Hammel, J. (2004) 'Developing and evaluating community based services through participatory action research: two case examples', *American Journal of Occupational Therapy*, **58**(1), 73–82.

Wadsworth, Y. (2001) 'The mirror, the magnifying glass, the compass and the map: facilitating participatory action research', in P. Reason and H. Bradbury (eds), *Handbook of Action Research: Participative inquiry and practice*, London: Sage.

Wimpenny, K., Forsyth, K., Jones, C., Evans, E. and Colley, J. (2006) 'Thinking with theory to develop practice', *British Journal of Occupational Therapy*, **69**(6), 423–8.

Chapter 11

Deliberative inquiry

Heather Kanuka

Introduction

In the early 1960s criticisms began to be levelled against many of the established, rule-governed methodologies adopted in science research. Perhaps Cronbach (1975) was the first researcher to argue that our empirical research may be doomed to failure because we simply cannot pile up generalizations fast enough to adapt our treatments to the myriad of variables inherent in any given instance. More recently, Reeves (1995) argued that many time-honoured research methodologies have little social relevance precisely because they do not reflect the real world messiness of everyday problems under investigation, and therefore offer minimal contributions to our disciplines. On this point, Reeves (1999) argues for 'socially responsible' research. Indeed, we live in a continually evolving world, comprised of human beings who are complicated, resulting in messy environments – or what Schön (1983) referred to as the swampy lowlands of professional practice.

A key element to generating socially responsible research is the use of more emergent methodologies that are effective at addressing the 'real world' messiness that researchers encounter routinely. On this point, Shulman (see also Cronbach and Suppes, 1969; Reeves, 1995: 8) argues that:

> disciplined inquiry does not necessarily follow well-established, formal procedures. Some of the most excellent inquiry is free-ranging and speculative in its initial stages, trying what might seem to be bizarre combinations of ideas and procedures, or restlessly casting about for ideas'.
>
> (Shulman, 1997)

In this chapter, I describe the circumstances that resulted in an emergent methodology, eventually referred to as a 'deliberative inquiry'. This explanation is followed with a description of the processes involved in conducting a deliberative inquiry (aims, participants, data collection, and data analysis), reflections on this method's advantages and limitations, and a précis on the value of a deliberative inquiry as a research method for examining consensus on complex issues under investigation. In particular, the deliberative inquiry can be an effective research methodology that facilitates the formation of a group opinion through a series of narrative cases and structured discussion.

Conditions resulting in the development of deliberative inquiry

Over the course of my career, I have collected large amounts of data resulting in outcomes on what works in the contexts within which the data were collected. Upon reflection on these research projects, I was finding that mainstream data gathering processes, such as survey research and individual interviews were somewhat restrictive and not effectively or efficiently achieving the research objectives. Specifically, the objectives of my research were evolving to a point where existing data-gathering techniques and methods were not able to meet two fundamental aims: (1) to gain consensus from a group of experts on a focused topic, and (2) to provide a space where differences in opinions could be discussed and debated, resulting in an assessment of whether consensus could be negotiated.

For example, in the third year of a longitudinal study, I was finding that the data were becoming increasingly difficult to analyse. While the data were consistent between partici-pants with respect to the changes occurring over time, they were dramatically inconsistent on whether these changes were viewed as positive or negative. Within these polarized posi-tions a need arose to establish where consensus of opinions actually existed, as well as to determine where there was room for discussion in-between. While group interviews (such as the focus group method) could have addressed the need for group discussion about the diversity of participant perspectives, focus groups do not aim to explore where consensus exists. Alternatively, consensus techniques (such as the Delphi technique) could have addressed the need to obtain consensus (or at least determine where consensus exists), but do not aim to facilitate group discussion. Hence, both methodologies were promising in addressing one aspect of the research problem, but neither was sufficient in and of itself. The following sections in this chapter provide a broader discussion on the use of a deliberative inquiry to address this particular type of research problem.

When a focus group is not enough

A focus group is a unique kind of interview, in that it collects data from a number of people in a manner that is non-quantitative (Cohen *et al.*, 2005; Cresswell, 2005; Gall *et al.*, 2007; Neuman, 2000). Focus groups are widely used for both exploration and confirmation, and are particularly effective for collecting data about attitudes, perceptions and opinions. However, while focus groups are a functional research method for clarifying the complexities of the problem or issue under investigation, they are not intended to reach a consensus among participants, to determine a plan of action or to generate solutions and decisions (Stewart and Shamdasani, 1998). Rather, focus groups are uniquely effective at gaining a more in-depth understanding of the topic and hence a better definition of the research problem(s). As such, in cases where the researcher has a need to determine where consensus exists with participants through discussion, the most significant limitation of the focus group method is that the aim of a focus group is to gain greater understanding on a topic, not to determine where there is agreement between and among participants.

When aspects of consensus techniques might be useful

When there is a need to collect expert opinions to provide further insights into a research problem, as well as a need to determine where agreement exists, consensus techniques can be useful. The Delphi technique, for example, solicits the opinion(s) of experts (usually in some sort of individual format) on an important issue or question to establish consensus (Linstone and Turoff, 2002). An important aspect of consensus techniques is the facilitation and encouragement of individuals to share the reasoning, rationale or logic of their opinions. Participant opinions are usually shared through written responses to questions in an indi-vidual survey-type format, with agreement determined through an interquartile mean. An inevitable certainty of consensus techniques is that non-consensus will occur on one or more of the topics. One view of this occurrence is that honest disagreement is often a good sign of progress (Anderson and Kanuka, 2003). However, the resulting outcome, irrespective of whether or not an opinion synthesis occurs, may be more defensible than other methodologies due specifically to the acknowledgment and accommodation of opposing opinions (Kanuka, 2002).

Merging the advantages of the focus group method and consensus techniques: deliberative inquiry

In my work, I realized a need to move the research objectives from a level of rhetoric to a level of practice where, through deliberation, the research findings would confront verity and view. As aspects of both the focus group method and Delphi technique were capable of addressing the research problem described earlier, I made a decision to combine these methods, resulting in a hybrid technique that I eventually came to refer to as a 'deliberative inquiry'. Unlike other consensus methods (such as nominal group and Delphi technique), a deliberative inquiry is not aimed at forcing a consensus on the issues under investigation. Instead, the aim is to deliberate about the issues as perceived by diverse stakeholders, and provide an opportunity to challenge ideas, reveal misconceptions and establish where mutual understandings exist. Indeed, I chose the term 'deliberative' because I asked the participants to deliberate with each other about the issues arising from a previous study, and arrive at a consensus on the impact of these issues.

This hybrid of research methods can most accurately be described as a method for exploring individual consensus through group dialogue. To achieve this, the deliberative inquiry method draws on specific characteristics from both the focus group and the Delphi techniques. Similar to a focus group, a deliberative inquiry involves a unique kind of group interview, in that it gathers data from a number of people in a manner that is non-quantitative; it is also similar to consensus techniques in that it requires participants to deliberate on issue(s) to explore where there is convergence of opinions.

Many important research questions lend themselves to group and consensus-building research techniques because the questions have no single, self-evident or universal answer. For example, a good research problem for a deliberative inquiry is when the researcher needs to draw out the participants' experiences and opinions and compare them with other similar experiences. The research question should be one where the researcher needs to obtain participants' opinions on an important but controversial idea or view of a complex problem. Hence, the nature of the research question dictates the use of a deliberative inquiry. A deliberative inquiry is also useful for revealing the complexities of a problem or issue under investigation. Specifically, a deliberative inquiry can be effective at stimulating in-depth exploration of a topic or issue when (1) there is a need for greater depth and understanding about the problem under investigation and (2) polarized views exist. Within these researcher needs, an important assumption embedded in a deliberative inquiry is the belief that the opinions we hold can be formed and changed, and that they arise from discussions with others. Hence, deliberative inquiries are effective at gathering data in an open and group context, where individual members consider their opinions against the opinions of others.

Aims of a deliberative inquiry

The primary aim of a deliberative inquiry is to facilitate a structured group communication process that explores where consensus exists with experts in the field. Similar to the Delphi technique (see for example Linstone and Turoff, 1975), a deliberative inquiry is useful when the research problem does not lend itself to well-defined systematic research methods, but can collect useful data from subjective deliberation by experts in a group setting. The success of a deliberative inquiry is dependent upon the researcher's ability to select participants with diverse backgrounds, views and expertise on the topic under investigation. In my own experience, I have found that bringing the participants together and deliberating on their diverse and polarized opinions provides the opening I need to determine where consensus exists and where it does not, as well as why these polarized opinions are held so passionately in the first place. I also find it provides an opportunity to collect data that clearly identify the nature and extent of opinion divergence. The results from a deliberative inquiry, then, may be more trustworthy than other methodologies because of the acknowledgment and accommodation of opposing opinions.

Assumptions underpinning a deliberative inquiry

The main assumption underpinning a deliberative inquiry is a belief that the decisions we make are socially constructed and grow out of discussions with other people. Bringing together carefully selected participants to deliberate about specific issues or problems can be an effective method to collect data, as the group's deliberations allow participants to react to and build upon the responses of other group members. When effectively moderated, the group effect results in determining whether consensus can be reached on the issue or problem under investigation – consensus that typically is not clarified through individual interviews, or specifically sought in focus group interviews. Further, a deliberative inquiry has the ability to eliminate incorrect or extreme opinions, making it possible to assess where there are consistent, shared views. Drawing upon the assumption that the decisions we make are socially constructed and grow out of discussions with other people, a related underpinning belief is that deliberative inquiries are effective at gathering data in a group context, where individual members consider their opinions against the opinions of others.

Participants

The success of a deliberative inquiry is dependent upon the diversity, expertise and experience of the participants; it uses aspects of participant selections from both consensus techniques and focus groups. When using either focus groups or consensus techniques, the panel participants are purposely selected because they are informed, interested and capable of providing high-quality verity and views about the issues(s) under investigation. Selecting expert participants is key to an effective deliberation because throughout the process, they will draw first on their own experiences and opinions and then build upon that knowledge by considering the opinions and expertise of others. A deliberative inquiry, similar to the Delphi technique, also requires participants to be selected who are interested stakeholders with broad research and practical expertise in the topic under investigation. Unlike a focus group, participants need to be selected carefully to ensure diversity is represented.

Moderator

With the aim of establishing both consensus and divergence of expert opinion, a deliberative inquiry requires stakeholders who have expertise in the topics and/or issues. As with a focus group, a deliberative inquiry requires an experienced group facilitator with expertise in the issue(s) under investigation. An important aspect of a deliberative inquiry is that the process necessitates the participants not just talking about the issue(s), but also carefully weighing the alternative possibilities posed by others and the consequences of those alternatives. To achieve this, the moderator is critical to eliciting meaningful information from each of the participants in a manner that remains respectful and safe when non-consensus arises.

Throughout the deliberation, it is important that the moderator be sensitive to each participant's perspectives in a manner that will encourage them to openly share their ideas and perspectives. While a group deliberation makes possible data collection that would be impossible in other formats, a shortcoming is that this format makes it difficult to prevent one group member from dominating the discussion, and thus shaping the entire deliberation. Additionally, some participants might be uncomfortable sharing personal opinions in a group format. To address these difficulties, the moderator needs to take an active role in mediating the deliberations, encouraging participation by all and curbing domination by a few, while ensuring a trusting and respectful environment is maintained throughout the process. Using a skilled moderator and carefully selected experts can result in credible and rich data that reveals the extent to which relatively consistent, shared views exist among participants, as well as identifying inconsistent and/or polarized views.

Doing the deliberative inquiry

The deliberative inquiry is ideally suited when the researcher needs to build on prior research, because the data has revealed polarized opinions on one or more issues or problems. The deliberative inquiry is most effectively facilitated when it is introduced by a moderator (who is not the researcher) to the group of participants, wrapped around a narrative case or cases that illustrate the diversity of opinions, with the researcher giving the participants the case or cases prior to the meeting. When forming the narrative cases, it is best to present the problem first, accompanied by opposing opinions on the pertinent issues, followed by open-ended questions for the participants to consider prior to the meeting with the group. A full explanation of the purpose of the study and a description of the deliberative inquiry process are also required prior to the meeting.

When the participants are brought together, the moderator should open the process first by presenting the theoretical framework for the study. This should then be followed by presenting the narrative cases based on background information or research outcomes. The moderator will portray both the issue and most importantly the polarized views. The participants are then asked by the moderator to share opinions and views on the open-ended questions presented in the cases, followed by guided deliberation with the other participants on the diverse perspectives presented.

In terms of ethics, all participants need to be informed that confidentiality and anonymity cannot be provided. All participants need to be provided with a consent form which states that the research will be conducted in a group format and the data will not be confidential and/or anonymous between and among the group participants. While it is possible to have the group participants sign an ethics form requesting confidentially of the deliberative inquiry, this is not realistic and the ethics forms should reflect this.

Data collection and data analysis

Data collection should be done using videotape. While it is possible to use an audio tape, audio data are difficult for a transcriber to manage when there are many participants, since it often can be difficult to determine the speaker's identity when there are numerous participants involved. Once transcribed, a member check should follow for clarity and accuracy.

Merriam (2001: 178) describes data analysis as the process of meaning making: 'consolidating, reducing, and interpreting what people have said and what the researcher has seen and read'. With a goal of constructing categories or themes that capture recurring patterns in the data, Merriam's recommendations are well suited for guiding data analysis in a deliberative inquiry. Using the constant comparative method of data analysis, categories can be created that reflect the purpose of the research as well as being exhaustive, mutually exclusive, sensitizing and conceptually congruent. Category construction should begin with the first set of notes (Merriam, 2001). Notations can be made by potentially relevant bits of data related to the alignment (or not) of perspectives. After working through the notes, 'like' comments/agreement can be grouped together, resulting in a running list of groups or themes created. The next set of data can be treated in a similar way, and then this list of notes and groupings should be compared with the first set. The result will be a set of categories derived from the data.

Separate thematic analyses, followed by debriefing meetings should also be conducted to avoid researcher privileging, maintain trustworthiness of the data, and detect potential biases or inconsistent conclusions. To maintain trustworthiness and credibility of the research process, an audit trail comprised of field notes, memos and observer comments should be established (Bogdan and Biklen, 2003). Peer debriefing meetings with research assistants can also avoid researcher privileging, as well as point out potential biases or inconsistent conclusions.

Advantages and limitations

The deliberation process works best when the participants are able to view their opinions in relation to those of the rest of the group, and are then given an opportunity to make a case and defend their opinions. The resulting dialogue allows individuals (and the group) to alter and refine their opinions, leading to an informed consensus. A deliberative inquiry has the capacity to garner rich and credible qualitative data. It can also provide quality controls on data collection, as participants jointly question and eliminate false or extreme views. The result is a proclivity to inquire about the most important topics and issues, and to assess the extent to which a relatively consistent, shared view exists among participants – as well as to identify inconsistent views. The participants in a deliberative inquiry should be carefully selected individuals who are informed, interested and capable of proving high-quality opinions on the topic under investigation. The expert panel of participants draws on their own expertise, while deliberating with other panel members about their opinions. This creates an environment for 'social cognition' which can result in collecting data that cannot be collected from individuals. The deliberation process, then, can offer researchers significant insights into the research problems they are working through, via the collective expertise of the expert panel members who have diverse backgrounds. Further, although a deliberative inquiry may not result in consensus, it does create an environment in which opposing views can be expressed both democratically and with respect, through the structured discussion format.

A marked advantage of the deliberative inquiry method over other consensus techniques is that it allows participants to react to and build on responses, in a group format. With an experienced moderator, the result is a stimulating effect on group behaviour, resulting in data or ideas that cannot be collected through individual interviews. Moreover, because the deliberative inquiry tends to provide checks and balances among group members to eliminate false or extreme views, it provides an opportunity for the researcher to determine the extent of consistent and shared views. Given these characteristics, conducting a deliberative inquiry can result in a robust method for collecting data on issues that attract polarized views.

Similar to many time-honoured qualitative methods, a challenge and a limitation of using a deliberative inquiry is that it represents feedback from a theoretical sample rather than from a randomly selected population (Glaser and Strauss, 1967). Typical of qualitative research, the data are also often diffuse and hard to manage, making data analysis demanding and complicated. As such, the results from a deliberative inquiry should not be generalized to other larger populations. Further, no guarantees of confidentiality or anonymity are possible because participants interact with each other face-to-face. In addition, a group setting can lead on occasion to uncomfortable power struggles associated with status differences among participants. Finally, because this research method requires bringing together expert participants who may be from geographically dispersed areas, it can be an expensive approach to data collection.

Closing precis

Good research is time-consuming and hard to do. However, it takes more than hard work and time to conduct research that makes a significant contribution; it takes a desire for researchers to explore the important problems and to recognize that these important questions are complicated (Reeves, 1999). A key element to generating significantly useful research is utilizing more emergent methodology that can effectively address the 'real world' messiness that researchers routinely encounter.

The method proposed in this chapter is in response to a need to explore emergent methods resulting from the excessive use of traditional data collection methods that are predictably used in the social sciences and humanities (for example, questionnaires, interviews, observation, reflective journaling, document analysis and field notes). While many existing methods are well accepted, recognized and effective at exploring, discovering and furthering understandings of the issues and phenomena under investigation, there are other non-mainstream methods that can also be effective at responding to research questions – and under certain circumstances can be effective at responding to the unique issues and problems in the social sciences, humanities and education in need of further investigation. This chapter provides a description of an emergent methodology, the deliberative inquiry, as a research method for examining complex issues and determining where consensus exists.

References

Anderson, T. and Kanuka, H. (2003) *E-research: Methods, strategies, and issues*, Boston, MA: Allyn & Bacon.

Bogdan, R. C. and Biklen, S. K. (2003) *Qualitative Research for Education: An introduction to theory and methods*, 4th edn, Boston, MA: Allyn & Bacon.

Cohen, L., Manion, L. and Morrison, K. (2005) *Research Methods in Education*, 5th edn, New York: RoutledgeFalmer.

Cresswell, J. W. (2005) *Educational Research: Planning, Conducting and evaluating quantitative and qualitative research*, Upper Saddle River, NJ: Pearson Merrill Prentice Hall.

Cronbach, L. J. (1975) 'Beyond the two disciplines of scientific psychology', *American Psychologist*, 30, 671–84.

Cronbach, L. J. and Suppes, P. (1969) *Research for Tomorrow's Schools: Disciplined inquiry for education*, London: Macmillan.

Gall, M. D., Gall, J. P. and Borg, W. R. (2007) *Educational Research: An introduction*, 8th edn, New York: Pearson.

Glaser, B. G. and Strauss, A. L. (1967) *The Discovery of Grounded Theory: Strategies for qualitative research*, New York: Aldine.

Kanuka, H. (2002) 'Guiding principles for facilitating higher levels of Web-based distance learning in post-secondary settings', *Distance Education*, **3**(1), 163–82.

Linstone, H. A. and Turoff, M. (1975) *The Delphi Method: Techniques and applications*, Reading, MA: Addison-Wesley.

Linstone, H. A. and Turoff, M. (2002) *The Delphi Method: Techniques and applications* (online) <http://www.is.njit.edu/pubs/delphibook/> (accessed 16 Nov 2009).

Merriam, S. B. (2001) *Qualitative Research and Case Study Application in Education*, San Francisco: Jossey-Bass.

Neuman, W. L. (2000) *Social Research Methods: Qualitative and quantitative approaches*, 4th edn, Boston, MA: Allyn & Bacon.

Reeves, T. C. (1995) 'Questioning the questions of instructional technology research', in M. R. Simonson and M. Anderson (eds), *Proceedings of the Annual Conference of the Association for Educational Communications and Technology, Research and Theory Division*, Anaheim, CA: American Educational Research Association.

Reeves, T. C. (1999) 'Rigorous and socially responsible interactive learning research', Association for the Advancement of Computing in Education (online) <http://www.aace.org/pubs/jilr/intro.html> (accessed September 2006).

Schön, D. A. (1983) *The Reflective Practitioner: How professionals think in action*, New York: Basic Books.

Shulman, L. S. (1997) 'Disciplines of inquiry in education: a new overview', in R. M. Jaegar (ed.), *Complementary Methods for Research in Education*, 2nd edn, Washington: American Educational Research Association.

Stewart, D. W. and Shamdasani, P. N. (1998) 'Focus group research: exploration and discovery', in L. Bickman and D. J. Rog (eds), *Handbook of Applied Social Research Methods*, London: Sage.

Chapter 12

Qualitative research synthesis

The scholarship of integration in practice

Claire Howell Major and Maggi Savin-Baden

Introduction

The question of what can be done to make the best and most effective use of best evidence is something that has remained problematic for those in the field of qualitative research. Since the mid-1980s there have been many attempts to try to combine qualitative findings in ways that are useful and informative, most notably the work of Noblit and Hare (1988). However, most attempts to date have resulted in approaches that are specializations, complex and refined in both application and technique, and for many are difficult to adopt. Qualitative research synthesis enables researchers to summarize existing studies in ways that are informative to policy makers and practitioners, and also enables the knowledge gained through such studies to be more widely available to others. It is an approach that is methodologically grounded and rigorous since it seeks to answer a specific research question through combining qualitative studies that use thick description and that are located in broadly the same tradition. This chapter will describe and argue for qualitative research synthesis, an approach that uses qualitative methods to combine the results from qualitative studies. Through our description we outline our methodologically grounded approach for analyzing, synthesizing and interpreting existing qualitative studies, and provide specific details and examples of how the approach works in practice. This approach will thus make the findings of existing qualitative research studies more accessible to those who make decisions, both practitioners and policy makers.

Qualitative research synthesis

At its most fundamental level, qualitative research synthesis is an approach in which findings from existing qualitative studies are integrated using qualitative methods. The purpose is to make sense of concepts, categories or themes that have recurred across a particular data set in order to develop a comprehensive picture of the findings. The approach requires adhering to a methodological, rigorous process while at the same time striving for transparency. While some evidence of attempts to integrate qualitative information appear earlier than the 1990s, real movement in the integration of qualitative information was catalyzed late in that decade by the provocatively titled publication of Noblit and Hare's classic text, *Meta-ethnography* (1998). In this text, the authors make a case for using an interpretive approach for integrating findings from existing interpretive studies. Noblit and Hare state that such an approach:

enables a rigorous procedure for deriving substantive interpretations about any set of ethnographic or interpretive studies. Like quantitative counterparts of meta-analysis (Glass *et al.*, 1981; Hunter *et al.*, 1982) and the integrative research review (Cooper, 1984), a meta-ethnography can be considered a complete study in itself. It compares and analyzes texts, creating new interpretations in the process. It is much more than what we usually mean by a literature review.

(Noblit and Hare, 1988: 9)

In their text, they outline their approach to synthesizing a small number (between two and five) of qualitative studies.

While Noblit and Hare are widely considered the fathers of using interpretive approaches to synthesizing interpretive research, many scholars have taken up the charge to integrate information from existing qualitative studies and to share their approaches as well as their products with others. These scholars hail from a range of disciplines, notably the health professions, but also from education, policy studies and organizational studies. These scholars have refined the original 'meta-ethnographic' approach over time, tending more and more toward interpretivism in their efforts, approaches that collectively can be referred to as 'qualitative research synthesis.'

Getting started in qualitative research synthesis

Once the decision to use qualitative research synthesis is made, the synthesist most often begins the process by formulating an appropriate research question and deciding what will count as data.

Formulating a question

The question is of critical importance in qualitative research synthesis, and likely stems from the synthesist's interests as well as from a problem of practice. The question should be clear and bounded, as is the case with primary qualitative research, as it will determine the knowledge that will be accumulated through the synthesis. Further, the question should be broad enough that a sufficient number of studies can be gathered during the search process, but it should be sufficiently narrow and focused so that the search for studies yields useful and useable information. Finally, the synthesist should strive to make the selection of the question a transparent process, as his or her biases necessarily drive its development.

Deciding what will count as data

A critical question among synthesists is what components of the original studies will be considered as data that may be included in the analysis phase of treating the data. Noblit and Hare were of the opinion that anything from the title to the discussion can be considered data, as they provide important clues to aid understanding. We tend to believe that findings, in particular rich, thick description provided in the findings sections of articles, serve as the primary data, while other aspects can be considered for helping to understand and interpret this data; they can be particularly useful for allowing for triangulation.

Searching for studies

Most synthesists set rigorous processes for searching for original studies to include in the synthesis, and they rigorously document these processes so that others can retrace their steps and repeat the search if needed. Among those processes are online database searching, including databases such as Academic Elite and ERIC. Synthesists also document their search strings, which are typically developed through a combination of divination of thesaurus descriptors, key words and Boolean logic. Most also review the bibliographies of the articles they uncover through online searching as well as through hand searching tables of contents of the most relevant journals on the topic.

Selecting the sample of original studies

Developing a sample of studies is a critical task, for those studies serve as the data for the analysis. Three steps are typically followed: deciding on and applying inclusion and exclusion criteria, establishing and implementing sampling procedures, and assessing the quality of potential studies. We describe these steps more fully in this section.

Deciding on inclusion and exclusion criteria

After searching for articles and developing an initial set for consideration, the set must be reviewed for applicability. This typically involves developing criteria for making decisions about which articles to include and exclude. Criteria typically involve factors such as topic, research question, date, research method and study participants. Most frequently, synthesists scan article abstracts to compare factors against inclusion and exclusion criteria. When the abstract does not contain sufficient information, it is necessary for the synthesist to consult the full article to make an initial determination.

Establishing a process for sampling

There is no universal agreement about how to sample studies. Some synthesists believe that it is necessary to develop a comprehensive sample and to synthesize findings from all relevant articles. We tend toward the more interpretivist camp, and believe that it is critical to develop the comprehensive sample initially, but that it is only necessary to continue to review articles until a temporary form of saturation is reached (that is, until themes begin to repeat and no new themes are generated). We believe it is critical to include a sufficient number of studies to allow for analysis, but not so many as to make analysis impossible. We find that between six and ten studies is the optimal number.

Ensuring quality

The last step in sample selection is ensuring the quality of the articles to be included. While it is important to include even weaker studies, as they may have something to add to the synthesis and interpretation, it is critical to exclude studies that are fatally flawed so as not to contaminate the data and lead to faulty conclusions. This assurance can be accomplished by an assessment of the congruence between research question, design, methods and efforts towards plausibility. We recommend that the synthesist develop a checklist, such as the one we included in Major and Savin-Baden (2010), for making such an assessment.

Treating data

In this section, we describe our three-phase process for data analysis, synthesis and interpretation. While our description is derived largely from our 2010 book, as well as from our 2007 article, in this section we use examples from Major's (2010) article titled 'Do virtual professors dream of electric students? College faculty experiences with online distance education,' to illustrate the processes. To provide some contextual information to aid understanding of the examples we include below, we cite Major's abstract:

> Faculty acceptance of distance learning plays an important role in its success or failure in higher education. Information about faculty experiences teaching online can improve understanding about this delivery mode's potential longevity in academe. Exploratory qualitative research has begun to uncover and unpack faculty experiences with online learning. Such studies provide a focused and detailed picture of faculty perceptions of teaching online. These studies, however, have not been considered for what they add to cumulative knowledge. The purpose of this research was to employ a rigorous and systematic approach to make meaning of these individual studies by considering them in aggregate. This article presents findings from a qualitative synthesis of university faculty experiences with online distance education. Results show that faculty members believe that teaching online changes the way that they approach and think about teaching, course design, time, instruction, and students. Results also drive suggestions for future research and for enhancing faculty experiences online.

Analysis: developing first-order themes

The first step of treating data in a synthesis is analysis, during which first-order themes are generated. The term "analysis" means to break apart into essential elements, in this case for the purpose of studying or investigating themes. Thus essentially what is done in this phase is to break apart findings from individual studies and examine their elements.

Description of processes

The first step of analysis involves simply identifying the findings in each of the studies. This involves reading and rereading the original studies, particularly the thick description provided, to locate those findings that data support. We recommend formalizing an assessment of each finding for credibility based upon whether it is (a) supported by clear data, (b) credible in the context, or (c) unsupported with evidence. We recommend using only those findings that are supported or credible. The next step involves finding themes across studies. This means reviewing all supported and credible findings for the themes that are embedded in them, and labeling them. This process may involve using the primary study author's labels of themes, it may involve developing new themes that the original authors could not identify (because they were looking at only their own data set), or it may involve a combination of the two. After themes are developed, text of the original articles is analysed for existence of those themes. Articles may be coded, much in the way that interview text is coded in primary qualitative research.

Example

In Major's work, for example, she initially listed all findings from articles and developed labels for them. She developed codes for the themes and coded the articles. She identified the following first order themes across studies:

- seeking to build a new online presence
- lessening of power and bias issues

- increasing of closeness with students
- learning from students
- increased access
- increased community building
- loss of visual cues and immediacy
- suffering of relationships
- missing the students.

These themes were directly related to her research questions of how faculty experiences change when teaching online.

Synthesis: developing second-order themes

Synthesis means to combine separate elements into a unified whole. In this phase, findings are aggregated then into a unified whole. This process is done with an eye toward providing a fresh perspective on the data, if one exists.

Description of processes

Moving from first-order themes to second-order themes is often a fairly straightforward process. It involves reading and rereading the studies, reading and rereading the first-order themes, and translating them into each other. While the process is straightforward, it is iterative, and movement must be allowed. Further, it is critical, as Noblit and Hare suggest, to allow for the possibility of failure. First-order themes may not translate into neat second-order themes, and they should not be forced. If they do not translate then an explanation of why may be offered.

Example

Major moves from first-order to second-order themes as shown in Figure 12.1. The process involves simple aggregation of the ideas. It also involves a process of inductive reasoning, and initial interpretive processes.

Interpretation: developing third-order themes

The third phase of data treatment is interpretation. Interpretation means to find the meaning or explanation of something. In this phase, third-order themes are developed through a process of critical thinking and inductive analysis.

Description of processes

Moving from second-order to third-order themes is complicated. In our book, we likened this phase to waiting for an 'epiphany' or a moment of revelation. The process requires reading and rereading initial studies, first-order themes and second-order themes. It requires being iterative, and allowing for movement of categories and themes. It requires being a reflexive scholar and allowing for the interpretation to emerge naturally. It also requires searching for the subtext, which is not always immediately apparent in the initial themes, making mental connections between the threads of themes and concepts.

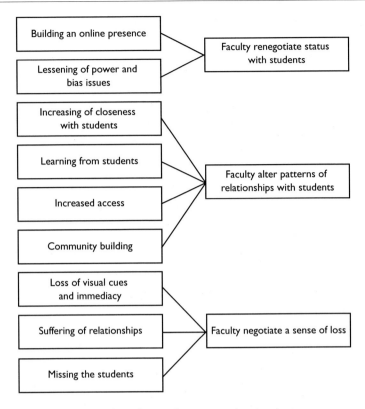

Figure 12.1 An example of moving from first-order to second-order themes

Example

In her work, Major moves from first-order analysis through second-order synthesis to third-order interpretation shown in Figure 12.2.

In her narrative, Major describes this changed relationship, posing the question of whether faculty want to reconstruct and renegotiate these relationships, and offering the hypothesis that it depends on whether faculty are able to move beyond technology as a tool for automation and standardization, into a position of viewing technology as a way to transform relationships, by being set free from ontological categories such as physical constraints of time and space.

Establishing plausibility

As we have noted, just as it is essential in primary qualitative research to provide some measure of accountability or to establish credibility, so too is it in qualitative research synthesis. We find, however, that traditional measures of validity or trustworthiness have some limitations in use with qualitative research synthesis. For this reason, in our book, we recommend a consideration of the concept of plausibility. Among the features of plausibility worth considering is the notion of locating realities. This involves a consideration of 'what seems to be true' given the context and those studies included in the investigation, as well as taking

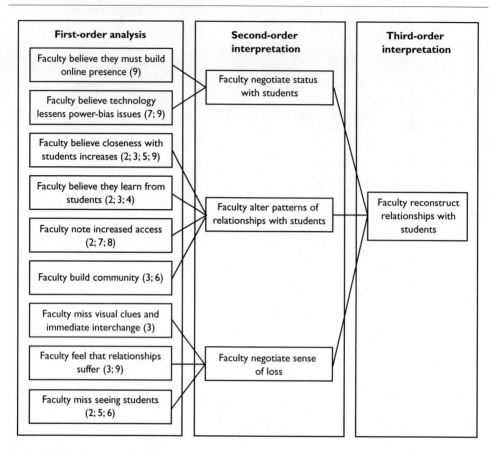

Figure 12.2 An example of moving from first, through second, to third-order interpretation

a critical stance in the questioning of what stakeholders consider as 'reality.' We also believe it to be critical for the synthesist to acknowledge their stance and to position themself against the data. We further argue that it is critical to locate the participants, their 'realities,' in the context of the original studies. Finally, we argue for clarity and transparency of processes and products attending the synthesis.

Presenting the synthesis

Presenting the synthesis can be a challenge, particularly for those planning to publish it. Doing an effective job requires comprehensiveness, but many journals have both space limitations and word count requirements. Moreover, potential members of the intended audience such as policy makers and practitioners want clear and considered information. For this reason, we argue for economy of presentation.

Economy of presentation may seem on the surface at odds with the goals of qualitative research, which requires contextual information for understanding as well as rich, thick description of data. We do not argue against that, but rather for trying in a synthesis to bridge the divide between quality narrative and the reality of existing constraints not only of space limitations but also of the reality of integrating findings from multiple interpretive studies. Thus we argue for economy of language in the narrative, being precise while providing sufficient details and the thick description necessary to paint a comprehensive picture of the findings for the intended audience. The strategic use of figures and tables to condense information into a usable but concise form for readers is also very beneficial.

Deciding to use qualitative research synthesis

There are several specific advantages for the potential synthesist that they should consider when deciding whether to use the approach. We acknowledge that there are those who take issue with the approach; we are sensitive to their concerns, and we attempt to respond to them directly. In this section, then, we list and explain some of the advantages as well as some of the potential pitfalls of qualitative research synthesis.

Advantages of the approach

There are many advantages of adopting qualitative research synthesis to integrate qualitative evidence. In the following few paragraphs, we highlight several key advantages of the approach.

Qualitative research synthesis provides a methodologically grounded approach to making sense of existing research

Traditional literature reviews have not been as effective at integrating information as arguably they could have been. One of the reasons is that there are few guidelines or processes for conducting literature reviews effectively. This dearth has led to imprecision in approaches and even faulty interpretations. The process of qualitative research synthesis, on the other hand, is methodologically rigorous. It mirrors the processes of original research, including rigorous sampling, analysis, and reporting. It also requires providing some measure of establishing the plausibility of the synthesis and the findings. This rigor helps to control for biases and to avoid errors of interpretation.

Qualitative research synthesis can help scholars make connections between studies

One difficulty with primary qualitative research is that often little connection is made between studies. Even early proponents of the method were worried that studies would become 'little islands' unto themselves, never to be linked or revisited (Glaser and Strauss, 1971: 181). Qualitative research synthesis targets this very problem by viewing results from multiple qualitative studies together in an attempt to see the larger picture that they reveal when viewed together.

Qualitative research synthesis can help scholars see gaps and omissions in the literature base

When scholars delve deeply into an existing literature base, they gain a sense of what has been done and what is yet to be done. This is arguably never so true as when using qualitative research synthesis, which unlike traditional literature reviews, begins with a specific research question. Scholars searching to answer a question with existing information become acutely aware of where the gaps and omissions are, not only topically but also methodologically – and they begin to have a clearer sense of how to fill those gaps.

Qualitative research synthesis can allow for theory building

Many qualitative researchers see it as their duty to build theory. Qualitative research synthesis allows for this in ways that no single study can alone. Indeed, the processes of qualitative research synthesis in some ways resemble those of grounded theory (which Noblit and Hare originally advocated), and the products tend to resemble practice, or situation specific, theory. These theories then may be tested or applied, which can help drive the development of fields and disciplines.

Qualitative research synthesis can put research findings into the hands of those who can make use of them

Increasingly, researchers have begun to see it as an obligation to influence practice and policy through their work. Qualitative research synthesis provides an important avenue for accomplishing this end, since it involves culling information from multiple sources and providing a layer of interpretation. This process makes the information more usable for practitioners and policy makers, who tend to want information that is a result of multiple studies, rather than from one single study alone. Moreover, these stakeholders tend to want the information distilled into a readily useable form.

The advantages to qualitative research synthesis are many and we have highlighted only a few in this section. But our purposes are twofold here, in that we intend not only to encourage use of the approach, but also to provide a rationale for selecting it. Indeed, in published syntheses, these advantages often are described in research methodology sections as a rationale for selecting the approach.

Potential pitfalls of qualitative research synthesis

Despite its apparent advantages, qualitative research synthesis is not without its critics. We acknowledge some of the most frequent criticisms and provide what we believe are adequate responses to them in the following few paragraphs.

Context is stripped through the process of synthesis

Some scholars believe that context, the mainstay of qualitative research, is stripped during the process of synthesis. They believe that rich, thick description is lost, and as a result that participant voices are marginalized. We believe that this need not be the case. Rather, the synthesist should strive to provide contextual information that retains the integrity of the original studies. Further, the synthesist should retain sufficient thick description to allow participant voices to be heard. It is admittedly a challenge to find the line between being succinct and retaining thick description while maintaining integrity, but it is a balance for which the synthesist must strive.

Synthesists are limited to questions that have already been asked and answered

We acknowledge that synthesists are limited to studying what is available in the form of published information. However, we assert that myriad questions have been asked, and that it is time to take stock of the information that has been gleaned through efforts to answer them before moving forward. Further, we suggest that synthesists can synthesize not only data, but also questions. Therefore they can seek to answer what in a sense is a meta-question.

Synthesists have not had input into the study design

We acknowledge that synthesists must rely on the work that other researchers have done, and are in some ways bound by extant research designs. However, we believe that the synthesist has control over the kinds of designs that he or she accepts, through the application of carefully constructed inclusion and exclusion criteria. Furthermore, the synthesist can eliminate studies that have a fatally flawed research design.

Synthesists do not have access to original transcripts and thus might understand things differently than original researchers

Some researchers believe that secondary analysis of data is a better approach for integrating information from multiple qualitative studies than qualitative research synthesis, because in secondary analysis the researcher has access to all of the original transcripts. While we acknowledge that having fuller strings of original data might be desirable in some instances, particularly when the original researcher did not present sufficient thick description for a reader to determine whether a finding is credible, what synthesists who employ qualitative research synthesis additionally possess are the interpretations of the original researcher. We believe that some clues and nuances cannot be captured in transcripts that the original researcher then supplies through interpretation, and that these additional interpretations in turn can aid the later synthesist's interpretation.

These are the most frequent criticisms of the approach that we have encountered, and again our intent for including them in our discussion of qualitative research synthesis is twofold. We want to provide the information not only so that potential synthesists can make informed decisions about selecting the approach, but also so that they can address criticisms directly in their own work. We recommend that those using this approach acknowledge the criticisms and suggest how they have sought to counter them.

Conclusion

Qualitative research synthesis, although methodologically grounded and rigorous, is an approach that should be undertaken only by those dedicated to the processes of integration and interpretation. Social science and professional fields need more professionals who are willing to undertake this complex task, or as Boyer suggests, who strive to 'give meaning to isolated facts, putting them in perspective' (Boyer, 1990: 18). Meeting such a challenge requires commitment and perseverance, at a similar level of dedication as those of primary research. It requires holding ourselves to the same standard as with discovery research, including having clear goals, adequate appropriate methods, significant results, effective presentation and reflective critique (as suggested by Glassick *et al.* (1997) in the follow-up to *Scholarship Reconsidered*, entitled *Scholarship Assessed: Evaluation of the professoriate*. If qualitative research synthesis is not undertaken with this same level of dedication and care, then the approach has the potential to do more harm than good. However, if it is in a format such as the scholarship of integration, then qualitative research synthesis has much to offer qualitative scholars who seek to combine and interpret existing evidence.

References

Boyer, E. L. (1990) *Scholarship Reconsidered: Priorities of the Professorate*, San Francisco, CA: Jossey-Bass.

Glaser, B. and Strauss, A. (1971) *Status Passage: A formal theory*, Chicago: Aldine-Atherton.

Glassick, C. E., Huber, M. T. and Maeroff, G. I. (1997) *Scholarship Assessed: Evaluation of the professoriate*, San Francisco: Jossey-Bass.

Major, C. H. (2010) 'Do virtual professors dream of electric students? College faculty experiences with online distance education', *Teachers College Record*, **112**(8).

Major, C. H. and Savin-Baden, M. (2010) *An Introduction to Qualitative Research Synthesis: Managing the information explosion in social science research*, London: Routledge.

Noblit, G. W. and Hare, R. D. (1988) *Meta-ethnography: Synthesizing qualitative studies*, Newbury Park, CA: Sage.

Savin-Baden, M. and Major, C. H. (2007) 'Using interpretive meta-ethnography to explore the relationship between innovative approaches to learning and innovative methods of pedagogical research', *Higher Education*, **54**(6), 833–52.

Part III

Places and spaces

Chapter 13

Locating space in qualitative research

Questioning culture through the corporeal

Paddy O'Toole

Introduction

Human beings inhabit various interwoven worlds. We clearly inhabit a corporeal or physical world, but we also inhabit a world of ideas, concepts and theory, and a world of interaction, practice and activity. In qualitative research the worlds of interaction, practice and activity, and concepts, ideas and theory have been privileged over the corporeal world (Dale and Burrell, 2009), as researchers attempt to investigate the complex interrelationships of human life, and contribute to the human understanding of these phenomena.

Qualitative research is concerned with building descriptions, explanations and theories that are rich, nuanced and comprehensive. This requires the qualitative researcher to probe beyond the superficial and the explicit. Qualitative researchers necessarily must focus their gaze on a bounded environment. This focus limits the research to what is manageable, what can be unpacked and viewed at an often short distance. To try to focus on too much means that there is a lack of focus; complexity is lost and the insights may be sparse and trite. By narrowing the researcher lens to an appropriately bounded range, the researcher can view phenomena in depth. At the same time, however, the representation of the phenomena under study is, at best, partial. To build a complete and 'accurate' representation is an inspirational aim. The qualitative researcher attempts to construct rich layers of meaning but is ultimately constrained by the impossibility of trying to fully explicate the tacit (Polanyi, 1962, 1967). At best, the researcher builds an integration of the tacit and explicit into a trustworthy and defensible account.

In this chapter, I argue that by including considerations of space to the research methods and thus the data collection and analysis, researchers gain yet another perspective that invites challenging questions, contested meaning and contradiction, which helps the researcher develop rich, nuanced explanations of social life and human complexity. The inductive approach outlined in this chapter is developed from a pragmatic perspective of ontology and epistemology, and a 'constant need to problematize [sic], a refusal to take anything for granted, to treat things as obvious and familiar' (Kociatkiewicz and Kostera, 1999: 37). Investigating space necessarily deals with the tacit and the unconscious understandings that perceptions of space invoke. By using heuristic principles derived from grounded theory method, I illustrate how researchers can make sense of the physical environment in terms of unpacking elements of organizational culture. 'Culture', in terms of the title of this chapter, refers specifically to organizational culture, which is defined by Schein as:

> A pattern of basic assumptions – invented, discovered or developed by a given group as it learns to cope with its problems of external adaptation and internal integration – that

has worked well enough to be considered valid, and therefore to be taught to new members as the correct way to perceive, think and feel in relation to these problems.

(Schein, 1985: 9)

In Schein's model of culture, artefacts, the corporeal aspects of an organization, are part of the manifestations of culture. The practice, rules and structures of the actors merge into the patterns of behaviour that we call 'culture'. In organizations, the various groups, often delineated by physical boundaries, will form separate cultures based on separate practice, learned experience and their experience of other groups (O'Toole, 2004).

The meaning of space in this chapter is confined to the physical realm, rather than the expanded definitions that include thinking spaces, virtual spaces and so on (Crang and Thrift, 2000). A basic determinant of physical space are boundaries such as walls, floors, ceilings and partitions, which are corporeal human constructs (Markus, 2006). The dispositions of space relate to such issues as where the boundaries are situated, the nature of the boundaries in terms of solidity, height and so on, and the juxtaposition of and distance between spaces. By bounding space, humans create constructs that can and do reflect and influence patterns of thinking and behaviour (Schein, 1985; Van Maanen and Barley, 1985). According to Gaver (1996: 113), 'social meanings are based on facts of the physical world'. Spaces may be negotiated, imposed or seized, and the boundaries of space, through their physical properties, may manifest power, community, status and identity. Too often, however, the gaze of the qualitative researcher passes over the disposition of physical space – it becomes the site of the research rather than part of the data analysed in the conduct of the research.

The investigation of space is explored using an approach based on grounded theory method (GTM), but which is also useful for a range of other qualitative methods. A significant connection between GTM and other qualitative methods is the inductive nature of qualitative methods in general. GTM is itself a series of inductive processes that produce theory that is embedded in the research context, rather than forcing the data to a predetermined speculative theory (Glaser, 1978). Any claim of undertaking a grounded approach, however, needs the caveat that any researcher will take into the research site assumptions and prior knowledge, thus the capacity for reflexively interrogating one's own place in the research is necessary (Finlay, 2002; Scourfield *et al.*, 2006).

GTM was created by Glaser and Strauss as a reaction to an increasing trend in sociological circles of testing theory, rather than generating theory (Glaser, 1978). According to Glaser (1978: 93), 'the goal of grounded theory is to generate a theory that accounts for a pattern of behaviour which is relevant and problematic for those involved'. The problem with GTM as first introduced by Glaser and Strauss was the vagueness regarding the practical procedures to be used. It seems that the efforts of authors to address this issue were the cause of the apparent schisms in the agreed methods (Glaser, 1992; Melia, 1996). Glaser, disturbed by what he found to be the 'inaccuracies' in a text produced by Strauss and Corbin (1990), produced several texts of his own, which have led to GTM according to Glaser, and GTM according to Strauss and Corbin. Charmaz has developed GTM further by creating a constructivist model that acknowledges the work of Strauss and Glaser, while more directly connecting GTM with the language and underlying assumptions of qualitative research (for example, Charmaz, 1994). This chapter will not describe how to use GTM in research projects; interested readers should refer to the excellent Charmaz (2006). A key feature of the researcher using GTM is the concurrence of data and analysis, with the researcher revisiting the data (and often the research context) to further develop the theory and ask further refined questions.

Although GTM can be used in quantitative research (Glaser, 1978), the inductive nature of GTM means that a strong overlap with other qualitative methods can be discerned in terms of the procedures used. Later in this chapter, the notion of theoretical bricolage is explored. Researchers may also act as bricoleurs in terms of using a variety of methodological tools to do the (research) job at hand (Patton, 1990). The approach set out in this chapter may help researchers expand their range of data collection and analysis tools when undertaking other research approaches that involve interacting with a site of human activity, such as ethnography or ethnomethodology.

This exposition concerning the place of space in research has been introduced through a brief background on the research approach from which many of the techniques later described were derived. I demonstrate and unpack a theoretical stance which is consistent with using an inductive approach to raise questions that contribute to the search for understanding the complexity of culture (O'Toole and Were, 2008). I determine that space may form part of the unit of analysis or be used as data to help build a representation pertaining to another unit of analysis, the latter being the focus of this chapter, and continue with the heuristic principles and practices that I believe facilitate involving aspects of space in research.

I conclude that although the boundaries of spaces are overt and corporeal, the deeper causes, reasons and explanations behind their manifestation may be tacit. Thus the researcher needs the wisdom to accept and even embrace uncertainty and supposition in investigations of space. The investigation of spatial dispositions, however, enables researchers to further explore, question and unpack the cultural richness of human interaction.

Unpacking the theoretical stance

The philosophical and theoretical stance of the researcher is a key issue in qualitative research (Denzin and Lincoln, 2000), and the stance that underlies this chapter is one of pragmatism. Pragmatism, popularized by William James, shuns rationalism, and rejects the belief that knowledge can be external and universal. For James (1987/1995), the notion of 'truth' rests on the practical consequences of belief. By tracing the practical consequences of belief, truth becomes more elastic and local. According to James:

> We say this theory solves ... [this problem] on the whole more satisfactorily than that theory; but that means more satisfactorily to ourselves, and individuals will emphasize their points of their satisfaction differently. To a certain degree, therefore, everything here is plastic.
>
> (James, 1987/1995: 1074)

In the pragmatist's view, according to James, the external reality is separated from the sensory perception of that reality, and thus also separated from the social construction of knowledge concerning that external reality. This separation of ontology and epistemology means a fundamental recognition that, although things can exist, knowledge about those things is socially constructed by human beings. Thus this approach, which should not be confused with empirical realism, posits that the world is not dependent on human cognitive structures to exist (Johnson and Duberley, 2000). For the researcher, this means that even when the actors involved in the investigation of space are available to the researcher, the understandings related to the corporeal surroundings will often be tacit and unconscious. In Davidson's (2009) study of domestic architecture, for example, she queries why her family still owns the house of Davidson's grandparents. When she voices personal bemusement over why her grandparents' house had been retained and maintained, her curiosity is left unsatisfied by those most nearly involved:

> This house had been vacant for four years and had hardly been altered. The water was still running. It was still furnished. In the front room, the rack full of my granddad's farmer hats stood untouched. I asked my dad what he thinks of the house. 'Nothing, I don't think of it.' ... I pressed my dad for a more satisfying answer ... My father says this house is of little consequence and shows more attachment to the hickory tree on a corner of the property, but I am not convinced.
>
> (Davidson, 2009: 333–4)

For Davidson's grandparents, the house is no longer a home. Her grandfather has died, her grandmother has moved into a nursing home. The maintenance of the house takes time, money and effort. Why keep the house? Davidson writes an engaging exposition that connects theoretical exploration with the undeniable fact of the retention of her grandparents' house. The fact remains, however, that her conclusions concerning the house cannot be confirmed. This particular occupation of space seems almost whimsical on the part of her family, and the reasons for their actions in keeping the house are clearly contested.

The example of Davidson's grandparents' house illustrates a basic paradox of qualitative research in general, and in the investigation of space and corporeal in particular. Qualitative research is concerned with the elicitation and construction of understanding (Lindlof, 1995), and understanding requires insights into relationships and entailments (Nickerson, 2008). From a broad understanding comes what we term 'wisdom', where wise persons construct mental representations that are coherent with other knowledge, at the same time understanding that knowledge itself is fallible (Nickerson, 2008; Meacham, 1990; Sternberg, 1990). For qualitative researchers, particularly those engaged in investigations of space, it is necessary to understand that confirmation of conclusions in relation to space (and other corporeal objects) will usually remain beyond the power of the researcher. Although methods and techniques such as interviews and member checking (for example, see Sandelowski, 1993) may elicit conscious decisions of actors in the research site regarding the disposition of space, the behaviours and assumptions that are constructed over time as the space is used and adapted may be and usually are beyond the capacity of actors to explicate (Hodder, 2000).

Understanding thus occurs as theoretical themes that emerge from analysis of the spatial data connect with the themes related to other data, such as interviews, observation and texts, and later with theories in the literature, in a coherent representation. Wisdom is needed both to make the connections that result in a coherent representation, and to accept that this representation is fallible and subject to revision and amendment. We cannot know the external reality of what we research. We can attempt to make a partial and fallible representation, and our knowledge claims need to include some acknowledgement of fallibility. The choice to include considerations of spatial disposition means that we as researchers are confronted with our own fallibility – how do we *know* that our conclusions concerning (for example) the interaction of space and culture, reflect and explain the activities and practice for a given research site? We as qualitative researchers need to accept that we cannot know, and the decisions that we make during the research need to reflect the understanding that we may build only the best representation we can.

The next section introduces how space may be included in a research study, with a concentration of using the investigation of space as a way of adding richness to the study's unit of analysis.

Using space to investigate culture

In incorporating space in research, two approaches can be used that relate to the entity that is the focus of the research: that is, the unit of analysis. The first uses space as the unit of analysis. The research question can be generalized to:

What (is or was) this space?

This approach sees the researcher problematizing the nature of the space itself. Davidson's work on domestic architecture, for example, was 'motivated by this personal question. ... Why, years after my grandfather's death and my grandmother's move into a nursing home, did my father and his siblings not sell or rent or tear down this house?' (Davidson, 2009: 333–4). This approach focuses squarely on the space and the material objects that inhabit the space. Corporeality manifests something, but the something is an unknown. Further investigation of the actors, interactions and events that populate the space and the corporeal manifestations is needed to build an explanatory representation. This type of research study is often related to fields and disciplines such as geography and material culture, and the literature is populated with various examples.

The second approach uses a context, event or social group as the unit of analysis. The question asked by researchers is then:

How does this space interact with the unit of analysis?

In this approach, investigations of space become part of the research methods rather than the unit of analysis, and this approach guides the rest of this chapter. Although true space is a vacuum without even, as Casey terms them, 'empty places' (Casey, 1993: xi), the notion of space in research sites such as organizations has developed into an understanding of bounded areas that are negotiated and contested. 'Making space' implies effort to push back either physically or metaphorically the boundaries that impede action, thinking or being.

Physical space deals with quantities, qualities and geometric relationships, such as distance and juxtaposition (Gieryn, 2000: 465). The importance of boundaries in defining the factual characteristics of quantity and geometric relationships can be foregrounded by considering what happens when such boundaries cannot be perceived or are swept away. An inability to perceive such boundaries may cause feelings of disorientation, of simply being lost without direction. Space can act as the 'bones' of place, a skeleton upon which meaning is built through objects and materials until space, place and things merge into a unit with meaning. The bounded space may be named, which further confirms occupation and meaning (de Certeau, 1984). This merging of space, place and things, and conversely the disorientation when the perception of the merger is lost, is graphically illustrated in Nossack's account of returning to the city of Hamburg after it was firebombed in 1943. 'What surrounded us did not remind us in any way of what was lost. It had nothing to do with it. It was something else, it was strangeness itself, it was the essentially not possible' (Nossack, 2004: 43). In this case, with all destroyed by the war, all had been lost. Not only the material objects that connect people to memories (O'Toole, 2006; O'Toole and Were, 2008), but also the boundaries that delineate meaning and connection.

If research is conducted within a building, then there are several forms of boundaries to observe. Casey (1993: 32) argued that 'A building condenses a culture in one place', and, giving the example of an early Greek temple, illustrates how the landscape in which a building is placed contributes to the meaning of the building and how the cultural attitudes towards the activities and purpose of the building develop. In terms of modern organizations, buildings may be situated within grounds that have their own boundary, with the external walls of the building constituting another boundary, and the internal walls constituting yet more boundaries.

Some key heuristic principles are useful in enabling the researcher to inductively think about space in terms of the data collection and analysis. The first principle lies in the often repeated remark of Glaser – 'All is data' (1978: 8). This principle causes a widening of perception to include more in data collection than simply interactions and practice. In the first approach, where space and corporeality is the unit of analysis, the researcher is centrally involved with the space and corporeal artefacts. In the second approach, however, where space becomes part of the data collection, it is easy for spatial dispositions to become lost among other data. As people move about organizations, they unconsciously demonstrate access and lack of access in terms of physical space, perceive the visible and audible, and look and listen through permeable walls and partitions. Including corporeal manifestations of space and boundaries, and the way people interact with these manifestations, creates another layer of richness and further possibilities for investigation.

Researchers need to cultivate sensitivity to spatial dispositions, and to actors' interaction and engagement with those dispositions. In organizations, for example, actors move through spaces, look over partitions, hear conversation through empty space and through boundaries, and are excluded or included via boundaries. Instead of focusing only on the actors, researchers can focus on the ways that actors are influenced by the presence or absence of boundaries, the power they have over the erection and demolition of boundaries, and signs of change that are manifested by and in regard to boundaries.

On a more technical level, it is useful to record floor plans and take photographs of the relevant spaces. The degree of accuracy in recording of floor plans will depend on the nature of the publication and the focus of the research. If the floor plan itself becomes an important part of the evidence supporting your argument, it is worthwhile using a computer-aided design package to depict a high-quality drawing of the plan. If the floor plan simply acts a supporting piece of data, then a hand-drawn depiction will be adequate – the depiction simply has to remind the researcher of the characteristics of the space, and would be viewed in conjunction with the photographs anyway. I have found that it is more effective to take photographs of spatial dispositions without people in them. The addition of actors obscures or diverts attention from the space, and in many cases would require permission from the actors for ethical reasons. Although photographs with actors may be useful records of events and interactions, these phenomena can be captured by field notes. These records – that is, floor plans, photographs and field notes – will act as a catalyst to thinking about how spatial dispositions reflect and influence cultural patterns within the research site, perhaps indicated by the use of the second principle.

The second principle relates to the need for constant comparison during data collection and analysis. Constant comparison is a GTM technique that serves to sensitize the researcher to features of the research site. Constantly comparing events, incidents and features of the physical environments draws attention to anomalies and exceptions, practice versus unusual behaviour, tacit understandings of the research participants and so on. In one organization where I conducted research, an employee was observed telling her co-workers to stay out of her cubicle in an increasingly exasperated tone, as she covered the papers on her desk with her arms. Her cubicle, like many others, was comprised of partitions that enabled most colleagues to see over them and to freely enter her work area. Part of her work, however, required calculating monthly payments to senior managers in the organization, a task that required conditions of strict confidentiality. The inconsistency between the privacy needed for her work, and the lack of privacy afforded by the actual space, which was allocated on the basis of the employee's status, gave a clue to an inconsistency with regard to the perceptions of the culture. The culture, according to most actors within the organization, was egalitarian. The inconstancy between her work needs and the allocated space was the first of a number of instances that pointed to a less egalitarian workplace than was generally believed. If this organization was an egalitarian workplace, surely someone undertaking confidential work would be allocated an office. As a pattern of events, or even when one outstanding event emerges in the data, researchers may commence comparing their insights with the theory in the literature.

The third principle relates to constant comparison and the literature review. In GTM the literature review occurs after the data collection, and is focused by the data collection. In practice, a continual review of the literature takes place in other qualitative approaches as well, even though a comprehensive review may occur before conducting the data collection. As the researcher builds a representation, concepts derived from external sources must earn their way into the emerging theory. This need to fit the literature to the data rather than vice versa resonates with the notion of bricolage, causing the researcher to transcend disciplinary boundaries in a search to explain 'what is going on with this data?' a question that, according to Glaser (1978), should be asked repeatedly by researchers. In terms of the spatial world, comparing a variety of theoretical propositions to context enables the researcher to find the closest fit between theory and context, and to explore what fails to fit. An inductive approach to research is compatible with the pragmatist's philosophy. According to James (1987/1995: 1072), 'Theories thus become instruments, not answers to enigmas, in which we can rest.' Rather than using theories as ideologies, this approach uses theories as tools with which the data can be sorted, synthesized and compared, with the theories as a point of comparison. The theories come from outside the research site, and thus have to win a place in terms of the developing theory.

An analytic separation of spatial dispositions from the rich substance of place and things can be illuminating in terms of perceiving the research site with clarity, investigating how space influences human activity and how human activity has determined space. Space itself becomes a palimpsest upon which human activity is drawn, erased and drawn again (de Certeau, 1984). Casey (1993: 7) notes that 'time is the order of *successive* things' (italics in text). Thus the investigation of space becomes associated with a sense of the temporal. What is going on with this space *at this time*? Are changes discernible? What do these changes indicate? How do and did spatial dispositions reflect or belie social structures? Where an investigation of space through a lens of power occurs, there are various questions that can be asked to unpack the issues surrounding a particular space. Who has the right to possess or occupy this space? To whom is this space visible? To whom is access granted? Who has the power to change this space? All of these questions deal with access, either physical access or access in terms of visibility and audibility. Thus, each theoretical lens gives rise to further questions with which to interrogate the data.

In one study incorporating space (O'Toole and Were, 2008), a blocked door in a room dedicated to product repairs is noticed. (All is data.) The door was the only blocked door in the organization. It was a very solidly blocked door. This barring of access was not discerned in any other place in the organization. (Constant comparison.) The investigation of the blocked door helped make sense of other data collected. It gave a focus to almost random events and snatches of conversation. As a picture emerged, specific data could be sought out to add depth to my understanding. It was concluded that:

> The blocked door is a physical manifestation of a change in political dominance and signals the decline of a group that the organization formerly privileged. The blocked door denied access to everyone, but the block was aimed at the people in R&D. In this research study, the blocked door acts as an indicator or signpost that warrants further enquiry. Making sense of the blocked door in terms of the organization's culture and political structure, and piecing together the data provided by interviews, conversations and observations, as well as the door, resulted in a picture of the political development of the organization.
>
> (O'Toole and Were, 2008: 625)

One occupation group (Research and Development) whose practice involved creativity and some chaos, had been displaced in primacy by another occupational group (Production Engineers) that brought order into the organization. The blocked door, through denying access by imposing a more rigid boundary, was a way of imposing order on the displaced occupational group. Thus the blocked door leads to the conclusion that the increasing organization of a workplace changes the culture through the changes of attitudes concerning acceptable behaviour. One group gains dominance over another group because the demand for increased production on the part of the owners of the organization's capital creates a force for greater organization. By reference to the literature and other data, a rich explanation of how political groups within organizations are aided by forces for organization emerges.

Conclusion

The inclusion of space in the focus of the qualitative researcher enables a rich, nuanced and varied perspective, and can engender insights that contribute to our theoretical understanding. The nature of space in terms of being made up of quantities, qualities and geometric properties, however, means that our interrogation has to be indirect. The heuristic principles that I have outlined in this chapter can guide the researcher through the plethora of sensory experiences that such research engenders, but does not guarantee infallibility. Many of the conclusions and consequent theory dealing with space and human society can thus be categorized as plausible and reasonable, rather than factual. In addition, in organizations and in other research contexts, the explicit reasons why certain boundaries are retained, while others are destroyed, the ways that spaces can have influence over and be influenced by culture, become lost as individual actors come and go.

The dispositions of space thus are a signpost and a site of action, and the 'voice' of these spatial dispositions is what we perceive it to be. Is this, however, a weakness in the research? We can certainly strengthen our investigations by using alternative data sources, and draw a picture that resolves contradictions and contested accounts, but is this enough? The acknowledgement of the uncertainty that accompanies research, I would argue, is a strength. Indicators, such as a spatial disposition, means that there is more to be found, while a supposedly established fact can lead to a mindset of complacency. A recognition of the ubiquitous nature of uncertainty calls on the researcher to grapple with the uncertainty, to understand the limits of knowledge and to construct part of the framework of knowledge that stands until something stronger comes along. In qualitative research, our methods for dealing with uncertainty lie in the richness, the detail and the depth of our explanations and the wisdom to accept our fallibility. To include the voice of the spatial adds to that richness, detail and depth, while exercising that wisdom.

References

Casey, E. (1993) *Getting Back into Place: Towards a renewed understanding of the place-world*, Bloomington, IN: Indiana University Press.

Charmaz, K. (1994) 'The Grounded Theory Method: an explication and interpretation', pp. 95–115 in B. G. Glaser (ed.), *More Grounded Theory Methodology: A reader*, Mill Valley, CA: Sociology Press.

Charmaz, K. (2006) *Constructing Grounded Theory: a practical guide through qualitative analysis*, London: Sage.

Crang, M. and Thrift, N. (2000) 'Introduction', pp. 1–31 in M. Crang and N. Thrift (eds), *Thinking Space*, New York: Routledge.

Dale, K. and Burrell G. (2009) *The Spaces of Organisation and the Organisation of Space: Power, identity and materiality at work*, Basingstoke: Palgrave Macmillan.

Davidson, T. (2009) 'Remembering houses: the role of domestic architecture in the structuring of memory', *Space and Culture*, 12: 332–42.

De Certeau, M. (1984) *The Practice of Everyday Life*, Berkeley: University of California.

Denzin, N. K. and Lincoln, Y. S. (2000) *The Handbook of Qualitative Research*, Thousand Oaks, CA: Sage.

Finlay, L. (2002) 'Negotiating the swamp: the operation and challenge of reflexivity in research practice', *Qualitative Research*, 2(2), 209–30.

Gaver, W. W. (1996) 'Situating action II: affordances for interaction: the social is material for design', *Ecological Psychology*, 8(2), 111–29.

Gieryn, T. F. (2000) 'A space for place in sociology', *Annual Review of Sociology*, 26, 463–96.

Glaser, B. G. (1978) *Theoretical Sensitivity: Advances in the methodology of grounded theory*, Mill Valley, CA: Sociology Press.

Glaser, B. G. (1992) *Emergence vs. Forcing: basics of grounded theory analysis*, Mill Valley, CA: Sociology Press.

Hodder, I. (2000) 'The interpretation of documents and material culture', pp. 703–15 in N. K. Denzin and Y. S. Lincoln (eds), *Handbook of Qualitative Research*, London: Sage.

James, W. (1987/1995) 'Pragmatism', pp. 203–14 in P. K. Moser and A. van der Nat (eds), *Human Knowledge: Classical and Contemporary Approaches*, New York: Oxford University Press.

Johnson, P. and Duberley J. (2000) *Understanding Management Research: An introduction to epistemology*, London: Sage.

Kociatkiewicz, J. and Kostera, M. (1999) 'The anthropology of empty spaces', *Qualitative Sociology*, 22(1), 37–50.

Lindlof, T. R. (1995) *Qualitative Communication Research Methods*, Thousand Oaks, CA: Sage.

Markus, T. A. (2006) 'Built space and power', pp. 129–42 in S. R. Clegg and M. Kornberger (eds), *Space, Organizations and Management Theory*, Malmö, Sweden: Liber & Copenhagen Business School Press.

Meacham, J. A. (1990) 'The loss of wisdom', pp. 181–211 in R. J. Sternberg (ed.), *Wisdom: Its nature, origins, and development*, Cambridge: Cambridge University Press.

Melia, K. M. (1996) 'Rediscovering Glaser', *Qualitative Health Research*, **6**(3), 368–78.

Nickerson, R. S. (ed.) (2008) *Aspects of Rationality: Reflections on what it means to be rational and whether we are*, Psychology Press (ebook online) <http://www.flinders.eblib.com/EBLWeb/patron?target=patron&extendedid=P_332837_0&> (accessed 15 October 2009).

Nossack, H. E. (2004) *The End: Hamburg 1943*, trans., J. Agee, Chicago: University of Chicago Press.

O'Toole, P. (2004) *Retaining Knowledge through Organizational Action*, Adelaide: Shannon Research Press.

O'Toole, P. (2006) 'Learning through the physical environment in the workplace', pp. 204–20 in B. Basu (ed.), *Organizational Learning: Perspectives and practices*, Hyderabad, India: ICFAI University Press.

O'Toole, P. and Were P. (2008) 'Observing places: using space and material culture in qualitative research', *Qualitative Research*, **8**(5), 621–39.

Patton, M. Q. (1990) *Qualitative Evaluation and Research Methods*, Newbury Park, CA: Sage.

Polanyi, M. (1962) *Personal Knowledge: Towards a post-critical philosophy*, London: Routledge & Kegan Paul.

Polanyi, M. (1967) *The Tacit Dimension*, London: Routledge & Kegan Paul.

Sandelowski, M. (1993) 'Rigor or rigor mortis', *Advanced Nursing Science*, **16**(2), 1–8.

Schein, E. (1985) *Organizational Culture and Leadership*, San Francisco. CA: Jossey-Bass.

Scourfield, J., Dicks, B., Holland, S., Drakeford, M. and Davies, A. (2006) 'The significance of place in middle childhood: qualitative research from Wales', *British Journal of Sociology*, **57**(4), 57–595.

Sternberg, R. J. (ed.) (1990) *Wisdom: Its nature, origins, and development*, Cambridge: Cambridge University Press.

Strauss, A. L. and Corbin, J. M. (1990) *Basics of Qualitative Research: Grounded theory procedures and techniques*, Newbury Park, CA: Sage.

Van Maanen, J. and Barley, S. R. (1985) 'Cultural Organization: fragments of a theory', pp. 31–53 in P. J. Frost, L. F. Moore, M. R. Louis, C. C. Lundberg and J. Martin (eds), *Organizational Culture*, Beverley Hills, CA: Sage.

Chapter 14

Listening spaces

Connecting diverse voices for social action and change

Theresa Lorenzo

Introduction

> It is important to believe that change can happen.
>
> (Coleridge, 1993: 86)

Research involving people and relationships, both individual and group, needs to be aware that essentially people relate to each other as human beings who come with different experiences, values, assumptions and expectations of self and others. My stance as a researcher is shaped by the nature of the relationship that exists between the participants and oneself, both individually and within a group. Narrative action reflection (NAR) workshops were created as a research method and strategy for social change, which arose from a realization that there was a need for a participatory method that combined action learning cycles and narrative inquiry. Such an approach would generate data about collective experiences of oppression and marginalization. The research process needs to address, and be cognisant of, the experiences of segregation, inequality, poverty, discrimination and oppression experienced by the participants; the daily uncertainties within a context characterized by poverty and marginalization. The process of challenging oppression requires particular forms of shared wisdom. Stories are shared as a collective, rather than on a one-to-one basis. These listening spaces allow multiple voices around different themes to emerge, which then enable participants to identify individual and collective actions over time.

This chapter draws on experiences of participatory research with disabled women living in informal settlements in Cape Town, South Africa, about their experience of poverty and discrimination in relation to race, gender and disability. Informal settlements are undefined temporary human settlements that are developed by displaced people who have no formal housing since they cannot afford to build a bricks and mortar house. The settlement consists of shacks made from sheets of corrugated iron, cardboard and wood. There are no formal municipal services and neither piped water nor sanitation in the homes. The chapter details ways in which NAR workshops promote a network of listening spaces that lead to an acquisition of inner strength and outward social action. These spaces allow participants to learn the power of listening. The approach is illustrated in the changes that the women reported, related to disability identities and removal of personal and environmental barriers. We identified ways of working in relationships to build inclusive, supportive communities and strategies that nurture emotional well-being. The final section of the paper explores my own views on the uncertainties and transitions in using NAR workshops.

Narrative action reflection workshops

NAR workshops are a combination of storytelling, narrative inquiry and action learning used to explore actions of participants linked to development and transformation for social change (Lorenzo, 2005). The conceptualization and processes of the NAR workshops were based on my training and experience in using Freire's transformative education approaches (Freire, 1974) and the power of storytelling, which gave me confidence in the potential of people to participate and commit to taking action. The workshops are informed by Reason's (1998) work on human inquiry, in that the workshops could be used as a data-gathering method in participatory action research or cooperative inquiry, depending on the overall methodology. The workshops therefore incorporate the use of storytelling and creative activities as *data triggers* (see Table 14.1).

Table 14.1 Data-generation methods and process

DATA PRODUCTION			
Data generation	*Data triggers*	*Facilitation techniques*	*Data capturing methods*
Storytelling groups	Drawings	Small group discussions	Videotaping Audiotaping Scribing
Narrative action reflection workshops	Drawings Clay work Clay sculptures Singing Music Movement Drama Critical incident stories Writing songs Writing poems	Buzz groups Pairing Small group discussions (maximum of eight people in a group) Plenary groups Brainstorming	Field notes Photographs

Reflective journal

Data: transcripts of videotapes, audiotapes; fieldnotes and commentary on photographs

Verification
of data

Data analysis	*Data interpretation*
Six-step analysis of 'triggers' (Hope and Timmel, 1995) Thematic analysis (Rubin and Rubin, 1995) Reflective stance approach (Meulenberg-Buskens, 1999)	Literature Consultative dialogues

Telling and listening to stories enables researchers and participants to discover the emotions and meaning of human actions for social and political change (Slim and Thompson, 1993; Clandinin and Connelly, 2000; Krog *et al.*, 2009). Action learning encompasses reflecting on actions based on the assumption that people learn from experience that then informs planning (Taylor *et al.*, 1998). Strong feelings need to be brought to the surface, so as to break through the deadly sense of apathy and powerlessness which paralyses marginalized people. Writing on the situation of poor people in the new South Africa, Barberton (1998) contends that the nature of action spaces is transformative and democratic, as they encourage people to think about and debate how the challenge of poverty and democracy is achieved by doing some things differently. These spaces push the boundaries and question policies, enabling people to initiate projects or programmes. The workshops occur at regular intervals over a period of time determined by the research team and participants. The details of steps in the process follow.

Methods in practice: the process

There are four phases in using NAR workshops when they are being used as a research method and strategy for change (Lorenzo, 2005).

Phase 1 is about *Setting the Scene*. It starts with an initial storytelling group of no more than eight to ten participants so that they are not rushed in sharing their stories. Depending on the size of the sample, there will probably be more than one storytelling group. Each participant uses a creative medium such as drawing a picture to tell their story related to the research question. The stories are analysed to identify the generative themes (what people feel strongly about), so as to engage participants in critical thinking about their situations. Then a workshop is organized where all participants from the different areas come together to plan the next phase of action.

Phase 2 is about *Action Planning*, which consists of a follow-up workshop for all participants from the storytelling workshops to come together for a reflective process of looking at how they felt telling their stories, what might have occurred since telling and listening to the stories, and how they would like to take the process forward. The researcher generates a set of questions for the participants to consider how they would like to explore the themes that emerge from their stories, so that initial domains of actions can be planned. New participants may join the process at this point as they hear about it from the other participants. It requires the researchers to allow the participants to manage the inclusion/exclusion dynamic as part of learning about power. The researchers and participants decide on how often they would like to meet for NAR workshops, which comprise action learning cycles over an identified period of time.

Phase 3 consists of the *Implementation of Action Learning Cycles*, which is at the heart of NAR workshops for gathering data of collective experiences as well as being a strategy for change. Each NAR workshop will have a specific theme identified from the analysis of transcripts of the previous workshop. An icebreaker introduces the theme for a workshop. The theme is presented in the form of creative activities or games as data triggers to pose the essence of the issue from the generative theme. The activity creates an atmosphere where participants feel comfortable in exploring difficult concerns. Taylor and colleagues (1998) argue that identifying the right question at the beginning of each action learning cycle is the most important place to start in the process of learning. The purpose of the trigger is to create some distance from the everyday-life event, so that participants are able to dialogue to discover the root causes of the problems and how these issues affect their lives without becoming defensive (Hope and Timmel, 1995; Dorr, 2006). The use of diverse methods (see Table 14.1) derived from vernacular traditions helps create active listening spaces. Different techniques are utilized in the workshops to facilitate participation, especially of quieter members (see Table 14.1). They follow a six-step analysis (Hope and Timmel, 1995: 18):

1   Description of the code [trigger] – What did you see happening?
2   First analysis – Why do you think this happened?
3   Real life – Does this happen in your own life?
4   Related problems – How do you see it happening in your own life?
5   Root causes of problems – Why do you think this happens?
6   Planning actions – what do you think you could do to make a difference/change things?

In small-group discussions a scribe needs to keep brief notes to use in reporting back. After reporting back from small-group discussions, a dialogue then facilitates in-depth reflection where the participants begin to formulate an understanding of the root causes of the issue. Before the end of the workshop, each participant identifies at least one action they will take between workshops, individually or collectively, so as to facilitate change, even in small ways. In the subsequent workshop, participants are asked to reflect on actions taken by responding to the following:

> What did we plan to do? What helped us do what we wanted to do?
> What did we achieve? What problems or difficulties did we see?
> What changes did we see? What did we learn?
> What would we do differently next time?
> What is our next step?
> Who is going to do what? When? How?

Following a period of workshops, a further workshop occurs in which participants reflect on changes that have occurred in their everyday lives, again being creative by working with clay or writing songs and poems. In this way, the cycle of acting, reflecting, learning and planning continues to generate supportive listening spaces and momentum for change.

Phase 4 involves the *Dissemination of Findings*. The nature of action learning cycles in NAR workshops produces benefits and outcomes during the process and not only at the end. These cycles enable simultaneous dissemination of findings as opportunities present themselves. Alternative and creative dissemination strategies can be utilized, such as printing T-shirts with the findings to raise public awareness, or writing songs and poems which participants can then perform at different community events and workshops for other community-based organizations. Traditional, institutional avenues such as seminars to postgraduate students at universities involving the participants, poster and paper presentations at relevant conferences, journal articles and newspaper reports are also employed.

The process described above will be illuminated using an example of NAR workshops with disabled women in informal settlements in Cape Town, so as to illustrate some outcomes of personal and social change that occurred.

Workshops in practice: creating a network of listening and action spaces

A collaborative project was initiated to explore how disabled women living in poor communities could equalize opportunities for human development and social change. The partners were Disabled People South Africa (DPSA), South African Christian Leadership Assembly

(SACLA) Health Project (a primary health care non-government organization) and a university occupational therapy department. NAR was adopted to encourage the disabled women to generate new consciousness and understanding related to the barriers faced and strategies used for their development. NAR workshops occurred on a monthly basis over a two and a half year period. As I am a white non-disabled woman researcher working cross-culturally in a context where the white person had been the oppressor, I chose to work with two African isi-Xhosa women: my co-facilitator was a disabled women, who was the provincial chair of the Disabled Women's Development Programme of DPSA, and my research assistant was a young occupational therapist. SACLA had trained the unemployed mothers of disabled children as community rehabilitation workers (CRWs), in order to provide rehabilitation services through home visits as well as community disability awareness raising.

The CRWs in five informal settlements organized the women to come together for initial storytelling groups. They remained involved in the study throughout as they organized the times and venues for workshops with the women. The themes were identified by the research team from analysis of women's stories and subsequent workshop transcripts (see Figures 14.1–3). Table 14.2 is an example of the programme for a workshop.

Figure 14.1 Narrative action workshops as a method and a strategy

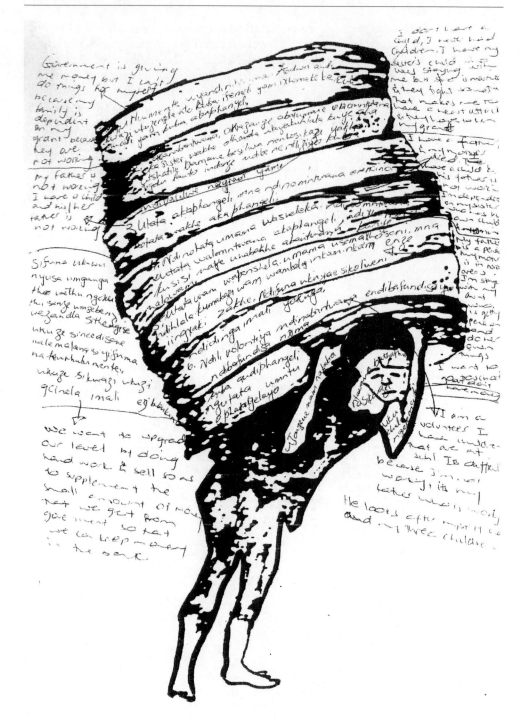

Figure 14.2 Trigger I – A woman burdened by her load

Figure 14.3 Trigger 2 – A woman managing/happy with her load

Table 14.2 Example of a workshop programme

Time	Theme: Affection: Exploring Your Family's Attitudes to Disability
9:30 – 10:30	• Tea and arrival, opening by prayer
10:30 – 10:50	• Welcoming and introduction
10:50 – 11:00	• Icebreaker : 'You and your neighbour' brainstorm
11:00 – 11:00	• Feedback
11:30 – 12:30	• Main activity: 'Disability and your family: looking at your load'
	The participants are shown pictures of two women and are asked to write down reasons why one women looks burdened (woman carry tyres) and anther looks able to cope with the load they are carrying (a pot and child) (see Figures 14.2 and 14.3). After writing reasons on the two pictures, the women are asked to relate them to their daily lives:
	• What is the nature of your load in your family?
	• How does your load in your family stop your social and economic development?
	• How does your load foster your social and economic development?
	• What will change the situation for you?
12:30 – 13:00	• Feedback
13:00 – 13:30	• Evaluation
13:30 – 14:30	• LUNCH!!

The complex interconnections between poverty and disability were tackled in the listening and action spaces. The outcomes from a series of workshops are presented here to illustrate the changes that occurred for the women and the research team.

Listening spaces: foster self-confidence, new friendships and healing

As the women began to express their emotional changes, listening spaces were recognized as a valuable resource and skill that everyone was able to acquire without needing vast material resources. They reclaimed their strong voices. Trust, support and cooperation were built, as revealed in Siphokazi's story:

> I was excited to tell my story in the workshop, as I wanted help from the facilitators. I was brave enough to ask them if I could talk with them after the meeting. I did not know how to cope. It was difficult for me to get to the monthly workshops because the taxis did not stop for me. I usually arrived late. But I had a lot to share and I listened to the other women. I did not know what to expect from the workshops, but I wanted to learn how to make money and start a small business. So I was determined to go to the training workshops on catering organized by SACLA. I felt very proud when I received a certificate at the end of the course. I went around showing my neighbours what I had made and let them taste it. They were very surprised. I felt GREAT! I am singing and dancing now. Especially now that I'm cooking, I even bring for the neighbour so that she can see Siphokazi can cook.

Their experiences echoed the words of Gueye (1999), that no future or African Renaissance could be envisaged if people felt psychologically defeated because they had lost their confidence in themselves and their ability to change their situation. Through small-group discussion, there was a growing self-awareness about their ability to provide for themselves and their families again as they re-engaged in familiar roles:

> We didn't know what to do after being disabled. The job of women in the community is to make the traditional African beer that is drunk by the men at special ceremonies. We were very excited when one of the women made a clay sculpture of the pot from which the men drink different African brews. The pot reminded other women of what they could do. When we sat down and thought about our future, we realized we could make 'mqombothi' [African beer] and sell it. We realized that in this group we would succeed. We could make 'marewu' [sour milk] in this calabash whilst we're still alive so that we can succeed. So this group gave us life and a name in our community.

Women identified an emerging need to unmask and confront domestic violence and exploitation that occurred in their homes. They had tried to fight the violence alone. The workshops enabled them to break through the silent spaces they occupied, and receive support and solutions from those with similar experiences. The power of listening helped to heal the strained relationships between the women, their siblings, spouses and children. The energy, enthusiasm, vigour and animation that developed were often tangible through the women's spontaneous singing, dancing and testimonies of change. While listening constitutes an action space in itself, collective action spaces linked to skills development provided opportunities where the women organized and learned new skills together.

Action spaces: catalysts for collective change, generating power and risk taking

DPSA prioritized the development of community-based support systems to provide an organized power base from which women could build a partnership (Finkelstein, 1993; Cilliers, 2004; Cockburn, 2003). Risk taking also grew as the women discovered new strategies to meet their needs:

> I've learnt a lot in these workshops. I couldn't talk before so I think that this group has helped me a lot. Another problem we recognized in our area is that disabled people are taken for granted.... I began to see how things had changed, as women found courage to speak out about their needs. We talked with the community leaders there but no one seemed to care. They only care about us when it's time for voting.

The women identified barriers that included insufficient awareness and information about disability issues. Information sharing was a key strategy to create group cohesion for collective action. The idea of changing attitudes to disability also extended to ways in which their family members could assist in the sustainability of their small-business initiatives. Small groups discussed this together:

> I was also in the group that went to the catering workshops as part of skills development in business. I got a certificate now so that I can get a job in catering and do something with my hands. I didn't know that I could be taught and become educated. I see how I was able to change inside from believing that I could not manage to work. Now I am

able to make mats that I learned about at Philani Nutrition Centre [an NGO in Khay-elitsha, an informal settlement in Cape Town, that provides nutrition programmes for children and skills development in income-generation for mothers and women].

Changing disability identity: from 'penalty' to possibility

The womens' narratives revealed the tensions between losses, as a consequence of their impairment and context, and agency as new possibilities and opportunities opened up (Lorenzo, 2003, 2004). Women broke through isolation (sometimes self-imposed) by getting to know each other through various interactions during workshops and community events. The narratives demonstrated that perceptions and misconceptions about disability were changed (Lorenzo *et al.*, 2002). These tensions speak to disability as an ever-present part of society. Siphokazi witnessed the changes through women telling their stories:

> I was excited about the changes that occurred for me from going to the workshops. When I'm in workshops I see myself as a woman with dignity. I never believed in myself. One young woman in the group was excited since she was now able to perm her hair using her grant. So she felt more beautiful as she could be like her friends. Before I never talked about my disability, but now that I'm talking, I'm even respected by the taxi drivers. The taxi will stop and wait until I am settled in because they know I'm their best customer.

The 'gifts of friendship' that were nurtured enabled women to overcome their struggles as 'belonging signposts the route towards becoming' (Hudson, 1995: 80). In the rest of the chapter, I intend to share different facets of uncertainties and transitions that we experienced, related to the capacity to change, inclusion and ensuring rigour.

Capturing uncertainties and transitions in running NAR workshops

As the only person in the group who could not understand or speak isi-Xhosa fluently, I was at a disadvantage. We had made a conscious decision there would be minimal interpretation during the workshops. This meant that we did not interrupt the process of deep sharing that occurred, as meanings then invariably end up lost. I also missed out on the informal conversations and joking. Thus, I had to manage a high degree of uncertainty. It was frustrating to be unable to engage actively during the workshops, and to have to wait until either the translation of the transcripts for analysis, or the planning meeting to get clarity or deeper understanding. It made me aware of the power of language and how difficult it is to let of go of control, as one feels redundant (Krog *et al.*, 2009). The NAR workshops raised tensions related to the uncertainties and transitions of change, inclusion and rigour that the research team needed to manage. These three aspects will be explored in more depth now.

Uncertainties of capacity to change

The listening spaces engaged participants in a critical analysis of their situations, which facilitated identification of the root causes of problems. They provided many opportunities to tackle the difficult or unconscious blocks to our own development. Our role as researchers was pivotal in helping participants to reflect on the root causes of problems by gaining a deeper understanding of social and political forces, so as to identify relevant actions for social change in their everyday lives, even in small ways. Through reflecting in a non-threatening, collaborative way, they generated collective action spaces to overcome their dependency on 'outsiders' to change things. At times, something that was said 'innocently' triggered a reaction to painful memories or feelings of mistrust. We had to be cognisant that dark emotions which are difficult to change are faced with resistance (Hudson, 1995), which was potentially draining of emotional energy for both researchers and participants. The workshops allowed us as researchers to act as the role models of care receivers, which enabled participants to shift from their own familiar, known roles as care receivers to become catalysts of change through problem solving, learning and planning actions. Through exploring their fears and anxieties, the participants were able to move beyond stagnation to goal-directed action that contributed to their personal transformation and social change.

While the NAR workshops generated proactivity, sometimes we felt demoralized and pessimistic about any significant long-term change occurring. As research facilitators, we were overwhelmed and felt hopeless when faced with experiences of discrimination, marginalization and impoverishment, but at least we had some reprieve when moving in and out of the context. The flows between excitement, self-doubt, anxiety and stress revealed the tensions that occurred. We had to mediate these tensions so that everyone learned the skills of conflict management, which is an essential skill in development practice (Taylor, 2003). Roodt (1995) advises that confrontation involves bringing the dynamics of avoidance behaviour to conscious awareness and facilitating ownership of responsibility for self-empowerment.

Uncertainties of inclusion

The processes of inclusion or exclusion are inherently linked to issues of power – who makes decisions about who participates, and how one gets access to information and resources. Participation involves looking at a shift in power and working in partnerships. Power in this sense is seen as a description of a relation, not a 'thing' that people 'have' (Nelson and Wright, 1995). Sustained empowerment and self-development happens when the participants are given the 'space and freedom to fail and learn from their failures on their own' (Coleridge, 1993: 113). NAR workshops enabled the researchers to resolve the power dynamic of inclusion/exclusion in practice. The listening and collective action spaces fostered opportunities for inclusion as they generated a willingness to learn and grow from different experiences. Inclusive development was feasible as these spaces contributed to participants working together effectively to voice their needs and achieve their desires. Flexibility in the workshops provided space to explore the dynamics of power in experiences of dependence, helplessness and vulnerability. All actors had to learn the importance of embracing mistakes by listening, observing, asking questions and reflecting on everyday practice to become active participants rather than passive recipients.

As researchers I believe we need to remain open to the participants' questions, and be accountable to the group in decision-making processes. Ensuring accountability contributed to the sustainability of the participants' initiatives. Listening spaces encouraged continuous reflection and exploration of different perceptions of power between professionals and disabled people's organizations, civil structures and services providers, similar to participatory research with community disability entrepreneurship projects (Lorenzo, 2005; van Niekerk *et al.*, 2006; Lorenzo, *et al.*, 2007). In this way, an attitude of 'cognitive respect' (Chambers, 1993) on the part of the research facilitators (perceived as the more educated and more influential) towards participants is encouraged. The challenge is to maintain the rigour of the research process.

Uncertainties of ensuring rigour

The structure of NAR workshops allows researchers to explore experiences of participants systematically, yet with flexibility and depth. For example, accurately capturing the continuous cycles of actions, reflections, lessons learned and planning to ensure sustained change is a challenge, as participation was unpredictable. It was difficult to record the multiple processes that took place. At times, the NAR workshops felt too slow and time-consuming, which raised the question of whether the participants truly benefited from the process. We had to reassure ourselves that in being present and creating spaces for participants to voice their experiences and act, we were 'doing' something that was meaningful for and beneficial to them. There was continuous movement between the inner world of each participant, and the outer, collective world in which they lived. We were sensitive to the cultural norms of the group, although also challenged them at times.

I learned to ask as much about the silences and silencing of the women as about what was voiced. Their attendance at the workshops was not always consistent. I found myself repeatedly confronted with questions related to the sustainability of our efforts:

- What is needed to sustain participants economically and socially?
- Do we have the ability to sustain their initiatives in business development in a context of poverty?
- Are we able to do justice in recording the findings to the process of change that we ourselves undergo as researchers?

While the chapter has described the NAR workshops with disabled women, the method can also be used in the training of CRWs, and equipping undergraduate and postgraduate students with skills in development practice. They can also be used with organizations of disabled people and parents of disabled children and service providers, in building partnerships for service delivery and development.

Conclusion: key reflections

Listening spaces allow multiple voices around different themes to emerge, which then enable participants to identify possible actions over time, so that a network of listening and action spaces is created, leading to collective action. Self and group reflection on action helps to build momentum for personal and collective changes. However, researchers must be prepared to hold the uncertainties and not expect predetermined outcomes. The power of listening and action generated through the creativity of the NAR workshops, which helps capture the complexities of participants' experiences and their resilience, inner strength and spirituality of struggle, is aptly stated by Bryan and Cameron:

> When we choose to see situations as opportunities, when we look within for answers and guidance, we find our outer world reflects our inner conditions. As we become more gentle and harmonious so do our outer worlds. As we become more adventurous and expansive, so do our worlds. We are co-creators not victims of circumstances.
>
> (Bryan and Cameron, 1998: 253)

References

Barberton, C. (1998) 'Introduction', pp. 3–10 in C. Barberton, M. Blake, and H. Kotze (eds), *Creating Action Space: The challenge of poverty and democracy in South Africa*, Cape Town: David Philip (DPSA).

Bryan, M. and Cameron, J. (1998) *The Artist's Way at Work*, London: Pan.

Chambers, R. (1993) *Challenging the Professions: Frontiers for rural development*, London: Intermediate Technology.

Clandinin, D. J. and Connelly, F. M. (2000) *Narrative Inquiry: Experience and story in qualitative research*, San Francisco, CA: Jossey-Bass.

Cilliers, L. (ed.) (2004) *Disability Policy in Action: South Africa's Integrated National Disability Strategy explained*, Cape Town: DPSA.

Cockburn, A. (2003) *Growing the Grassroots: A handbook for people with disabilities who serve as local government councilors*, Cape Town: DPSA.

Coleridge, P. (1993) *Disability, Liberation and Development*, UK: Oxfam.

Dorr, D. (2006) *Spirituality of Leadership: Inspiration, empowerment, intuition and discernment*, Dublin: Columba Press.

Finkelstein, V. (1993) 'Disability: a social challenge or an administrative responsibility', pp. 34–43 in J. Swain, V. Finkelstein, S. French and M. Oliver (eds), *Disabling Barriers – Enabling Environment*, London: Sage.

Freire, P. (1974) *Education: The practice of freedom*, London: Writers and Readers Co-operative.

Gueye, S. P. (1999) 'African renaissance as an historical challenge', pp. 243–64 in M. W. Makgoba (ed.), *African Renaissance*, Sandton: Mafube.

Hope, A. and Timmel, S. (1995) *Training for Transformation: A handbook for community workers*, rev. edn, Zimbabwe: Mambo Press.

Hudson, T. (1995) *Signposts to Spirituality: Towards a closer walk with God*, Cape Town: Struik Christian Books.

Krog, A., Mpolweni, N. and Ratele, K. (2009) *There Was This Goat: Investigating the Truth Commission testimony of Notrose Nobomvu Konile*, Durban: UKZN Press

Lorenzo, T., Saunders, C., January, M. and Mdlokolo, P. (eds) (2002) *On the Road of Hope: Stories told by disabled women in Khayelitsha*, Cape Town: Division of Occupational Therapy, University of Cape Town.

Lorenzo, T. (2003) 'No African renaissance without disabled women: a new way of looking at social and economic development of disabled women in South Africa', *Disability and Society*, **18**(6), 759–78.

Lorenzo, T. (2004) 'Equalising opportunities for occupational engagement: disabled women's stories', pp. 85–102 in R. Watson and L. Swartz (eds), *Transformation Through Occupation*, London: Whurr.

Lorenzo, T. (2005) 'We don't see ourselves as different: a web of possibilities for disabled women', unpublished doctoral dissertation, University of Cape Town, South Africa.

Lorenzo, T., Van Niekerk, L. and Mdlokolo, P. (2007) 'Economic empowerment and black disabled entrepreneurs: negotiating partnerships in Cape Town, South Africa', *Disability and Rehabilitation*, **29**(5), 429–36.

Meulenberg-Buskens, E. (1999) *Leadership and Facilitation in Participatory Research and Action*, Cape Town: Research for the Future.

Nelson, N. and Wright, S. (eds) (1995) *Power and Participatory Development: Theory and practice*, London: Intermediate Technology.

Reason, P. (1998) 'Three approaches to participative inquiry', pp. 261–91 in N. K. Denzin and Y. S. Lincoln (eds), *Strategies of Qualitative Inquiry*, Thousand Oaks, CA: Sage.

Roodt, E. (1995) *Lifeskills: A resource book for facilitators*, Braamfontein: Nolwazi Educational Publishers.

Rubin, H. J. and Rubin, I. S. (1995) *Qualitative Interviewing: The art of hearing data*, London: Sage.

Slim, H. and Thompson, P. (1993) *Listening for a Change: Oral testimony and development*, London: Panos.

Taylor, J., Marais, D. and Heyns, S. (1998) *Community Participation and Financial Sustainability*, Action Learning Series – Case Studies and Lessons from Development Practice, Cape Town: Juta.

Taylor, J. (2003) *Organisations and Development – Towards building a practice*, Cape Town: CDRA.

Van Niekerk, L., Lorenzo, T. and Mdlokolo, P. (2006) 'Understanding partnerships in developing disabled entrepreneurs through Participatory Action Research', *Disability and Rehabilitation*, **28**(5), 323–31.

Chapter 15

The politics of space in qualitative research

Aaron M. Kuntz

Reflection

On a spring, Thursday afternoon I left my campus office, descended the horseshoe staircase and made my way to the car. I walked under giant trees that outpaced my age by decades, passed memorials to the American Civil War, and settled in for a quick trip across town. From campus, I made my way across railroad tracks and into a parking space across the street from a sawmill, directly in front of an old, windowless bar. On other days, I kept driving, barely noticing the landmarks as I traversed the familiar pathway home. On Thursdays I elected to stop, leave my car and enter an atmosphere lit by the neon lights of beer signs and pinball machines. In this space I was greeted with wary suspicion – not coming often enough to be a regular, my accent and mannerisms revealing my geographical misplacement. I stopped at the bar to break up routinized movement in comfortable spaces, to become attuned to the feeling of being out of place. The act of inquiry requires sensitivity to space, an ongoing reflective process that informs and extends beyond the analysis of data, that make 'facile gestures difficult' (Foucault,1988: 134).

To paraphrase Harvey, if I question what the academic building, sawmill or windowless bar means, 'then the only way I can answer is to think in relational terms' (2006: 125). Though I often pass the memorials without consciously recalling the Civil War, I am never freed from the history of this campus, nor the way in which I, as a New England Yankee, am implicated by history.

Driving home I am never divorced from my material surroundings. I exist in dynamic relation with the world, contributing to and affected by multiple productions of meaning that bind the social with the material, refusing easy distinction between objects and the meanings they evoke. And yet, in qualitative work discursive understandings of the world are often isolated from the material, as though I could separate my interpretations of my work at the university from place and practice. Space is socially produced and contributes to human meaning-making in often unexpected and relatively unexplored ways, yet we often overlook space in qualitative inquiry. Throughout this chapter I advocate for spatial analyses as part and parcel with all investigations into social ways of knowing, as dynamically interactive with how we view and engage with the world. More than insisting on the inclusion of the spatial within qualitative inquiry, I argue for specific considerations of space as relationally productive.

Introduction

This chapter offers the analysis of space as a critical, though often unexamined, aspect of qualitative inquiry. It is also a call to return to more materialist methodologies, ways of studying the social world that recognize the implications of the material, embodied environment on meaning-making. At times, texts that emphasize qualitative research methods stress overly discursive interpretation at the expense of the material, as though we are unaffected by our material surroundings or embodied experiences. If our research presents a discursive reality as divorced from the material, a significant aspect of meaning-making remains underdeveloped, with consequences for how we represent the human experience in the studies we enact. Further, ignoring the material, embodied implications of meaning-making sustains the Cartesian duality that poststructural theorists have taken pains to problematize. Instead of replicating the overly simplistic mind–body division of human experience, we might begin from the ontological assumption that the linguistic realm is implicated by the physical: the discursive is affected by and affects our material worlds. Thus, even thematic analyses of language have material and embodied implications. To develop the implications of materialist methodologies in qualitative inquiry, I incorporate insights from critical geography, a field of study that assumes space as always in-process, produced by numerous discourses and politically laden.

Integrating spatiality raises numerous issues that might otherwise remain unacknowledged or unexplored in qualitative research. I begin this chapter by explicating contemporary theorizations of space, arguing that spatial interpretations are latent in all research and especially important to qualitative inquiry. I then examine space in relation to *time, embodiment* and *daily practices*. Within these three sections I offer theoretical and methodological considerations for qualitative inquiry. Finally, I conclude by offering examples of how spatial analyses imbue qualitative research with dynamic meaning and insight, provocations that might otherwise remain unresolved. Simply put, if qualitative research is to address the uncertain, messy business of social interaction and meaning-making, it must wrestle with space. Moreover, if we are to study social processes in space, we must use a qualitative approach that accounts for material–discursive interactions.

Definitional issues

What is space? What are its connections to place, to time? Several scholars have sought to define space in order to bring forth the recognition that space matters to our understandings of the world in which we live. Space as an active contributor to meaning-making directly counters the unexamined and normative representation of space as passive background against which the stuff of social meaning is made. Several scholars critique previous scholarship for assumptions of space as an 'empty backdrop' to, or simple 'container' of social interaction (for example Baynham, 2003; Harvey, 2006; Massey, 1994; Soja, 1989). 'Space' is conceptually invisible, always there but never acknowledged and so never interrogated. Space is assumption. Space is rendered neutral, reified. We work around and in it, but are otherwise unaffected. Against such a definition, one might understand space as contributing to meaning-making and as, itself, produced. If, as I suggest, assertions about the nature of space – what it is, what it does – are unavoidable in research, then one goal of this chapter is to make our spatial assumptions less covert, more visible in our scholarship and more up for debate.

Here, I refer to space to include both *material places* (buildings, the four walls of a classroom and so on) and *social spaces* (the meanings we make of our material surroundings). Yet I do so with hesitancy, recognizing that such conceptual clarity often oversimplifies the layered interconnections of space and place, the material and the social. Additionally, I understand *daily practices* as material activities and learned behaviour enacted to achieve some anticipated outcome. The *body* I connect with Heidegger's (2001) notion of the corporeal, those physical properties (eyes, fingers, skin and so on) that form our material bodies. *Embodiment* exists as the interaction of the body, material places and social spaces toward the development of meaning.

Also, following Cary's notion of embeddedness, I assert the political nature of spatiality:

> This is a call for the study of how we are normalized, how we are embedded within local institutions and how we engage in and negotiate the production of legitimate knowledge. This embeddedness excludes certain ways of being and erases the bodies of those students, teachers, parents, custodians and others who are considered deviant, or outside the norm.... It is important to reveal the discourses themselves and how this knowing impacts the lives and possibilities of being for those we 'know'.
>
> (Cary, 2006: 3)

Examining the 'embeddedness' of the political subject brings the commonsensical to light, makes strange the underwhelmingly familiar, specifically, the means by which we produce and appropriate legitimated knowledge, as well as the erasure of illegitimate others through processes of normalization. In short, analyses that recognize space as a productive process engage in research as social critique. The self-evident becomes strange and we critically engage with the 'geography of "common sense"' (Harvey, 2006: 85) as it develops within neoliberal contexts. Qualitative researchers begin to question normalized conceptions of context, setting or environment, and the consequences of such assignation.

Take for instance the home-office in which I write these pages. As someone hailing from New England now working in Alabama, I often refer to it as the 'mudroom' we converted into my working office. My southern neighbours refuse the term 'mudroom' (a Yankee term, I'm told) and simply say 'side entry' or 'servants' entrance'. So I sit in my home-office/mudroom/side entry/servants' entrance and log onto SKYPE to perform a virtual interview with someone in Australia about faculty work practices and wonder about the spaces I inhabit. All of these are situated within the same four walls, two doors – with the same material artifacts. Of course, there is the virtual space, where my voice meets another's through a labyrinth of fibre-optic cables and electromagnetic connection. To which do we assign meaning and in what contexts? How do these socially constructed contexts overlap and intermingle with my material body as I hunch over my laptop, frowning at my screen, interpreting the words of another housed in a foreign space yet linked to my own? What, in this context, is space? How specific can we make our definitions to promote conversation while remaining open to revision and continual reflection?

All of this points to the fact that the study of space is far from benign. Indeed, attempts to stabilize or fix spatial meaning might themselves be investigated as layered sites of social contexts (Massey, 1994): whose account of particular spaces becomes legitimate, is given priority as the normalizing definition? Whose is lost? In what ways do our own research practices recreate essentialized notions of space, and how might we work actively to disrupt such hegemonic activities? As a means to eschew normalized definitions and investigate productively the role of space in our scholarship, I present three entry points in debates on spatiality and social meaning-making: time, embodiment and daily practices.

Space and time

In part, a consequence of hesitating to fully integrate the spatial into qualitative inquiry, time has been privileged in our conceptions of the lived world (Baynham, 2003; Casey, 1997). One element directly linked to the development of Modernity is the separation of time from space (Giddens, 1990; Lefebvre, 1991). Time, in Western thought, has become commodified repeatedly, a measured outcome often implicated in the push towards increased efficiency. Further, as time has played a role in marking stages of development, it displaces spatial representations of human existence. We measure ourselves against ticking clocks, speed measured not by distance, but by time. My own professional viability, for example, is set against a standard tenure track. Importantly, though the metaphor of a tenure track seems spatial initially, it quickly takes on a temporal order of progression. *Tenure track* become *tenure clock*. If you are on the track, you are on the clock. Should I take a position at another institution the tenure clock will most likely continue its objective pace unabated unless I choose (or am forced to choose) to have the clock reset. Nonetheless, the clock beats on, regardless of my spatial placement in one institution or another; ordered, measurable time.

Against the prioritization of time at the expense of space, an interdisciplinary array of scholars assert a 'spatial turn' is critical (Massey, 1994; Soja, 1989) and question the very separation of space and time, pointing to the way in which a theoretical analysis of space links implicitly to perceptions of time (Massey, 2005). How might qualitative inquiry incorporate space and time as an interrelational process rather than two separate terms or one term defined by the other? What are the implications? One main implication is the removal of linearly progressive time and statically immobile space, two privileged interpretations that have combined to produce what Baynham has termed 'single, homogeneous notions of time and space' (2003: 347). Often, qualitative scholars seek to produce a coherent narrative of research findings and participants' perceptions, one that shows progressive change over time set against the backdrop of isolated spatial contexts. In this way, participants and research findings change with time, altering perspectives through experiences within a temporal world, spatial change being an indicator of time's progress. Yet the human condition rarely follows such an ordered representation – we sit in our offices and cars, surrounded by contemporary environments, made meaningful through the insertion of memory, past experiences shaping the meaning we make of the world in which we live. We encounter different narrative forms of space and time, at times conflicting and contradictory. How might we produce new narratives through relational interpretations of time and space? In such a scenario we might map out social narratives, showing their production within a multitude of overlapping and sometimes contradictory spatial and temporal ways of knowing. What new meanings will be generated through the production of spatial ways of knowing within historically informed contexts?

If we conceive of both space and time as socially configured, we have the opportunity to examine how they are produced within our research, how we and the participants with whom we work reproduce and deviate from normalized conceptions of time and space as objective, quantifiable entities. Further, these spatial and temporal ways of knowing produce specific effects – how we understand ourselves, others and meaning-making. Recognizing time and space as overlapping social processes reminds us that our own research is itself a production, a re-creative process of meaning making. From what historically situated discourses do our conceptions of space draw? Returning to processes of narration, Baynham (2003) notes how problematizing contemporary notions of time and space within narratives causes scholars to ask newly productive questions. Instead of simply asking, 'How are narratives oriented in space and time?' (a question that assumes space and time as static backdrops to the direction of the narrative), we might ask, 'How are spaces and times ... involved in the construction of narrative?' (Baynham, 2003: 352), imbuing both entities with productive value.

Space and embodiment

Key to understanding how we encounter the spaces in which we live as embodied subjects is conceptualizing the many ways in which our material bodies intermix with, encounter and produce meaning through multiple overlapping environments. As Pillow writes, 'bodies bear the marks of our culture, practices, and policies' (2000: 214). Because conceptions of the spatial are intimately linked to our bodies' movement through space, one cannot conceive of the body absent from its spatial orientations.

Like those who separate space from place for conceptual clarity, Heidegger (2001) distinguishes the physical form or the corporeal, from the perceiving body. In this way the body extends beyond its skin expanding beyond the corporeal limit (Aho, 2005). Heidegger's distinction between the corporeal and the body raises important issues regarding the body's dimensionality, particularly in interaction with interrelational time–space. Though we often understand our bodies as contained by the skin, is the air we breathe part of our body? Are the things we see part of our embodied processes? Like the spatial environments in which we live our lives, the body is not so easily defined, not so cleanly understood as a container. Here, the body has no distinct boundaries that separate it from an outside environment – instead, our bodies remain intricately connected, blurring into multiple contexts, inhabiting and contributing to multiple spaces. Yet social norms are often enacted upon assertions of finite bodies laying claim to particular spaces.

In the West, we typically object to impositions upon personal space, for example, a culturally known area around our bodies that buffers us from others. To extend the example, we might see how we engage in processes of accumulation to expand the protective spaces that literally surround our bodies – wealthier citizens are afforded larger zones of space, living in gated communities that reinforce the social and material distance from those who do not share such privileges. In this sense the body becomes what Harvey (2006) terms an 'accumulation strategy', its very presence testimony to the social processes that give it definition.

Heidegger emphasizes that the perceiving body is oriented within space, and thus embodiment finds meaning within spatial contexts. Similarly, Merleau-Ponty (1962) links the physical body with perception, emphasizing that we come to know through perception which in turn is mediated by bodily experience. Further, for Merleau-Ponty language itself draws from embodied experiences: 'if the words "enclose" and "between" have a meaning for us, it is because they derive from our experience as embodied subjects' (1962: 236). Thus, experiences are interpreted by embodied subjects, affecting the very language we use to render them knowable. In this way perceptions of bodily experiences are historical, affected by the sociohistorical contexts in which they take place. As a consequence, to study the body and conceptions of embodiment, it remains crucial to study how the body and space are reproduced by particular social and historical practices. In this sense, the spatially oriented body serves 'as a site of information and practice, of regulation, power, and resistance' (Pillow, 2000: 214).

To locate the body within qualitative inquiry requires that we recognize our own impact on the studies we enact. As Ellingson notes, researchers' bodies 'unavoidably influence all aspects of the research process' and 'all researchers have bodies that should be acknowledged' (2006: 298). Through presenting embodied experiences as influencing our studies – their design, implementation and findings – we can collapse the artificial separation of the researcher and the study, our bodies from our experiences of the social world. We might ask, 'How do my bodily experiences impact my assumptions about human experiences? How do these assumptions, in turn, shape my research questions and methods – what can be known and how might we come to such knowledge?' Further, it remains important to maintain the recognition that we gain meaning by moving bodily through material environments. As such, our qualitative studies cannot simply operate at the level of the linguistic. We must begin to examine inherent links between perception, embodied experiences, particular spaces and habitual practices.

Space and daily practices

In my own work, space, time and embodiment are examined productively through the close analysis of daily practices. Since these social processes often escape notice by their subtle 'everydayness', it remains important to examine their effects in daily actions of meaning-making. Key to understanding the productive elements of the spatial is the close analysis of those daily practices invoked and practised by individuals with material effects, in material contexts.

This interest in the close analysis of daily practices draws from the work of Foucault, who advocates for an analytical focus not on 'institutions', 'theories' or 'ideology', but *practices* – with the aim of grasping the conditions which make these acceptable at a given moment'(1991: 75; original emphasis). In this sense, examinations of daily practices reveal larger social processes that make such practices possible – even logical – within particular sociohistorical contexts. More specifically, daily practices might be examined for the means by which they interact with particularly spatialized ways of knowing. Harvey addresses the intersection of daily practices and spatial analyses quite well:

> there are no philosophical answers to philosophical questions that arise over the nature of space-the answers lie in human practice. The question 'what is space?' is therefore replaced by the question 'how is it that different human practices create and make use of different conceptualizations of space?

(Harvey, 2006: 126)

For Harvey, our interpretations of space are distilled into everyday practices, activities that have a hand in the production of spatial ways of knowing. As Harvey later adds, 'We may not even notice the material qualities of spatial orderings incorporated into daily life because we adhere to unexamined routines. Yet it is through those daily material routines that we absorb a certain sense of how spatial representations work' (2006: 132). Building on the previous section, we might extend Harvey's analysis by noting that human practices are embodied, never losing their connection to the material world. Analyses of daily practices reveal how normative conceptions of space and time are articulated through the body, made manifest by embodied activities.

The trick for researchers examining the spatial as it develops within daily practices is to make strange the familiar, to engage critically with our everyday assumptions. Hidden within these seemingly innocuous movements are layers of meaning, practices that draw from, anticipate and recreate social ways of knowing. In our everyday practices the relational properties that make up the spatial coalesce, bringing forth constellations of meaning. If we are to take the close examination of daily practices seriously as qualitative scholars, we must recognize the inherent spatial relations they contain. As Massey writes, 'The "lived reality of our daily lives" is utterly dispersed, unlocalised, in its sources and in its repercussions' (2005: 184). Thus locally contingent daily practices remain inextricably linked to larger and more multifarious spatial processes.

Spatial implications for inquiry

Often, when I first walk into a classroom I am struck by the many ways in which the class is already produced before I cross the door's threshold. The material place of the room was imagined (or, more likely, replicated) by some designer's hand as the building was renovated. Builders constructed the room, adhering to specified standards and codes regarding load-bearing walls, electrical outlets and emergency exits. Someone furnished the room with particular chairs, desks, tables, a lectern, computer and whiteboard, those commonsensical tools needed for everyday pedagogical practices. At some point, a caretaker came through and straightened the rows from previous classes, positioning them facing the 'front' of the room by the whiteboard, emptied the bins, and removed all non-essential signage or other postings. Students entered and arranged themselves in their chairs, oriented towards the empty front part of the room where I am expected to appear and settle, classroom tools at my disposal. I enter and wonder, 'How would I research this class, this space?' 'How would I make sense of all of this?' The point is that this 'class' has been reproduced many times over, imagined and recreated across time and space. This class brings together the multiple issues discussed in this chapter thus far: spatial and temporal ordering; embodiment (of students, teachers, architects and other labourers); the reproduction of the intersecting daily practices of multiple constituencies; all ultimately caught up in an array of endlessly productive relational discourses. Suddenly, the question of 'what is a class?' is problematized, given layers of meaning.

Yet space is anything but predictable. Space cannot be designed or built with predictable outcomes (Hernes, 2004). Architects design, administrators imagine and workers construct buildings and other material spaces with particular intentions regarding their use, only to find designed material environments appropriated in unexpected ways, altered for newly interpreted social practices. As space takes on such a protean morphology, analyses that foreground the spatial prove especially fruitful, though never easy. Hernes offers several questions to researchers interested in the production of space in their own research:

> A main question is evidently what spaces matter, as the number is potentially infinite and any selection might seem about as viable as any other. Another question ... is *how* a space matters. A third question relates to the *dynamics* of the space; how and when does it appear, and how does it evolve.
>
> (Hernes, 2004: 66; original emphasis)

Foregrounding fluid, changing and productive understandings of space, qualitative researchers might examine not just what spaces matter, but to whom, and how such spatial importance is made known or articulated. Which spaces are overlooked, assumed to not matter, and therefore escape notice? These latter spaces might be the interstices, the small gaps between mattering spaces, where one can get a toehold for provoking larger change in how meaning is made or recognized as legitimate.

Spatial presentations remain unavoidable in our research, and we must take pains to examine critically the implications of space upon how we represent ourselves others, and the vast array of social processes that have a hand in the production of meaning-making. As O'Toole and Were write, 'To include space ... in our data collection and analysis is to include a rich source of insight that gives the researcher a deeper perception of the intangible and tacit through an examination of the corporeal and present' (2008: 631). Space remains a contributing factor to human meaning-making, one that potentially reveals the implications of particular social processes overlapping and intersecting in particular ways. The analysis of space is, in the end, both inherently messy and full of critical potential. How we (re)produce space in often unconscious ways informs our daily practices, the way in which we live our lives through embodied experiences in our social world. Critically examining these daily practices offers possibilities for more intentionally changing – (re)producing – our embodied social spaces.

Conclusion

This chapter was designed to provoke qualitative scholars to critically recognize the impact of the spatial on their research. I have made suggestions for epistemological and methodological concerns in how we have come to consider time, embodiment and daily practices in qualitative inquiry. Like other social processes, spatial ways of knowing are socially constructed and provide evidences for how we make sense of and inhabit the world in which we live. Consequently, ignoring the impact of space on meaning-making, or rendering space as a static backdrop against which meaning is produced, flattens important aspects of qualitative inquiry.

Recognizing the impact of space on meaning-making ultimately causes qualitative scholars to ask different questions of their research: how can we incorporate spatial ways of knowing into our research? How do our abstract concepts and use of metaphors call forth or derive from embodied interpretations of experience? What kinds of data or modes of study are available to us as we incorporate space into our research? How do we account for material and social ways of knowing in our methodologies? How do our participants acknowledge or render absent their own bodies as they make sense of the world in which they live? How do spaces change through the interaction of embodied subjects and learned daily practices? How can we understand these changes within the historical processes of our social meaning-making? Addressing these questions and more will make available important ways of knowing that are all too often unacknowledged in our contemporary practices of research and teaching.

References

Aho, K. (2005) 'The missing dialogue between Heidegger and Merleau-Ponty: On the importance of the Zollikon seminars', *Body AND Society*, 11, 1–23.

Baynham, M. (2003) 'Narratives in space and time: Beyond 'backdrop' accounts of narrative orientation', *Narrative Inquiry*, 13, 347–66.

Cary, L. J. (2006) *Curriculum Spaces: Discourse, postmodern theory and educational research*, New York: Peter Lang.

Casey, E. S. (1997) *The Fate of Place: A philosophical history*, Berkeley, CA: University of California Press.

Ellingson, L. (2006) 'Embodied knowledge: Writing researchers' bodies into qualitative health research', *Qualitative Health Research*, **16**(2), 298–310.

Foucault, M. (1988) 'Practicing criticism', pp. 152–8 in L. Kritzman (ed.), *Politics, Philosophy, Culture: Interviews and other writings 1977 – 1984*, New York: Routledge.

Foucault, M. (1991) 'Questions of method', pp. 73–86 in G. Burchell, C. Gordon and P. Miller (eds), *The Foucault Effect: Studies in Governmentality*, Chicago: University of Chicago Press.

Giddens, A. (1990) *The Consequences of Modernity*, Cambridge: Polity Press.

Harvey, D. (2006) *Spaces of Global Capitalism: Towards a theory of uneven geographical development*, New York: Verso.

Heidegger, M. (2001) *Zollikon Seminars: Protocols–conversations–letters*, trans. F. Mayr and R. Askay, Evanston, IL: Northwestern University Press.

Hernes, T. (2004) *The Spatial Construction of Organization*, Amsterdam: John Benjamins.

Lefebvre, H. (1991) *The Production of Space*, trans. D. Nicholson-Smith, Oxford: Blackwell.

Massey, D. (1994) *Space, Place, and Gender*, Minneapolis, MN: University of Minnesota Press.

Massey, D. (2005) *For Space*, Thousand Oaks, CA: Sage.

McDowell, L. (1999) *Gender, Identity, and Place: Understanding feminist geographies*, Minneapolis, MN: University of Minnesota Press.

Merleau-Ponty, M. (1962) *Phenomenology of Perception*, trans. C. Smith, London: Routledge.

O'Toole, P. and Were, P. (2008) 'Observing places: using space and material culture in qualitative research', *Qualitative Research*, 8, 616–34.

Pillow, W. S. (2000) 'Exposed methodology: The body as a deconstructive practice', pp. 199–220 in E. St. Pierre and W. Pillow (eds), *Working the Ruins: Feminist poststructural theory and methods in education*, New York: Routledge.

Soja, E. (1989) *Postmodern Geographies: The reassertion of space in critical social theory*, New York: Verso.

Chapter 16

Urban ethnography
Approaches, perspectives and challenges

Kristan M. Venegas and Adrian H. Huerta

Introduction

Urban ethnographies take place in the research spaces of the home, family, school, work and street amongst the uncertainty of city life. As other chapters within this text have shown, the reality of research spaces impacts how a researcher or research team might engage in design, implementation and reporting of results. In this chapter, we examine possible approaches, perspectives and challenges related to engaging in research in urban spaces. We rely on inter-disciplinary work that spans sociological, economic and educational fields. We acknowledge that our work, our experiences and perceptions of the work of others are transitory and context-bound. We contend that conducting research in modern urban spaces is different from engaging in research projects with other populations and cultures, such as indigenous (Tuhiwai Smith, 1999), rural or suburban groups (Lareau, 2003). There are overlaps with these research spaces related to issues of imperialism, colonization or mispresentations of voice, but the dynamic power structures within urban environs are nonetheless unique because of their particular focus on race and class-based inequalities.

In some cases, our suggestions and assertions may lead the reader to ask more questions, rather than provide finite answers. It can be argued that this sense of wanting to know more is part of the outcome of the research process, whether qualitative, ethnographic, urban or not. However, this uncertainty does not free us from attempting to provide meaningful structure and thoughtful conclusions. The chapter includes a discussion of common ethno-graphic tools used in urban ethnography, an evolving definition of urbanicity and a discus-sion of linking theoretical perspectives to urban ethnographic work. Our central argument is that urban spaces are different from other research spaces and therefore deserve a nuanced approach.

Defining urban spaces

For the purposes of our chapter, urban is defined as a social, cultural and physical space that is located within major city settings (in the context of our research, in the United States). Urban city dwellers may experience condensed housing conditions, limited access to quality education, health care and transportation, and increased exposure to violence. A number of residents live below the federal poverty line (Bourgois, 1995; Newman, 1999). The resi-dents are typically racially, ethnically and socio-economically diverse. Some urbanites may engage in underground economies to support themselves or families (Bourgois, 1995). Urbanites with stable economic situations have access to higher-quality education, health care, housing and transportation than less affluent counterparts (Bourgois, 1995). Urban environments are vividly enriched and sometimes segregated by cultural diversity through food, language, immigration and migration, and juxtaposed socio-economic differences within close proximity (Farr, 2006).

The sharp differences for residents in urban environments are illustrated by the overwhelming social inequities encountered by impoverished city dwellers (Bourgois, 1995). Some examples include harassment from local law enforcement, perpetual cycles of poverty, and limited educational opportunities because of decrepit facilities or lower scholastic expectations from instructors (Newman, 1999). Another common characteristic of urban spaces is the condensed and overcrowded residences that may house multiple family generations compacted in one unit; an arrangement that may be omnipresent in the neighbourhood. The physical space might raise the anxiety of researchers who because of their own economic and personal background are unfamiliar with the struggles of low-income urban environments.

The perpetual cycle of poverty is a difficult path from which to deviate, because of multiple social pressures and family responsibilities such as child care, low-wage employment and low educational achievement (Bourgois, 1995; Newman, 1999). Our focus in these communities with limited opportunities, voice and control of their environment is fundamental to extracting the experience through the lens of urban ethnographies. These living conditions also affect the ways in which the populations may or may not allow ethnographers to participate in understanding their lives.

Ethnographic researchers in urban spaces have the opportunity to record the multiple stories and experiences of marginalized communities. These encounters provide a location to gain an understanding of the space, power dynamics and relationships between participants. For researchers who are not native to urban spaces, their personal challenges include acquiring and understanding the area's social capital and culture, in order to be able to integrate into the community (Bourgois, 1995). This advanced understanding will then provide the foundation to understand residents' social norms and expectations.

Explaining our engagement within urban spaces, ethnography and contexts

To ground our claims and research stance, we include a brief discussion on our work as urban ethnographers. Venegas has sought to examine educational settings within urban environments in South Central and downtown Los Angeles, California and Las Vegas, Nevada, both in the United States. She has worked primarily with students, teachers, administrators, community advocates, college preparation programme staff and families in postsecondary, community-based, community college and university settings. She has striven to speak to research, policy and practice audiences. She comes to this work with her own lens as someone who grew up in the urban sprawl of Los Angeles County. She comes from a low-income family, was a first-generation college student, and attended schools in urban settings.

Huerta's inquiry has developed along two thematic strands. He is engaged in educational work as well, with a focus on the college access process for low-income Black and Latino males in Los Angeles and the persistence of urban Latinos in Midwest graduate schools in the United States. He has been influenced by his experiences as a youth in Las Vegas, Nevada. His early and continuing experiences within the Chicano movement and the influence of critical race theory within research and practice is of continual interest. The authors are connected in their work as ethnographers and as individuals who have a clear interest in issues of social justice. As a pair, we come to the development of this chapter with these lived experiences and social commitments in mind. In addition to our own work, we rely on respected examples from Farr (2006), Bourgois (1995), Duneier (1999), Newman (1999), Suskind (1998) and others to explore and explain how urban ethnography 'works' in practice and publishing. We acknowledge and assert the importance of the researcher as an ally, the researcher as participant, and the researcher as a vehicle for empowering while observing individuals in their social spaces.

Using ethnographic tools in urban spaces

Urban ethnography employs many of the typical interdisciplinary approaches used in other ethnographic work. Borne out of an anthropological approach, ethnography is systematic and features a detailed study of the social environment including physical spaces and customs. The use of participant observation, field notes and traditional interview are the basic tools of ethnography (Creswell, 2008). Urban ethnography has been viewed as a subfield of sociology, with a connection to both the Chicago School ethnographic approaches that emerged after the Second World War and the ethnographic cultural shifts in the 1960s. Urban ethnographers rely on these simple tools to understand and explain the social environment, but they may find themselves engaged in the work and lives of those they seek to study in a more complex way. Deep engagement in the social structure and an explicit valuing of cultural reproduction related to a particular space are part of a modern urban ethnographic style. Duneier (1999) found himself working as a magazine street vendor in his ethnographic work, *Sidewalk*. He began as a helper within this informal industry and later moved up the ranks and was enabled to run the magazine vendors' tables while they were away. Similarly, Bourgois (1995) served as a lookout for drug dealers in the urban spaces through which he collected data for his ethnographic work. Their data-collection process necessitated that they were deeply engaged in the lives and work they observed.

The level of intimacy and trust needed by urban ethnographers to gather solid data and produce a meaningful snapshot of their study space is a distinctive feature of an urban ethnographic approach. All the researchers who produced the studies mentioned here emphasize the importance of gaining trust and respect from urban study participants. To be sure, these issues appear in investigations of other social spaces, but arguably not in the same ways that one might experience when studying, for example, the corporate world or child-rearing practices of middle and upper-income families. Before moving into a more in-depth discussion of the role of the researcher within urban ethnographic work, Lichtman's (2006) 'ten critical elements of qualitative research' are noted here as a plausible foundation for thinking about the key pieces of qualitative work, regardless of the space that is to be studied. These research essentials are:

- the role of description, understanding, and interpretation
- the import of dynamism
- attention to the multiple ways of approaching the same study
- a decision to practise inductive thinking
- a commitment to a holistic investigation
- the need to gather a variety of data within the same natural setting
- the need for in-depth study

- the notion that qualitative research is not linear
- the acknowledgement of the importance of words, themes and writing
- an understanding of the role of the researcher within the research process.

Taken together, these fundamentals outline considerations and practices that are meaningful to the practice of ethnography. These suggestions are reflected in the work of others who study social settings (Lofland and Lofland, 1995; Weis and Fine, 2004) and provide a useful framework for thinking about developing one's own ethnographic approaches.

How might each of these facets of investigation affect the kinds of work that would be produced in an urban environment? What additional time commitments, social commitments and personal risks come into play when working within urban contexts? While professional training and the constraints of our university institutional review boards provide guidance, rules and limitations, our own sense of connection to the researched muddy the professional waters. The need for in-depth study and openness to inductive reasoning may challenge these boundaries. Such considerations are especially salient given the risks and commitments of studying people and culture within the urban context. Urban ethnographic exploration, especially work within educational contexts, has been further characterized as applied, reformist or prescriptive (Yon, 2003). Weis and Fine (2004) suggest that these approaches are connected to a mission of social justice. If either Yon or Weis and Fine's assertions are true, researcher reflexivity is central to conducting and sharing the results of an urban ethnography study.

The role of the researcher

Garnering the necessary relationships with gatekeepers or urban insiders to gain access with desired study participants eases the transition into the environment and provides necessary social connections. Some researchers choose to move into their study location. This decision provides unlimited access to their participants, which allows them to cultivate meaningful and deep relationships. For example, in her work with Mexican transnational immigrants in Chicago, USA, Farr (2006) highlights her intimate relationship with Mexican women in Chicago, Illinois, USA and a small village in Michoacán, Mexico. This shifting of spaces allowed access to daily activities, cultural phenomena and gender roles. These interactions were only possible through steady and unanticipated interactions.

Once the researcher enters an urban space, they need to gauge their relationship with the community members. These connections can be measured on a continuum, and are contingent on the researchers' progress with community agents. Developing contacts within urban spaces may pose challenges for researchers if they do not share the same ethnic or racial background, socio-economic status or personal background. The depth of a researcher's relationship with their participants is contingent on understanding one's social position. Exploring the environmental conditions of marginalized space should be conducted with caution because of the influence and perceptions of the area using a middle-class or upper-class educated lens (Dillabough, 2008). Where a person with middle-class sensibility might see untenable living conditions, a person from a less economically privileged background might find an improved state of being.

Second, researchers must be cognizant of their insider/outsider status. An insider is a native of that particular geographic area, culture or acutely aware of social norms, whereas an outsider does not possess any of the previous listed characteristics. Bourgois (1995) and

Farr (2006) assert that their researcher status should not be misused because of the sensitive nature of their position. Researchers as newcomers and outsiders can easily be shunned and lose access to their study participants should they cross the tacit urban boundaries of respect and culture. Moreover, insider/outsider status is impacted by the conflict in value system and possible challenges to personal cultural beliefs (Weis and Fine, 2004).

Third, the power dynamics between researcher and participants impact the stories recorded, the meaning created from their participants' experiences, and cultural reference points such as the academic and the streets. Researchers should be mindful of stories published, as they create the meaning behind the voices and experiences of urban residents. This is notably significant when exploring the stories of urban rationally marginalized communities. There may be additional challenges to the researchers in deciphering the participants' interviews, if their responses are infused with multiple personal adversities that are not immediately shared with the researcher. When engaging with urban participants who lack secondary and post-secondary education, complications may occur with verbal communication, because of the researchers' use of educated language that may surpass participants' academic acumen (Bourgois, 1995; Newman, 1999).

Theoretical perspectives in urban ethnography

Other chapters in this book have thoughtfully engaged in the discussion of truth, stance and other aspects of positioning oneself within research paradigms. Rather than dwell on these philosophical differences, we discuss the use of both theoretical frameworks and social research models (by which is meant, postmodern approaches) within urban ethnographic work. Some urban ethnographic researchers emphasize the use of grounded theory or phenomenological approaches to position their work. No one theory or epistemological standpoint fits any one or all urban spaces. The goal is to select a standpoint that allows one 'to see' and understand the environment that is under investigation (Anfara and Mertz, 2006).

From our experience as researchers, we have engaged in research processes that were more loosely coupled to a particular theoretical stance. Venegas was a member of a research team that developed two major research studies on college access in urban schools over a period of seven years. She joined the team during year two and participated in a research project that focused on nine core tenets or beliefs about college access as the foundation for thinking about the development of protocol, research design and final analysis of data. These nine tenets grew through findings from previous research studies with the same evolving student population in the same urban spaces (Tierney, Colyar and Corwin, 2005; Tierney and Jun, 2001) The theoretical foundation for this investigation fits on the continuum of grounded theory. The grounded theoretical standpoint that guided the research did link to this particular data, yet it did not emerge solely from this data set (Lichtman, 2006). However, the coding practices that are essential to the grounded theory process were closely connected to the final analysis and writing of results.

Phenomenology is the study of the experiences of individuals who have lived through similar events and circumstances. We might also claim that the individuals might engage in these events within the same space. As such, the social environment can be explored carefully in terms of culture and space. It is not uncommon for ethnographers to engage in phenomenological inquiry based on personal observation from their lived experience. Venegas has conducted ethnographic research following multiple phenomenological questions within the same public and private spaces throughout South Central Los Angeles. Space is a significant aspect of this work because interactions and observations take place within the urban milieu.

How might space or perceptions of space shape individuals who identify themselves as urban and experience their lives through this lens, even when they are outside their urban contexts? Huerta's experience as an urban Chicano researcher while completing a graduate degree at a large Midwestern university led him to further engage in a study of other urban Latino graduate students with similar experiences. Through his nuanced experiences, he began to understand that other Latino/Chicano male students from similar environments were facing similar trials.

There are three facets of the research design to consider as they relate to constructions of urbanicity, space and study participant perceptions. The first concern is that urbanicity, like many other social constructs, can exist within and without the experience of the context within 'real time'. A second possibility is that space does not necessarily have set boundaries. Third, and perhaps most importantly, an individual's perceptions about the space and time in which they dwell affect how they see themselves within their own environment. Some individuals may place themselves within a specific urban environment because they live that reality on a daily basis (Newman, 1999). Other individuals may place themselves within an urban context as a means of understanding their own identity, even though they may not be currently living in a defined urban context. Such an occurrence is essential to Huerta's work with urban graduate students; it emerges as a phenomenon that study participants share. Urbanicity and the study of urban contexts in this case are not confined to physical space; they also exist in the minds and described behaviours of the study participants.

Conclusion

Understanding urban populations in research means understanding the context of space, the history of a community and the current economic and sociopolitical conditions that impact residential experiences and cohesion (Cohen, 2006). The primary commitment of the researcher is to remain true to the ethnographic naturalism of a particular setting (Schwandt, 2007). As ethnographic researchers, we would also argue that an obligation to the people within the setting is equally as important within an urban environment. The research and research approaches that we have noted here emphasize the distinctive qualities of an urban ethnography, while making connections to more traditional methods. In this chapter, we have unpacked some of the issues that challenge the goals of gathering data within an urban environment: understanding context, connecting with study participants, selecting an appropriate method and showing respect for study participants. We have identified starting points for research design and data analysis, theoretical grounding, as well as an emphasis on the role and commitments of the research. Lichtman's (2006) ten suggestions, Anfara and Mertz's thoughts about utilizing theoretical perspectives (2006), and the examples given through our own work and the work of others serve as reference points for those engaging or reflecting on their practice as urban ethnographers.

Developing a clear voice while acknowledging one's own role within the research as an academic and a person are crucial points of consideration that deserve a final iteration. The choices that are made related to sharing the stories that are gathered through the ethnographic process also bring a set of important choices to light. Again, these conclusions are not made with ease; uncertainty can guide the onset of the writing process. Goodall (2008) and Madison (2007) frame these choices within an ethnographic lens as they consider the politics of narratives that share the experiences of those in marginalized urban spaces. They acknowledge that personal reflexivity is important, perhaps especially in the midst of practising a 'dangerous ethnography' that disrupts what we accept as true from political and social perspectives. Rogler (2008) shares his over forty-year journey with understanding and deciding to pursue and share narratives from his ethnographic work. In the end, he relies upon decades-old advice that encouraged him to study and share life 'as life itself,' rather than through manufactured experience (2008: 10). The decision to bring his research to life required a close understanding of his role and social commitments within the context of what he studies, and who he is as a person within the space in which he gathers his data. For the urban ethnographer, who chooses to represent the voice of the marginalized other in urban spaces, there is a need to consider the place of social justice and the impact of their work in moving a particular agenda forward or keeping it in the same place.

References

Anafara, V. A. and Mertz, N. (2006) *Theoretical Frameworks in Qualitative Research*, Thousand Oaks, CA: Sage.

Bourgois, P. (1995) *In Search of Respect: Selling Crack in El Barrio*, Ithaca, NY: Cambridge University Press.

Cohen, J. L. (2006) 'Global links from the postindustrial heartland: Language, Internet use, and identity development among U.S.-born Mexican high school girls', pp. 3–32 in M. Farr (ed.), *Latino Language and Literacy in Ethnolinguistic Chicago*, Mahwah, NJ: Lawrence Erlbaum.

Creswell, J. (2008) *Research Design: Qualitative, quantitative and mixed method approaches*, 3rd edn, Thousand Oaks, CA: Sage.

Dillabough, J. (2008) 'Exploring historicity and temporality in social science methodology: a case for methodological and analytical justice', pp. 185–218 in K. Gallagher (ed.), *The Methodological Dilemma: Creative, critical, and collaborative approaches to qualitative research*, London: Routledge.

Duneier, M. (1999) *Sidewalk*, New York: Farrar, Straus & Giroux.

Farr, M. (2006) *Rancheros in Chicagoacán: Language and identity in a transnational community*, Austin: University of Texas Press.

Goodall, H. L. (2008) *Writing Qualitative Inquiry: Self, stories, and academic life*, Walnut Creek, CA: Left Coast Press.

Lareau, A. (2003) *Unequal Childhoods: Class, race and family life*, Berkley, CA: University of California Press.

Lichtman, M. (2006) *Qualitative Research in Education*, Thousand Oaks, CA: Sage.

Lofland, J. and Lofland, L. H. (1995) *Analyzing Social Settings: A guide to qualitative observation and analysis*, 3rd edn, Belmont, CA: Wadsworth.

Madison, S. (2007) 'Keynote address', 3rd International Congress on Qualitative Inquiry, Champaign-Urbana, IL.

Newman, K. (1999) *No Shame in My Game: The working poor in the inner city*, New York: Knopf/ Russell Sage Foundation.

Rogler, L. H. (2008) *Barrio Professors: Tales of naturalistic research*, Walnut Creek, CA: Left Coast Press.

Suskind, R. (1998) *A Hope in the Unseen: An American Odyssey from the inner city to the Ivy League*, New York: Broadway Books.

Schwandt, T. A. (2007) *The Sage Dictionary of Qualitative Inquiry*, 3rd edn, Thousand Oaks, CA: Sage.

Tierney, W. G., Colyar, J. and Corwin, Z. B. (2005) *Preparing for College: Nine elements of effective outreach*, Albany, NY: State University of New York Press.

Tierney, W. G. and Jun, A. (2001) 'A university helps prepare low-income youths for college: Tracking school success', *Journal of Higher Education*, 72(2), 205–25.

Tuhiwai Smith, L. (1999) *Decolonizing Methodologies: Research and indigenous peoples*, New York: Palgrave.

Weis, L. and Fine, M. (2004) *Working Method: Research and Social justice*, New York: Routledge.

Yon, D. A. (2003) 'Highlights and overview of the history of educational ethnography', *Annual Review of Anthropology*, 32, 411–29.

Chapter 17

Researching in immersive spaces

Maggi Savin-Baden, Lesley Gourlay and Cathy Tombs

Introduction

The rise in the use of technology for learning has resulted in increasing interest in the impact of the use of immersive spaces on staff and students in higher education. Further, research into immersive worlds is still relatively new. The impact of learning in such worlds in terms of students' conceptions of reality, their relationship between in-world and real-world behaviour and issues of representation, embodiment and immersion bear further research. This chapter draws on projects and studies that have used different research approaches in immersive spaces such as Second Life™, and a further project that evaluated the use of problem-based learning in immersive virtual worlds (IVWs). The chapter outlines research approaches that have worked well in such spaces, such as narrative inquiry and participatory action research (PAR). It also illustrates other approaches that have proved effective.

Immersive virtual worlds in context

IVWs such as Second Life, Activeworlds and There have become used increasingly in higher education not only as new teaching and learning spaces, but also as ones where both traditional and new forms of research are being adopted. Early work by authors such as Turkle (1995, 2005) and Haraway (1991) tended to focus on the relationship between humans and computers, with particular focus on the impact on our social, psychological and work lives. However, what is interesting is the shift from this early work which raises questions about comparing ourselves with computers, to the current position which would seem to relate not only to our dependency on computers but also a desire to instantiate ourselves and our characters through them. The result would seem to be that the body is increasingly seen as a liminal installation or artefact with media as a bodily extension. Thus we suggest that any investigation into these complex questions demands that the researcher do more than simply employ face-to-face interviewing techniques, as the complex and abstract experiences and orientations of participants are likely to require a more holistic approach to investigation, in order to explore them in any depth.

As emergent sites of both social and educational practice, online IVWs exhibit various features which render them both exciting and challenging domains of inquiry. These features demand new approaches to establishing relationships with research participants, data collection and interpretation. Perhaps the most striking feature of the IVWs is their moving, three-dimensional (3D) nature. Unlike the 2D 'flat' appearance of conventional webpages, IVWs are animated, and the participant has some sense of 'entering' a kinetic and visual environment which visually resembles a computer game. Participation in online IVWs such as Second Life (the immersive world currently used most widely in a variety of disciplinary settings) involves the creation and use of an *avatar* (Sanskrit for 'incarnation') – a moving graphic figure controlled by participants and used to interact with and explore the environment, and to communicate with other participants. Participants have a large degree of control over the name and visual appearance of their avatar, which can move around or even fly through the virtual world. Text chat is used to communicate with others, voice may be used, as are other forms of communication such as note cards, depending on the environment. As a result, participants must mobilize a multimodal set of semiotic resources for effective participation – that is, they may access a range of modes of meaning-making; verbal, kinetic and auditory, as opposed to merely textual. It would seem then that what is emerging is a 'grammar' of semiotic resources – a system of established signs with meanings used and understood by participants in the environment (Kress and van Leeuwen, 2006), examples being virtual clothing, hairstyles and other features such as movement, gait, gesture and proximity, which can be mobilized in order to construct and project an online identity. As a result, any attempt at a detailed understanding of communication and practices in these spaces requires an approach to data collection and analysis that can capture some of the complexity of these processes.

Research in immersive virtual worlds

The research to date in IVWs is complex and varied. Although there are many interesting studies and findings there does seem to be a methodological conundrum at play. For example, authors such as Hine (2005) have been steeped in the use of virtual ethnography, and manage to encompass in this work the sociological and methodological challenges of using a well-rehearsed approach (ethnography) in a new and complex space. Others have tended to shift real-world practices into IVWs and largely shy away from the methodological difficulties this poses, but in ways that have enabled possibly more appropriate 'viral' methodologies to emerge. (Carr and Oliver, 2009; Bayne, 2008). An example of this is Bayne's (2008) comparative analysis of the semiotics of a virtual learning environment and a collaborative wiki. She looks in particular at the visual features and organization of the two environments, and how they position participants and make ideological statements about education.

Although this is a somewhat polarized view, what it does bring to the fore is the importance of doing both – allowing methods and methodologies to emerge, with a nod towards viral learning, at the same time as using more established methodologies. An example of this is a strand of research that has looked at literacy practices in IVWs. This work bases its use of the term 'literacy' on the work of New Literacy Studies. This research focuses on not only the recognition but also the multimodal production of meaning-making, which makes it well suited for the complexities of the IVW context. This first section presents two studies that used real-world approaches to explore in-world experiences: the first used narrative inquiry, the second participatory action research.

Narrative inquiry

A study that used narrative inquiry was undertaken to explore staff experiences of learning and teaching in IVWs (Savin-Baden and Tombs, forthcoming; Savin-Baden, 2010). Narrative inquiry was used since stories are collected as a means of understanding experience as lived and told, through both research and literature (Clandinin and Connelly, 1994). It is seen in a variety of ways, and tends to transcend a number of different approaches and traditions, such as biography, autobiography, life story and more recently life course research. In terms of locating it in the broad spectrum of qualitative research, it tends to be positioned within a constructivist stance, with reflexivity, interpretivism and representation being primary features of the approach.

Although some researchers would argue that narratives are structured with a beginning, a middle and an end, held together by some kind of plot and resolution (Sarbin, 1986), the studies here indicated that a shift was required away from any kind of linearity. The narratives did not necessarily have a plot or structured story line, but were interruptions of reflection in a storied life. However, what is particularly important when researching IVWs is this concern over representation. Differences about the issue of representation seem to be one of the strong points of disagreement between qualitative researchers who hold different perspectives. This is not surprising, because to debate the issue of representation would usually draw into question the very processes with which the voices of participants are believed to be captured and presented. We consider that such opinions are, in turn, strongly influenced by views that are held about the nature of truths (see Chapter 4 by Van Niekerk and Savin-Baden). However, perhaps the most valuable way of illustrating the challenges of using narrative inquiry is through the exemplar below, which explores issues connected with undertaking narrative interviews in IVW research.

Narrative interviewing in immersive worlds

The study explored student and staff experiences' of learning in IVWs, and data were collected through three different types of data collection: face-to-face, telephone and in-world interviews. The purpose of the study was to understand the purpose and meaning behind the interviewee's decision to use learning in IVWs; to understand the emotions, thoughts and opinions of each individual (for more details on these see Savin-Baden and Tombs, forthcoming; Savin-Baden, 2010). While the primary aim of the study was to gather stories of users' educational experiences of virtual worlds such as Second Life, it was also extremely beneficial to compare and contrast the participants' responses based on which data collection technique was being used.

The majority of interviews took place in real life. However, in-world discussions provide benefits that face-to-face ones cannot, such as removing the boundaries of time, space and geography, and vastly reducing costs. Additionally, Boulos and Wheeler (2007) state that textual interaction facilitates the type of on-screen interaction, with its perceptions of distance and safety, that many find comfortable. When scheduling the interviews, participants were given the option of choosing whether to take part in-world, face to face or via telephone. Particular issues emerged relating to where interviews took place.

Despite the exact same questions being asked for all three types of interview, the responses were longer and contained more data in the real-life sessions. Curasi (2003) suggests that as online participants are able to read and reread their answers in text before responding, they may exercise more caution over what is said, and their responses may contain less spontaneity. While this transpires as what could be considered a 'written story' as opposed to a 'spoken story', the participant's response may be less genuine and more constricted than the real-life interviews. It could be suggested that if in-world interviews are conducted, voice chat would be better used for narrative inquiry, as the interviewer can gather more information from tones of voices and hesitations, to understand the participant's emotions and opinions better.

Andy and Tom were two students who were interviewed as part of the study, Andy in-world and Tom in real life:

> *Interviewer*: OK – did you ever express uncertainty about using [Second Life] SL or did you take to it straight away?
> *Andy*: Oh I'm always uncertain about it, but I think most people I've spoken to feel the same. That it's sort of its own world that you get sucked into, like if you tried to explain an SL project to someone who had never heard of SL they probably would be like 'wha?' (in-world interview)

> *Interviewer*: Did you or any of your course mates ever express uncertainty about using Second Life?
> *Tom*: Yes. It was more, it was more the first few weeks when you're looking at it, your internet connection's not the best in the world, and it's all, it's all jerky, things are popping in and out. But I suppose it's one of those things where if you're going to have something that's going to be so open, people can go in Second Life and build whatever they want, and pretty much do whatever they want, you're going to have a few problems. (face-to-face interview)

Consequently, from this research study in particular, it appeared that the collected data varied in accordance with whether the interview took place in a virtual world or in real life. Despite the nature of the information being in relation to IVWs, there was a large contrast in the standard of data gathered; the participants in Second Life provided much shorter statements than those questioned outside the virtual world. There could be any number of reasons for this, for example familiarity and comfort – if the user was still a novice in the virtual world, which a number of them were, they might not have felt entirely comfortable with their surroundings. It could also be suggested that it is much more difficult to tell your experiences as a story using text as opposed to talking; it is likely that because of the structured, very linear approach in-world, the participants gave little thought to recreating their experience as a story and instead simply focused on answering the prompting questions of the interviewer.

In addition, with the face-to-face interviews, it was also possible to determine when the participant was enthusiastic about a particular point in the discussion from tone of voice, facial expressions and hand gestures. This is far more difficult to distinguish in IVW interviews, especially those that are purely text-based. Participants who were more familiar and comfortable with the virtual world seemed to understand this difficulty, and hence made use of 'gestures' in Second Life, for example making their avatar nod their head when they agreed with something the interviewer said. However, while this was useful for distinguishing whether there was a reason for a hesitation in the participant's typing or knowing whether they understood the questions or not, it provided very little use for anything else; as a 'forced gesture' there could be no way of knowing whether an avatar's smile or frown was genuine or not. While non-verbal cues are easily used in face-to-face and even telephone interviews, comparable cues on the part of the interviewer could be missed in Second Life interviews; furthermore interjecting a murmur of agreement in text could be construed as interrupting, and might even have halted the interviewee mid-story if they considered the text to be a signal to stop. Therefore an interviewer in-world should take care to make use of appropriate visual gestures that encourage the participant.

Interviewing in Second Life is particularly useful where traditional real-life techniques may be problematic, for instance for those who have disabilities or are uncomfortable with social situations. As before, the fact that it removes the boundaries of time, geography and space, and vastly reduces costs, contributes to the appeal of in-world interviewing. However, it is important to note that where the benefits are great, there are disadvantages that need to be considered before undertaking such a method of data collection. Additionally, there are slight restrictions to using certain research methods that the researcher might not consider before embarking on in-world research. As discussed, the linear structure of text chat in Second Life might make it more difficult for the interviewee to create a narrative, and furthermore the interviewer needs to take extra care to ensure the participant knows they are listening and encouraging them to continue with their story of experience.

Participatory action research

An example of the use of PAR in immersive worlds research is the CURLIEW project. This is a study that is using PAR to examine staff and students' perspectives from a wide range of disciplines in Higher Education Institutions across the United Kingdom. It is investigating their conceptions of and decisions about the way in which they teach and learn at the socio-political boundaries of reality (http://cuba.coventry.ac.uk/leverhulme/). This study is focusing on the exploration of three main themes:

- students' experiences of learning in immersive worlds.
- pedagogical design.
- learner identity.

Negotiated participation and the development of shared understanding of practice are central to this project. In practice this has meant engaging people as active participants in the research process; and results in practical outcomes related to the work and learning of the participants. PAR originates from the fields of adult education, international development and the social sciences, and is seen by authors such as Kemmis and McTaggart (2000) as an inclusive form of inquiry. Thus PAR is not just a method of conducting research but rather an orientation towards research. It is an approach that has been used in cross-cultural contexts, and therefore would seem to be highly appropriate for spanning the boundaries of research into virtual and real-world studies and exploring the extent to which they converge and diverge (for example, Wallerstein and Duran, 2003). Such a research approach can:

- provide insights into how knowledge is created and/or understood, in terms of propositional knowledge, practical knowing and experiential knowing or knowing by encounter in virtual worlds
- locate and delineate 'thought-worlds' or unique interpretative repertoires of the participants involved in learning and teaching in virtual worlds
- explore the extent to which particular approaches to teaching and disciplinary differences help or hinder learning in immersive worlds
- delineate the likely sociopolitical impact of such learning on the higher education community through exploration of virtuality, veracity and values (Atkinson and Burden, 2007).

These two examples (narrative inquiry and PAR) are merely illustrative of the many well-established methodological approaches that are being adopted in IVW research. However, there are new stances and methodologies that are being adopted in order to examine, understand and reflect these environments more effectively.

Emergent methodologies and methods in immersive virtual worlds

The previous sections have described how established research methodologies have been applied and adapted to the context of IVWs. However, the particular features of IVWs demand that new approaches must be found which are not only congruent with the environment, but also find ways of examining the features and use of the environment itself. This is an emergent area of research, but where possible examples will be given of projects taking new approaches that attempt to capture the particular communicative and semiotic features of IVWs.

Virtual ethnography

The work of Hine (2000, 2005) in this field has been seminal in terms of seeking to understand from a sociological perspective what people 'do' on the internet. Her stance has not been to focus on immersion, as in more traditional ethnographic studies (for example, Geertz, 1973), but instead to suggest it is important not to assume that merely examining online actions and spaces makes it possible to understand what was or might be significant or meaningful. Thus virtual ethnography is seen as:

> ethnography of, in and through the virtual – we learn about the Internet by immersing ourselves in it and conducting our ethnography using it, as well as talking with people about it, watching them use it and seeing it manifest in other social settings.
>
> (Hine, 2000)

An example of this that relates to IVWs is Moore *et al.* (2006), who undertook a study of online immersive games. They employed video-based conversational analysis, a technique they suggest is grounded in virtual ethnography. The emphasis here, as above, is on gaining an 'insider' participant's perspective on the environment and practices within it. The researchers spent long periods of time playing the games under investigation and forming relationships with players. They point out that avatars display much less information about the state of the individual than real bodies when it comes to cues to manage turns at talk, the meanings conveyed by embodied activities, and the use of gaze for the purpose of gesturing. As they point out, a focus on social interaction is an emergent, under-researched field. A further example is the work of Boellstorff (2009), who spent two years as a 'resident' in Second Life, observing the day-to-day practices of users. His is the first ethnography of an IVW, and explores issues of identity and virtuality in social practice. This type of research may also inform and supplement smaller-scale work in IVWs.

Cognitive ethnography

This approach explores the cognitive processes that affect the work carried out within a setting, while recognizing in turn the effect that the material world and social context have on the actions carried out, and that the meanings attributed within the setting also affect the cognitive processes (Hollan *et al.*, 2000). The work of Steinkuehler is an example of this approach. In a two-year online study, she used cognitive ethnography to describe 'specific cultures in terms of cognitive practices, their basis, and their consequences' (Steinkuehler, 2007: 299). In doing so she analysed thousands of lines of transcribed observations of game play, player communications of various types and documents such as fan websites. She also conducted unstructured and semi-structured interviews with informants. Further examples of research in this vein include Black and Steinkuehler (2009), who investigated the digital literacy practices of young people, and the virtual literacy ethnography of Teen Second Life™ conducted by Gillen (2009).

Situated activity research

A further example of this type of attention to avatar-mediated interaction can be seen in Bennerstedt's (2008) study of gamers' practices in the online game World of Warcraft™. She draws on Goodwin's situated activity systems, which he defines as: 'how participants deploy the diverse resources provided by talk [...], sequential organization, posture, gaze, gesture, and consequential phenomena in the environment that is the focus of their work in order to accomplish the courses of action that constitute their life world' (Goodwin, 2000: 1519).

The emphasis here is on the analysis of various semiotic fields (Goodwin, 1994, 2000) – an intertwined range of semiotic resources used for meaning-making, including movement, speech, text and gesture. Bennerstedt looks at the virtual semiotic fields present in the immersive environment of the game, also taking an approach influenced by ethnomethodology (for example, Lindwall and Lymer, 2005). She used video recording and subsequent transcription to analyse how participants manage the discourse in this setting. In doing so, she uses interaction analysis to focus on the discursive practices and support for visual cues used by players.

Although these projects focus on games, the features of the environments are similar enough to make this type of approach highly relevant for the context of IVWs, in particular if the research aims for an understanding of communicative processes, arguably at the heart of what makes an IVW a collaborative environment.

Viral methodologies and connective ethnography

The notion of viral methodologies is that instead of methodologies being specifically 'located' in areas such as poststructuralism and constructivism, the underlying theories are seen as mutable and liquid. Although such methodologies are emergent and there is currently little written about them, they are based in the idea of viral learning (see for example the Downes website, http://www.downes.ca/). Such methodologies are interrupting theories and methods that change, are changed and are adapted according to researcher contexts, postionality and cultures. Such methodologies can be related to earlier work such as emergent design (Lincoln and Guba, 1985), but it is the viral quality that makes them different.

An example of such an approach is ethnographic connectivity. This method is one of those that have stemmed from the argument of such researchers as Leander and McKim (2003), who have suggested the need to move beyond place-based ethnography. The central idea here then is in combining online and offline ethnographic methodologies. An example of this is provided by Hine (2007), who argues against traditional ethnographic constructs such as position, place and identity, and instead engages with the complexities of how such constructs are further destabilized in research online. The focus here is on how connectivity relates to connection and mobility. Thus construction and deconstruction are examined as the ways in which diverse forms of communication are used to contextualize one another.

Discussion

The unique position of IVWs also arguably renders them as sites of ideological struggle regarding underlying values of education and participation, as a range of social actors seeks to appropriate the space for their own purposes. In the case of virtual islands established by universities in Second Life, senior management or marketing departments may see the virtual space as an opportunity to publicize the university and its courses, and also to discursively position the university itself as 'cutting edge'. This often leads to the building of a virtual version of an iconic building from the real-life university, and other markers of corporate identity. In contrast, educational practitioners may choose to develop the resource in ways which seek to challenge familiar modes of practice and representation from the face-to-face setting.

The features of the environment raise research questions regarding identity work being done by participants in the creation, maintenance and use of their avatar. These might focus on participants' relationships with their avatars, whether they are perceived as some kind of extension of the self: an 'alter-ego', 'mini-me', puppet, figure-shaped mouse pointer or a complex and shifting combination of various types of identification. The degree and nature of participant identification may arguably have a bearing on the extent of their commitment to the experience both emotionally and cognitively, and how they relate to other avatars and communities online. The concept of 'immersion' is a complex one involving notions of embodiment and various types of 'presence', with many authors using such terms inter-changeably.

Conclusions

These various approaches draw on different disciplinary roots, but what unites them is a focus on observation of practice, engagement with the setting and a focus on multimodality and communication. Bauman recently suggested:

> For the young, the main attraction of the virtual world derives from the absence of con-tradictions and cross-purposes that haunt the off-line life. Unlike its off-life alternative, the online world renders the infinite multiplication of contacts conceivable – both plau-sible and feasible. It does it through the weakening of bonds – in a stark opposition to its off-line counterpart, known to find its bearings in the continuous effort to strengthen the bonds.
>
> (Bauman, 2009: 10)

Yet such a stance would seem to ignore the complexity of research and learning in immersive virtual worlds and locate 'the young' and their identities in an essentialist way. It would seem that perhaps the way forward is one of connectivity across methodologies, stances and approaches to maximize the exploration and the spaces for investigation that IVWs appear to afford.

References

Atkinson, S. and Burden, K. (2007) 'Virtuality, veracity and values: Exploring between virtual and real worlds using the 3V model', in *ICT: Providing choices for learners and learning*, Proceedings OF Ascilite, Singapore 2007 (online) <http://www.ascilite.org.au/conferences/singapore07/procs/atkinson.pdf> (accessed 19 November 2009).

Bauman, Z. (2009) 'Education in the liquid-modern setting', Keynote presentation DPR8: Power and the Academy, in *8th Conference of the Discourse, Power, Resistance Series 6–8*, Manchester Metropolitan University (online) <http://www.esri.mmu.ac.uk/dpr/education.pdf> (accessed 20 November 2009).

Bayne, S. (2008) 'Higher education as a visual practice: seeing through the virtual learning environment', *Teaching in Higher Education*, 13(4), 395–410.

Bennerstedt, U. (2008) 'Sheeping, sapping and avatars-in-action: an in-screen perspective on online gameplay', pp. 28–52 in S. Mosberg Iversen (ed.), *Proceedings of the [Player] Conference, IT University of Copenhagen, Denmark, August 2008*, Copenhagen: Nørrebros Bogtryk ApS.

Black, R. W. and Steinkuehler, C. (2009) 'Literacy in virtual worlds', pp. 271–86 in L. Christenbury, R. Bomer and P. Smagorinsky (eds), *Handbook of Adolescent Literacy Research*, New York: Guilford.

Boellstorff, T. (2009) *Coming of Age in Second Life: An anthropologist explores the virtually human*, Princeton, NJ: Princeton University Press.

Boulos, M. N. K. and Wheeler, S. (2007) 'The emerging Web 2.0 social software: an enabling suite of sociable technologies in health and healthcare education', *Health Information and Libraries Journal*, 24(1), 2–23.

Carr, D. and Oliver M. (2009) 'Second Life, immersion and learning', in P. Zaphiris and C. S. Ang (eds), *Social Computing and Virtual Communities*, London: Taylor & Francis.

Clandinin, D. J. and Connelly, F. M. (1994) 'Personal experience methods', in N. K Denzin and Y. S. Lincoln (eds), *Handbook of Qualitative Research*, Thousand Oaks, CA: Sage.

Curasi, C. (2003) 'A critical exploration of face-to-face interviewing vs. computer-mediated interviewing', *International Journal of Market Research*, 42(2), 137–55.

Geertz, C. (1973) *The Interpretation of Cultures*, New York: Basic Books.

Gillen, J. (2009) 'Literacy practices in Schome Park: a virtual literacy ethnography', *Journal of Research in Reading*, 32(1), 55–74.

Goodwin, C. (1994) 'Professional vision', *American Anthropologist*, 96(3), 606–33.

Goodwin, C. (2000) 'Action and embodiment within situated human interaction', *Journal of Pragmatics*, 32: 1489–1522.

Haraway, D. (1991) *Simians, Cyborgs, and Women: The reinvention of nature*, London: Routledge.

Hine, C. (2000) *Virtual Ethnography*, London: Sage.

Hine, C. (2005) 'Internet research and the sociology of cyber-social-scientific knowledge', *The Information Society*, 21(4), 239–48.

Hine, C. (2007) 'Connective ethnography for the exploration of e-science', *Journal of Computer-Mediated Communication*, 12(2), article 14 (online) <http://jcmc.indiana.edu/vol12/issue2/hine.html> (accessed 20 November 2009).

Hollan, J. Hutchins, E. and Kirsh, D. (2000) 'Distributed cognition: toward a new foundation for human-computer interaction research', *ACM Transactions on Computer-Human Interaction*, 7(2), 174–96.

Kemmis, S. and McTaggart, R. (2000) 'Participatory action research', pp. 567–605 in N. K. Denzin and Y. S. Lincoln (eds), *Handbook of Qualitative Research*, Thousand Oaks, CA: Sage.

Kress, G. and van Leeuwen, T. (2006) *Reading Images: The grammar of visual design*, 2nd edn, London: Routledge.

Leander, K. M. and McKim, K. K. (2003) 'Tracing the everyday "sitings" of adolescents on the Internet: a strategic adaptation of ethnography across online and offline spaces', *Education, Communication and Information*, **3**(2), 211–40.

Lincoln, Y. S. and Guba, E. G. (1985) *Naturalistic Inquiry*, Newbury Park, CA: Sage.

Lindwall, O. and Lymer, G. (2005) 'Vulgar competence, ethnomethodological indifference and curricular design', in T. Koschmann, D. D. Suthers and T. W. Chan (eds), *Computer Support for Collaborative Learning: The next 10 years*, Mahwah, NJ: Lawrence Erlbaum Associates.

Moore, R. J., Ducheneaut, N. and Nickell, E. (2006) 'Doing virtually nothing: awareness and accountability in massively multiplayer online games', *Computer Supported Cooperative Work*, **16**(3), 265–305.

Sarbin, T. R. (ed.) (1986) *Narrative Psychology: The storied nature of human conduct*, New York: Praeger.

Savin-Baden, M. (forthcoming) 'Changelings and shape shifters? Identity play and pedagogical positioning of staff in immersive virtual worlds', *London Review of Education*.

Savin-Baden, M and Tombs, C. (forthcoming) 'Students' experiences of learning in immersive world environments', in R. Sharpe and H. Beetham (eds), *Listening to Learners in the Digital Age*, London: Routledge.

Steinkuehler, C. (2007) 'Massively multiplayer online gaming as a constellation of literacy practices', *E-learning*, **4**(3), 297–318.

Turkle, S. (1995) *Life on the Screen: Identity in the age of the Internet*, New York: Simon & Schuster.

Turkle, S. (2005) *The Second Self: Computers and the human spirit*, Cambridge, MA: MIT Press.

Wallerstein, N. and Duran, B. (2003) 'The conceptual, historical, and practice roots of community based participatory research and related participatory traditions', pp. 2 –52 in M. Minkler and N. Wallerstein (eds), Community-based Participatory Research for Health, San Francisco, CA: Jossey-Bass.

Afterword

Maggi Savin-Baden and Claire Howell Major

We began this book with a preface, in which we described the reasons that we undertook editing this volume. In particular, we described our work to develop a new approach to synthesizing qualitative evidence, qualitative research synthesis (Major and Savin-Baden, 2010; Savin-Baden and Major, 2007). The experience of learning and building something anew, particularly an approach that had us delving so deeply into the research processes that others used, led us to an understanding, as well as an appreciation, of the level of uncertainty that lies within the field of qualitative inquiry. There is uncertainty as to how to position oneself as a researcher, uncertainty about what specific methods and methodologies actually entail, and uncertainty about the contexts within which qualitative research is conducted. Uncertainty also leads to the necessity of making decisions, of making choices about how to conceptualize and carry out qualitative research.

While, as we noted in the Introduction, researchers have rejected the notion of objectivity and absolute truth, many have not yet considered the application of uncertainty to their own work. Yet as we have argued, engaging with this concept can lead to a kind of advancement. For example, periods of stuckness and liminality are apparent in academic writing. Recent research has explored the idea that there are moments of conceptual threshold crossing in the writing process (Kiley and Wisker, 2008; Savin-Baden, 2008). Such work focuses on 'stuck' moments (Lather, 1998) and explores the process of moving on: the shift into focused, formed articulation in writing (see Wisker and Savin-Baden, 2009). Further, it has been suggested in other work there might be different forms of stuckness, and that forms may differ between people, and their encounters with it may vary (Savin-Baden, 2007). Uncertainty too can be connected with a sense of being stuck. Thus engaging with it can lead to advancement of knowledge and wisdom, as thresholds are crossed and articulation becomes clearer.

This book has sought throughout its chapters to deal with issues of space, concepts, place, cultural difference and diversity, reconceptualization of the notion of texts, new research spaces and diverse and new methods for undertaking research. Yet we believe that these are uncomfortable spaces that should remain uncomfortable, since that is where learning can happen and a field may be advanced. It is for this reason that we undertook the project of this book, selecting chapters that highlight how others have grappled with difficult and important questions and shaped their own approaches to qualitative inquiry. Like the chapters here the endings of the book are full of uncertainty, but we hope the contributors have offered you wisdom for your journeys ahead.

References

Kiley, M. and Wisker, G. (2008, June 2008) '"Now you see it, now you don't": Identifying and supporting the achievement of doctoral work which embraces threshold concepts and crosses conceptual thresholds', paper presented at the Threshold concepts: From theory to practice conference, Queen's University, Kingston, Ontario, Canada.

Lather, P. (1998) 'Critical pedagogy and its complicities: a praxis of stuck places', *Educational Theory*, **48**(4), 487–98.

Major, C. H. and Savin-Baden, M. (2010) *An Introduction to Qualitative Research Synthesis: Managing the information explosion in social science research*, London: Routledge.

Savin-Baden, M. (2007) *Learning Spaces: Creating opportunities for knowledge creation in academic life*, Maidenhead: McGraw Hill.

Savin-Baden, M. (2008) 'Liquid learning and troublesome spaces: Journeys from the threshold?' in R. Land, J. Meyer and J. Smith (eds), *Threshold Concepts within the Disciplines*, Rotterdam: Sense.

Savin-Baden, M. and Major, C. H. (2007) 'Using interpretive meta-ethnography to explore the relationship between innovative approaches to learning and innovative methods of pedagogical research', *Higher Education*, **54**(6), 833–52.

Wisker, G. and Savin-Baden, M. (2009) 'Priceless conceptual thresholds: beyond the "stuck place" in writing', *London Review of Education*, 7(3), 235–47.

Glossary

Cognitive ethnography – an approach that explores the cognitive processes that affect the work carried out within a setting, while recognizing in turn the effect that the material world and social context have on the actions carried out, and that the meanings attributed within the setting also affect the cognitive processes (Hollan et al., 2000).

Conceptual or theoretical framework – an existing concept or proven theory that serves to guide study design as well as interpretations.

Confirmability – the idea that the researcher has remained neutral in data analysis and interpretation. It is based upon the notion that the researcher needs to demonstrate that results could be, and at times even should be, confirmed or corroborated by others.

Connective ethnography – this method is one of those that has stemmed from the argument of such researchers as Leander and McKim (2003), who have suggested the need to move beyond place-based ethnography. The central idea then is in combining online and offline ethnographic methodologies.

Consensus techniques – techniques that aim to achieve a convergence of opinion.

Credibility – the term credibility is centred on the idea that results are credible and therefore to be believed. It is the idea that the reader can have confidence in the data and their interpretation. The focus is on the trust which can be placed in the accuracy of data and the process by which it was acquired, the sense that it is believable and that confidence can be placed in it.

Daily practices – material activities and learned behaviours enacted to achieve some anticipated outcome.

Deliberation – a structured discussion on issues that have diverse opinions by experts. The aim of deliberating is to provide an opportunity to challenge ideas, and reveal misconceptions.

Deliberative inquiry – a hybrid of research methods (the focus group and the Delphi technique) which is most accurately described as a method for exploring consensus through group deliberation.

Dependability – the notion that research can be trusted over time. Dependability is derived from the more positivist perspective of reliability and replicability.

Embodiment – the interaction of the body, material places and social spaces towards the development of meaning.

Empirical studies – social science studies in which research findings are derived from evidence, rather than simply theory alone. The study, whether qualitative or qualitative, involves collecting data in the field.

Ethnodrama – a research-based play script consisting of dramatized, significant selections of narrative collected through interviews, field notes, journal entries and/or print and media artifacts, which may also include or consist solely of the playwright's autoethnographic reflections. Ethnodrama is groundwork for ethnotheatre, which employs theatrical production techniques to mount for an audience a live (or mediated) performance event of research participants' experiences and/or the researcher's interpretations of data.

Ethnography – a systematic way of gathering data using qualitative methods, including participant observation, interviewing, the collection of analysis of various documents or artifacts, individual narratives with a focus on the social environment including physical spaces, customs and culture.

Evaluative methods – methods used to study an organization or curriculum in a way that contributes to a review of policy and decision making within the organization. Thus qualitative methods are used which will enable the researcher and those involved to review the advantages and disadvantages of the programme under study and explore the problems and policies. The classic model used is illuminative evaluation, although there are many others.

Evidence-based practice – this began its development as evidence-based medicine and, as such, began from a very quantitative and 'hard science' perspective. It is currently used to refer to practices in health care that use a range of studies, both qualitative and quantitative, to inform the way practices are carried out. Thus it is an approach to treatment rather than a specific treatment.

Exclusion criteria – the criteria used to decide which studies will be excluded from the review.

Explanatory literature review – reviews that explore a particular topic with a view of offering an explanation of the issue under study. These do involve analysis, but the form generally is not specified, although at times there is a general mention of 'weight of evidence' criteria, in the sense that if a preponderance of evidence demonstrates a finding, it is considered credible.

Faculty – in the United States, teaching/research professionals in institutions of higher education who hold academic rank; used interchangeably with staff in the United Kingdom.

Focus group – a unique kind of interview, in that it collects data from a number of people in a manner that is non-quantitative.

Grey literature – in the context of social science literature, this means those works that do not appear in peer-reviewed journals, including conference proceedings and dissertations.

Grounded theory – a type of qualitative research in which theory is generated from data.

Hand searching – the process of locating articles by hand (often in a library) and checking articles to see whether they are relevant for a review.

Honesties – the idea that there needs to be a sense that what counts as trustworthiness and truth is a negotiated position in research.

Inclusion criteria – the criteria used to decide which studies will be included in a review.

Interpretivism – the perspective that knowledge, contexts, meanings and ideas are a matter of interpretation, thus researchers analyse the meaning people confer upon their own and others' actions.

Iterative – a cyclical procedure that involves revisiting issues, ideas and concerns related to research.

Literature review – a critical overview of literature in order to identify and make clear the current state of knowledge about a given topic.

Material place – physical surroundings (buildings, the four walls of a classroom and so on).

Member checking – a process for ensuring plausibility in which participants (in the case of synthesis subjects or authors) are contacted to ask whether data interpretations or findings are accurate.

Meta-analysis – a process through which statistical methods are used to analyse results from several studies on a given topic, often to determine effect size.

Meta-ethnography – an approach to synthesizing and interpreting findings from multiple qualitative studies. Noblitt and Hare (1988), from the field of education, developed this interpretive approach which has served as the basis for most qualitative approaches to synthesizing qualitative research.

Meta-synthesis – an approach to synthesis of qualitative studies (or qualitative and quantitative studies) that tends to be aggregative (as opposed to interpretive) in approach. However, the term is sometimes used interchangeably with meta-ethnography.

Moderator – a group facilitator with expertise in the issue(s) under investigation.

Multimodal resources – modes of meaning-making; verbal, kinetic and auditory, as opposed to merely textual.

Naturalistic inquiry – research that takes place in the natural setting, sees the researcher as the primary data collecting instrument, and is often characterized by the use of an emergent design.

Negotiated honesties – the idea that there needs to be a sense that what counts as trustworthiness and truth is a negotiated position in research.

Participant observation – studying people by participating in social interactions with them in order to observe and understand them.

Plausibility – a technique for ensuring rigour in qualitative research synthesis which involves locating the truths and the realities in the study, adopting a critical approach and acknowledging the complexities of managing 'truths' in research.

Positivism – a philosophical system which recognizes only positive facts and observable phenomena, thus the only reliable knowledge of any field of phenomena reduces to knowledge of particular instances of patterns. Therefore reality is single and tangible, research is value free and generalizations are possible.

Postpositivism – a philosophical approach which argues that realities are multiple, that research is value bound and is affected by time and context.

Practice profession – a field that helps to prepare students for work in a particular profession, including education, medicine and the law.

Practitioners – those who are employed in practice professions, such as medicine, law and education.

Primary research – a process through which a researcher engages in empirical research.

Primary studies – individual studies included in a review are referred to in this way before they are synthesized.

Problem-based learning – an approach to learning in which students engage with complex, real-world situations that have no one 'right' answer, and are the organizing focus for learning. Students work in teams to confront the problem, to identify learning gaps, and to develop viable solutions and gain new information through self-directed learning.

Qualitative research – a term that describes a developing field of inquiry and covers several research approaches that share a set of common characteristics. Those who use the approach frequently seek to understand human behaviour. They often are interested in the 'why' and 'how' questions, rather than the 'what'. Data collected and presented generally is thick in its description.

Qualitative research synthesis – an approach for integrating information from existing qualitative studies (Major and Savin-Baden, 2009).

Quantitative research – a field of inquiry that relies upon statistical techniques to analyse data.

Randomized control trials – an experimental study where subjects are randomly allocated to different control groups for the allocation of different interventions.

Reflexivity – seeking to continually challenge our biases and examining our stances, perspectives and views as researchers. This is not meant to be a notion of 'situating oneself' as formulaic as pronouncing a particular positioned identity connected with class, gender or race, but rather situating oneself in order to interpret data demands so as to engage with critical questions.

Research review – the use of a review of research to demonstrate information in a particular way, for example to develop a comprehensive picture of knowledge about a topic or issue.

Research synthesis – a stand-alone report that combines evidence in a way that aggregates information from a body of studies into a new whole.

Researcher bias – the acceptance that in qualitative studies bias exists and is understood as inevitable and important by most qualitative researchers. However, processes such as reflexivity can be adopted to gain 'a better set of biases'.

Second Life – a 3D virtual world created by LindenLab set in an internet-based world. Residents (in the forms of self-designed avatars) in this world interact with each other and can learn, socialize, participate in activities and buy and sell items with one another.

Semi-structured interview – a process that involves use of interviewing with an interview protocol that is somewhat set, but that also relies on open-ended questions to allow for spontaneity by the participant.

Situated Activity Research – the analysis of various semiotic fields (Goodwin, 1994, 2000) – an intertwined range of semiotic resources used for meaning-making, including movement, speech, text and gesture.

Social space – the meanings we make of our material surroundings.

Staff – a term used in the United Kingdom to denote professionals who hold rank as lecturers or professors, used interchangeably with faculty in the United States.

Stakeholders – a group or groups of people who have an interest in an issue, institution or other item.

Stance – one's attitude, belief or disposition towards a particular context, person or experience. It refers to a particular position one takes up in life towards something, at a particular point in time.

Synthesis – the process of reassembling parts into a comprehensive whole.

Synthesist – the person who engages in the process of conducting a synthesis of original qualitative studies; we use the term to mark a distinction from researchers, by whom we mean the primary investigators and authors of the studies included in the synthesis.

Thick description – this involves explanation of the context as well as the importance of interpretation. Thus it is not just reporting detail, but instead demands interpretation that goes beyond meaning and motivations.

Transferability – refers to the idea that findings may be applicable in similar situations. While transferability is generally considered the responsibility of the one who wishes to apply the results into new contexts, the researcher is generally expected to have provided sufficient information about context and assumptions to determine whether the research is transferable.

Transparency – ensuring research processes are documented and presented as rigorously as possible to make the research process clear.

Triangulation – the use of different types of methods, researchers and/or theories in a study in an attempt to maximize the validity of a study.

Trustworthiness – the process of checking with participants both the validity of data collected, and that data interpretations are agreed upon a shared truth. It is evidence of research accountability, and involves both integrity and rigour.

Validity – criteria for judging the soundness of qualitative research, thus strategies are developed to ensure there is some kind of qualifying check to ensure the research is sound and credible.

Verisimilitude – demonstrating the appearance of truth; the quality of seeming to be true, which is arguably a more realistic quest than uncovering 'truth'.

Viral methodologies – instead of methodologies being specifically 'located' in areas such as poststructuralism and constructivism, the underlying theories are seen as mutable and liquid.

Virtue – a term used to refer to an excellence of moral character representing a mean between extremes of behaviour.

Virtual ethnography – methodology that seeks to understand, from a sociological perspective what people 'do' on the internet (Hine, 2000, 2005).

Index